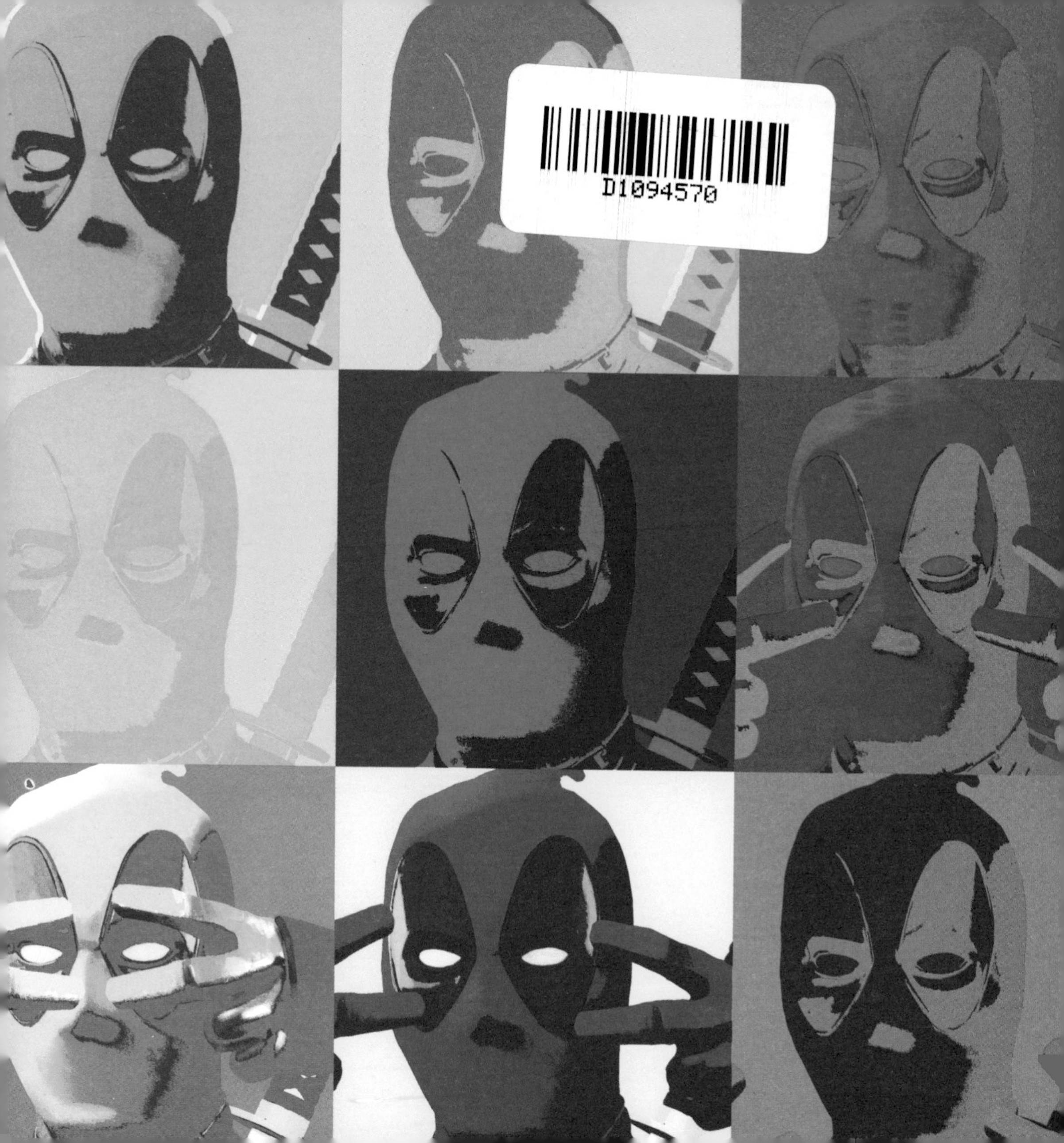

THE PHILOSOPHY OF
DEADPOOL

MARVEL

BONJOUR, MES AMIS! THAT'S FRENCH FOR WASSSSUUUUUPPPP! IT'S YOUR OLD PAL DP HERE IN ANOTHER FABULOUS BOOK ABOUT ME. FROM '90s MERCENARY TO KILL-THE-ENTIRE-MARVEL-UNIVERSE NUTJOB, THERE'S A LOT OF ME TO ENJOY. SO GET THOSE FINGERS PUMPED FOR SOME AWESOME PAGE-TURNING ACTION!

INSIDE IS AN ARRAY OF MY GOOD BITS, BAD BITS AND STRAIGHT-UP UGLY BITS, FILLED WITH SIMPLE WISDOMS THAT GET ME THROUGH LIFE WITHOUT WANTING TO KILL MYSELF (OR 23 BLIND ORPHANS, BUT THAT WAS ONE TIME!).

ANYHOO, SIT BACK, RELAX - LOCK THE BASEMENT DOOR - AND ENJOY...

Deadpool

The Philosophy of Deadpool
ISBN: 9781787731851

Editor: JAKE DEVINE
Designer: DAN BURA

Published by Titan Comics, A division of Titan Publishing Group, Ltd.
144 Southwark Street, London, SE1 0UP

A CIP CATALOGUE FOR THIS TITLE IS AVAILABLE FROM THE BRITISH LIBRARY

10 9 8 7 6 5 4 3 2 1

WWW.TITAN-COMICS.COM
BECOME A FAN ON FACEBOOK.COM/COMICSTITAN | FOLLOW US ON TWITTER @COMICSTITAN

THE PHILOSOPHY OF DEADPOOL

CONTENTS

MARVEL

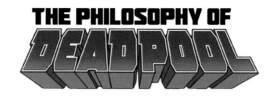

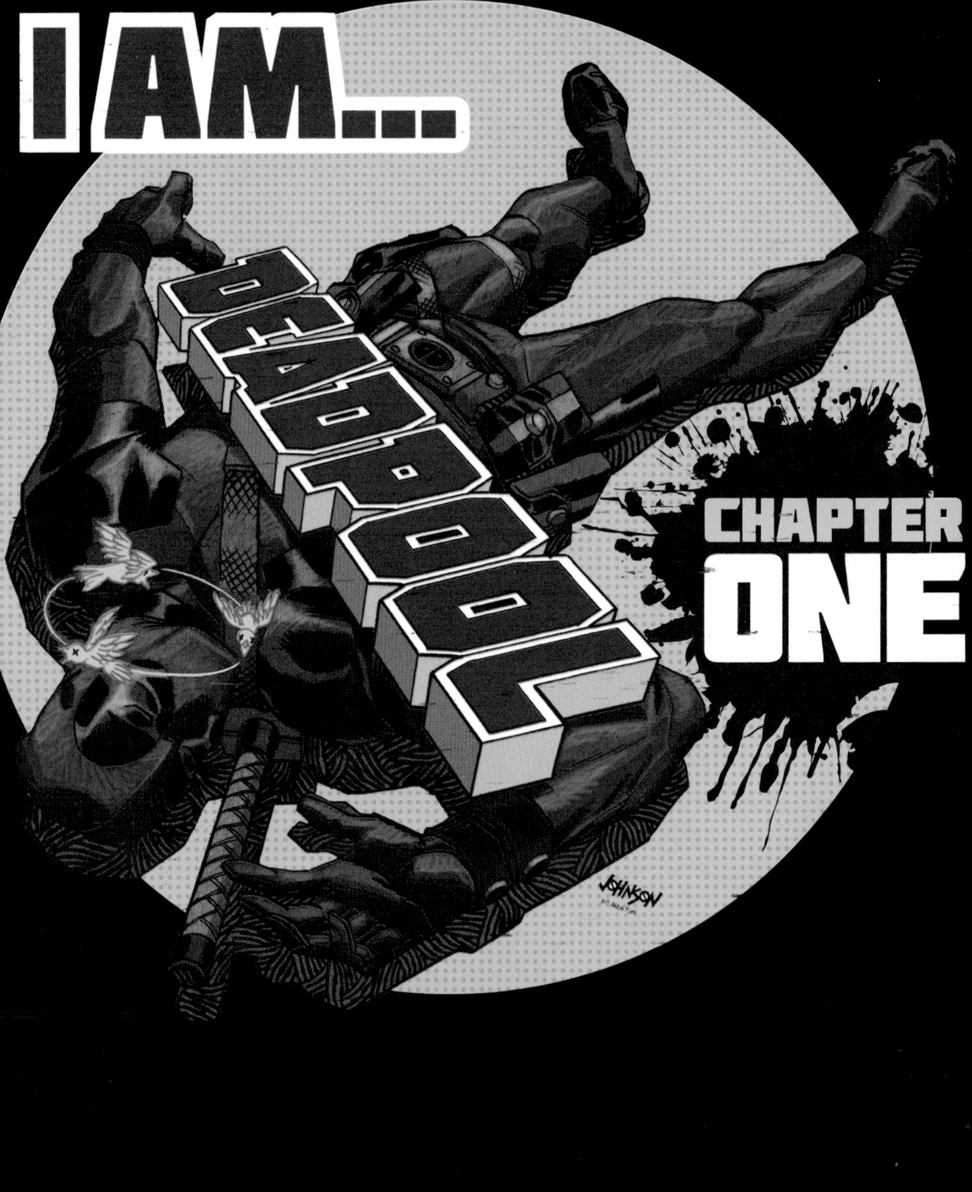
I AM...
DEADPOOL
CHAPTER
ONE
JOHNSON

I'VE BEEN CALLED PSYCHO, MERCENARY, CLOWN-FISH (OR WAS THAT NEMO?)... BUT I PREFER THE TERM: 'CLEANSER OF THE GENE-POOL'. I MAY BE A MASS-MURDERING HUMAN SALAMI, BUT I HAVE REAL CHARACTER!

JUST FOLLOW THE GOODY-TWO-SHOES ROUTINE THAT MAKES ME A TRUE COMIC BOOK SUPERHERO - YOU'LL SEE.

01: A NOBLE CREED.

"IT'S LIKE MY MUTANT POWER IS TO *KILL* PEOPLE WHETHER I WANT TO OR NOT!"

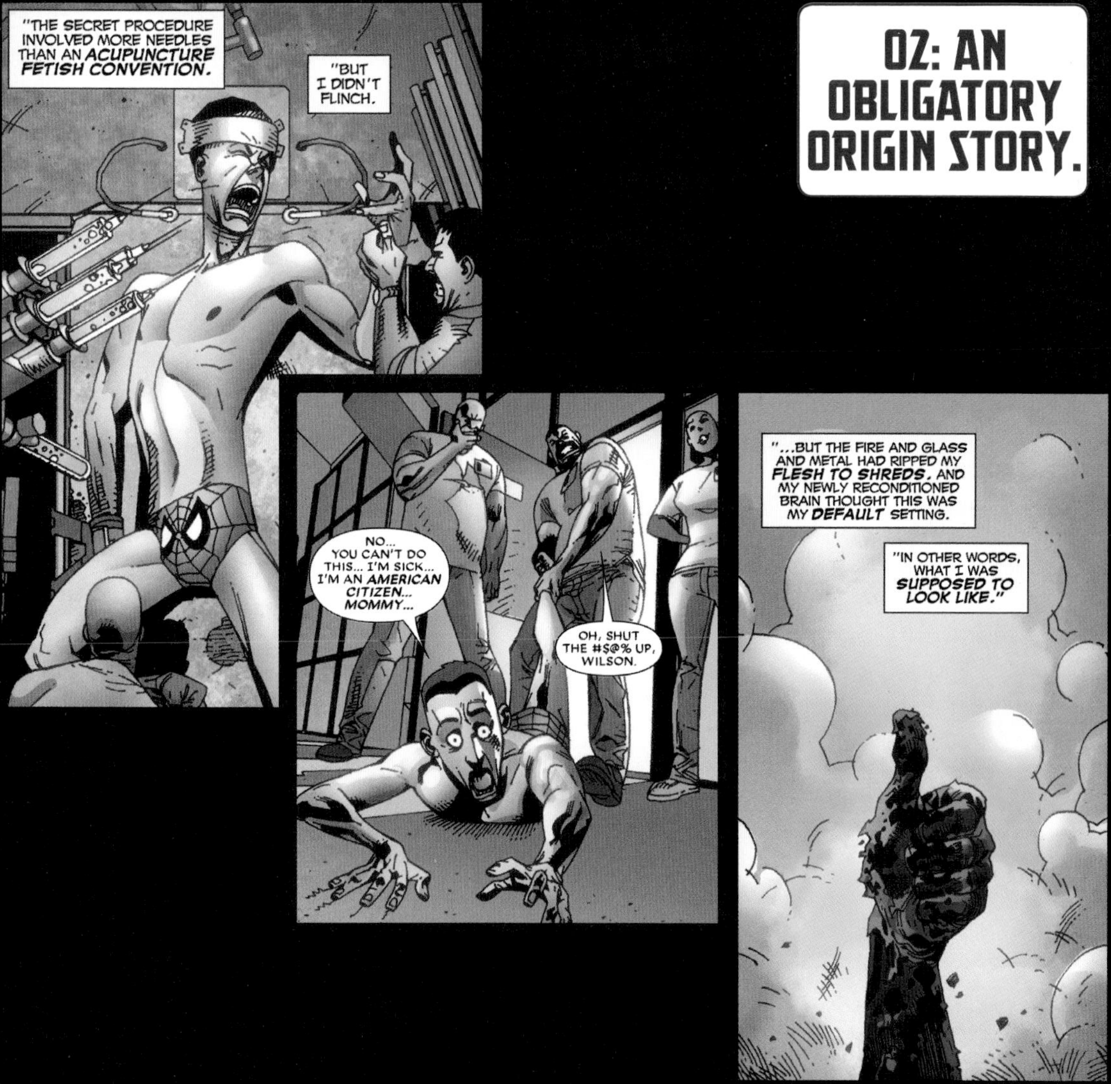
OZ: AN OBLIGATORY ORIGIN STORY.
"THE SECRET PROCEDURE INVOLVED MORE NEEDLES THAN AN ACUPUNCTURE FETISH CONVENTION.
"BUT I DIDN'T FLINCH.
NO... YOU CAN'T DO THIS... I'M SICK... I'M AN AMERICAN CITIZEN... MOMMY...
OH, SHUT THE #$@% UP, WILSON.
"...BUT THE FIRE AND GLASS AND METAL HAD RIPPED MY FLESH TO SHREDS. AND MY NEWLY RECONDITIONED BRAIN THOUGHT THIS WAS MY DEFAULT SETTING.
"IN OTHER WORDS, WHAT I WAS SUPPOSED TO LOOK LIKE."

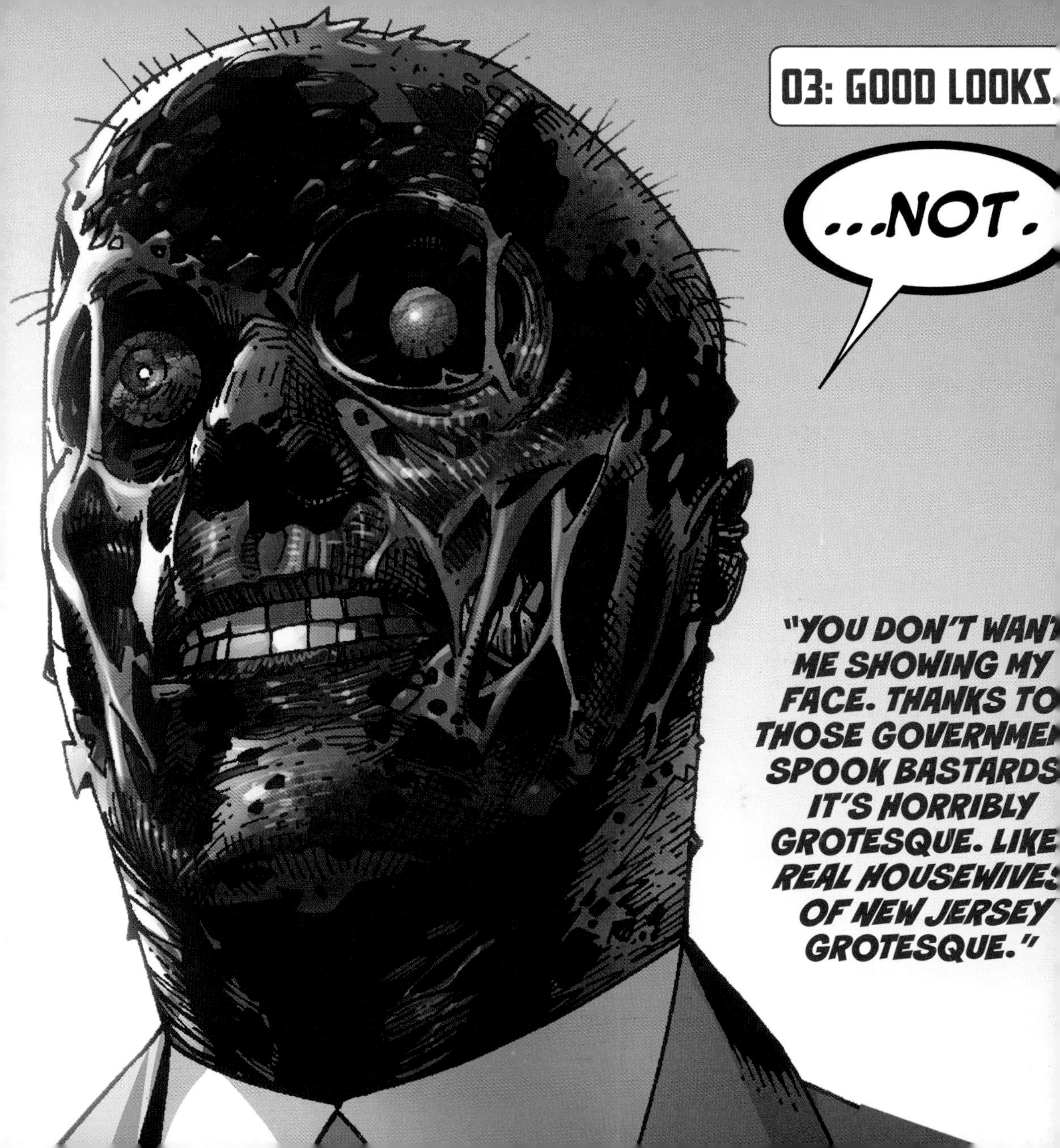
03: GOOD LOOKS.
...NOT.
"YOU DON'T WANT ME SHOWING MY FACE. THANKS TO THOSE GOVERNME SPOOK BASTARDS IT'S HORRIBLY GROTESQUE. LIKE REAL HOUSEWIVE OF NEW JERSEY GROTESQUE."

04: A FORGIVING NATURE.

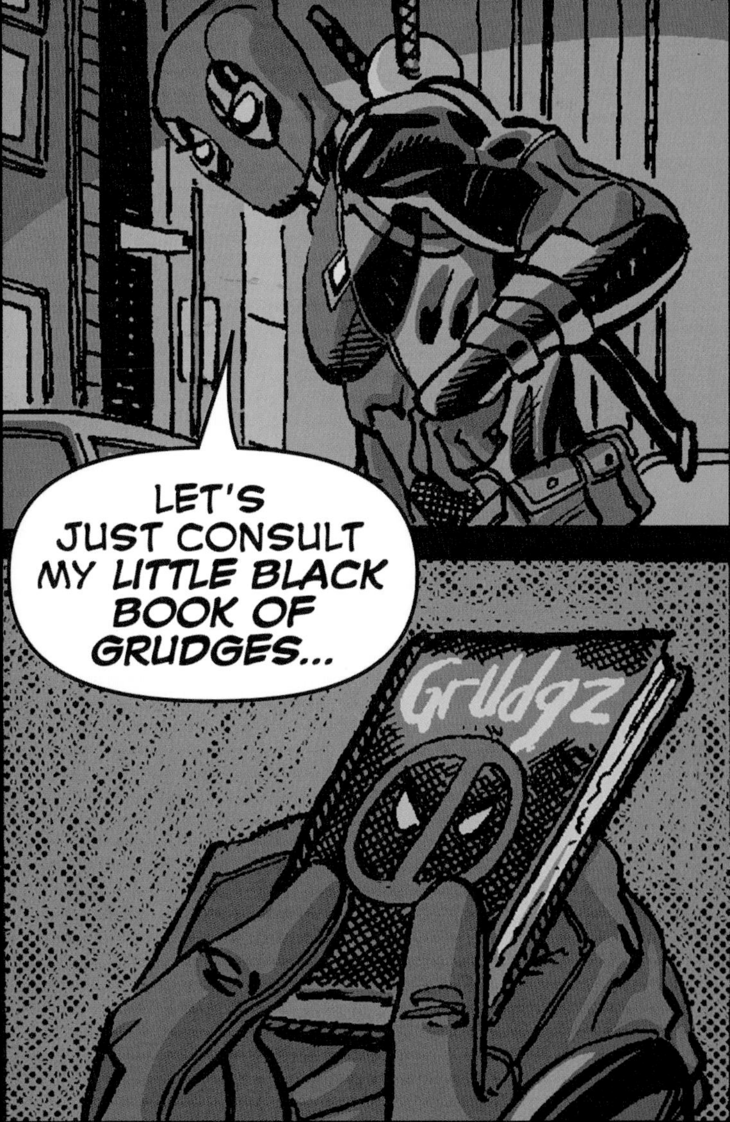
LET'S JUST CONSULT MY *LITTLE BLACK BOOK OF GRUDGES...*
Grudgz

05: UNLIMITED POWERS.

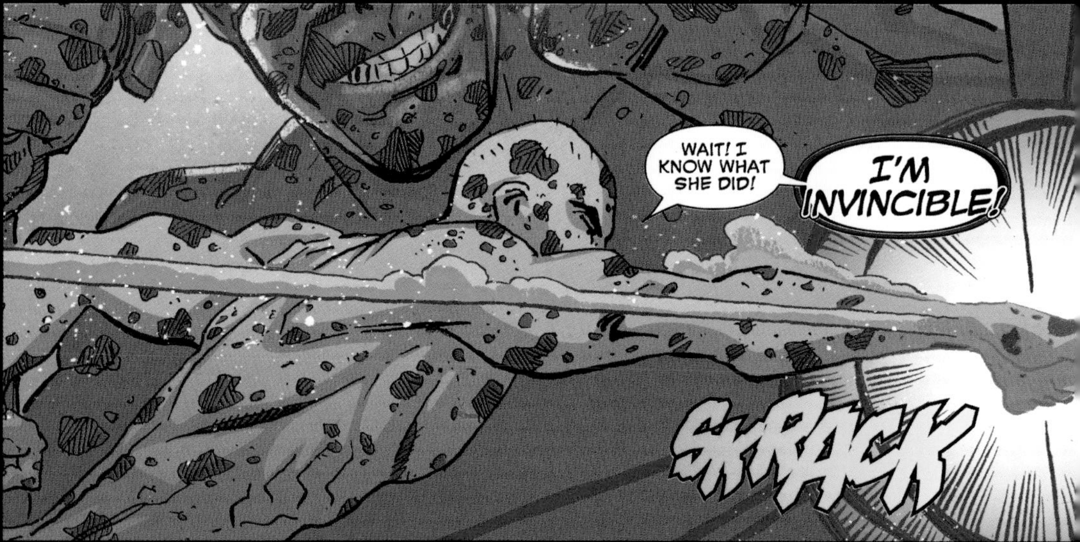
WAIT! I KNOW WHAT SHE DID!
I'M INVINCIBLE!
SKRACK

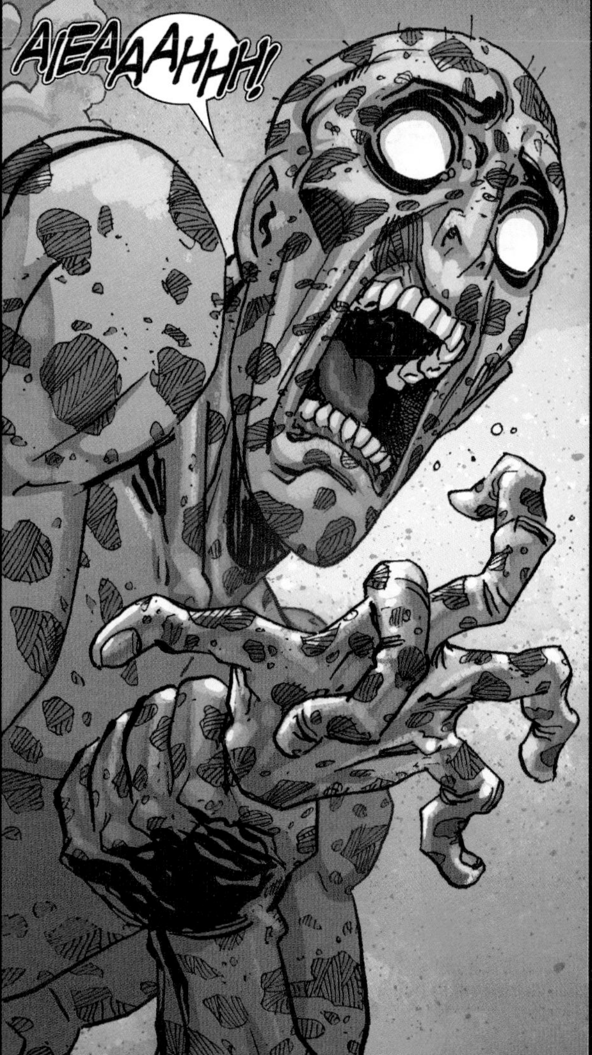
AIEAAAHHH!

06: COOL TOYS AND GADGETS.

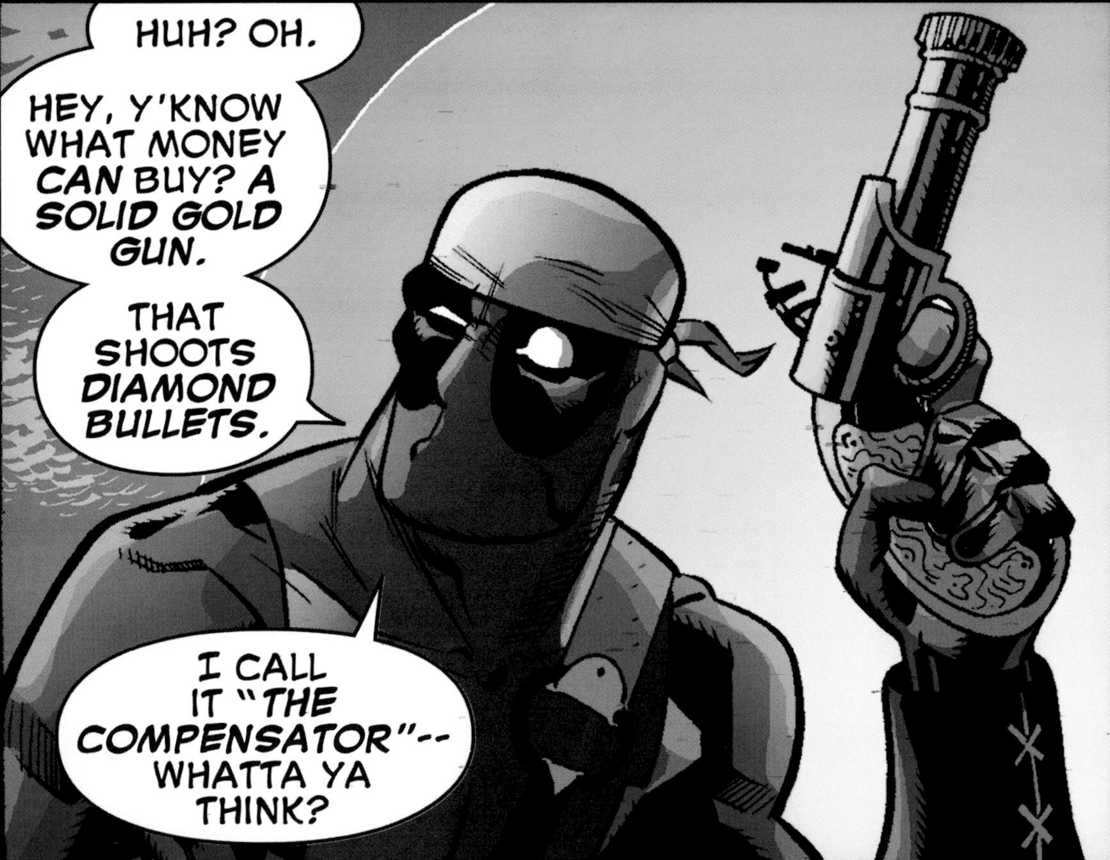
HUH? OH.
HEY, Y'KNOW WHAT MONEY *CAN* BUY? A *SOLID GOLD* GUN.
THAT SHOOTS *DIAMOND* BULLETS.
I CALL IT "*THE COMPENSATOR*"-- WHATTA YA THINK?

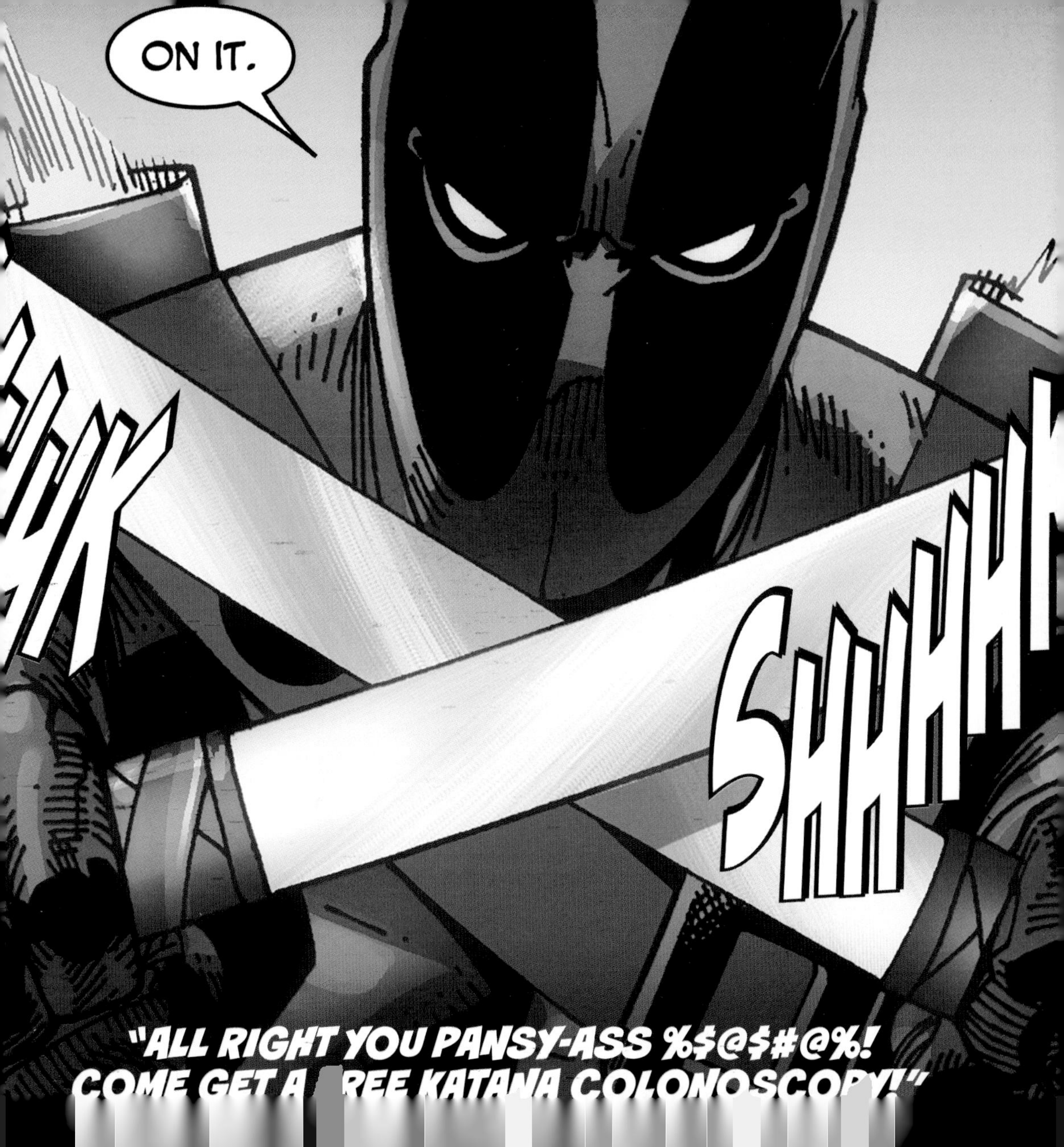
ON IT.
"ALL RIGHT YOU PANSY-ASS %$@$#@%!
COME GET A REE KATANA COLONOSCOPY!"

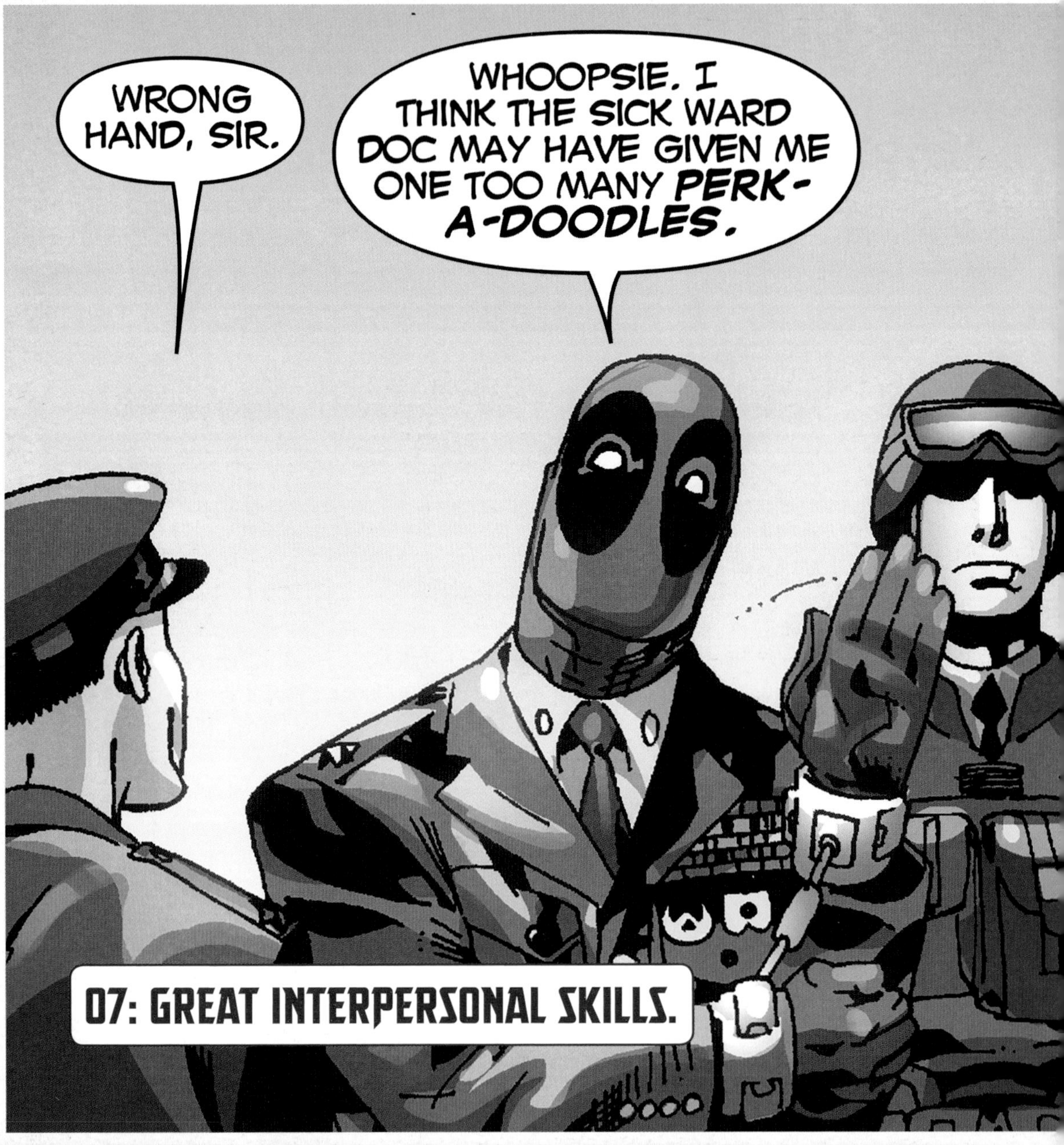
WRONG HAND, SIR.
WHOOPSIE. I THINK THE SICK WARD DOC MAY HAVE GIVEN ME ONE TOO MANY PERK-A-DOODLES.
07: GREAT INTERPERSONAL SKILLS.

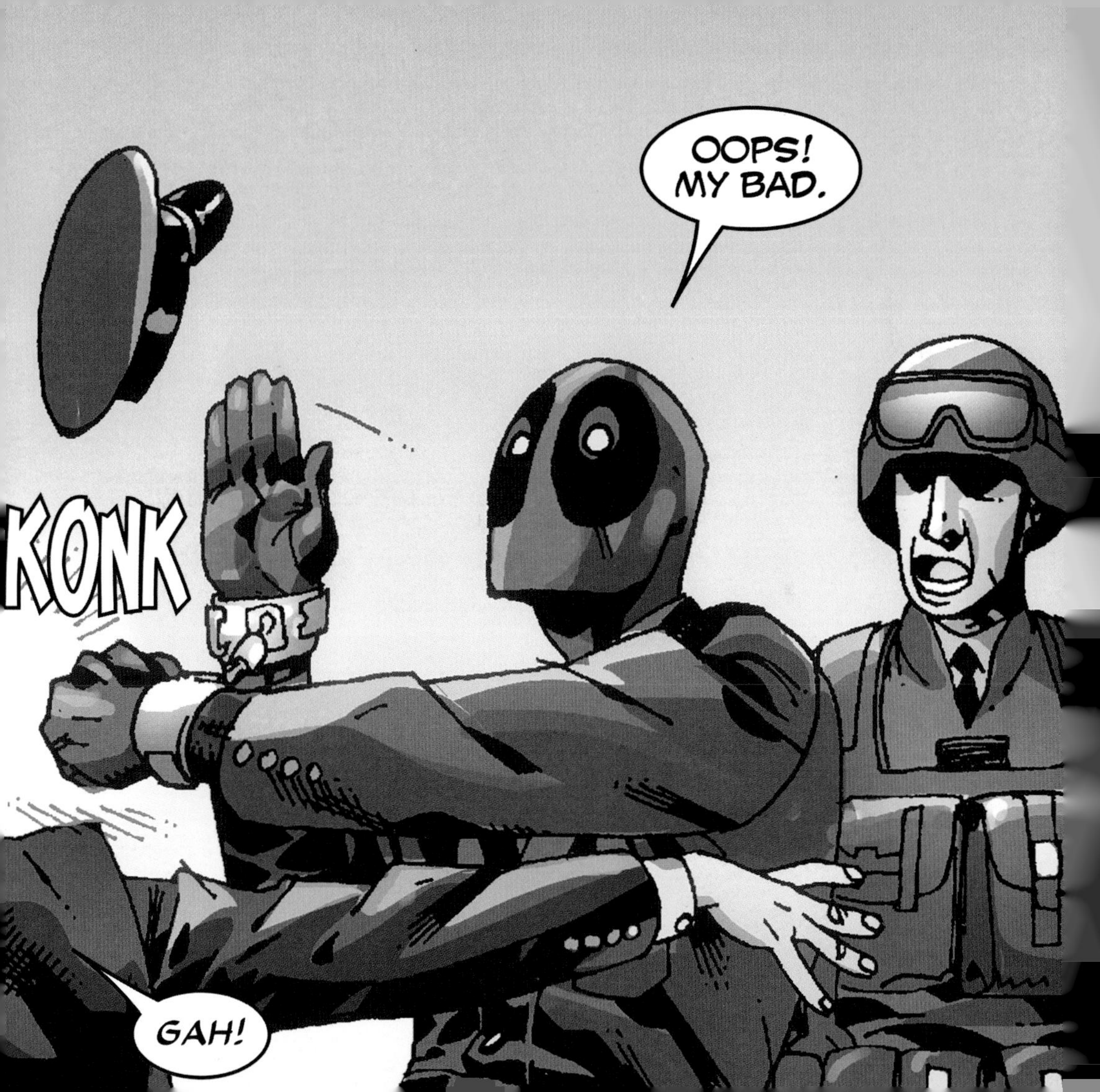
KONK
OOPS! MY BAD.
GAH!

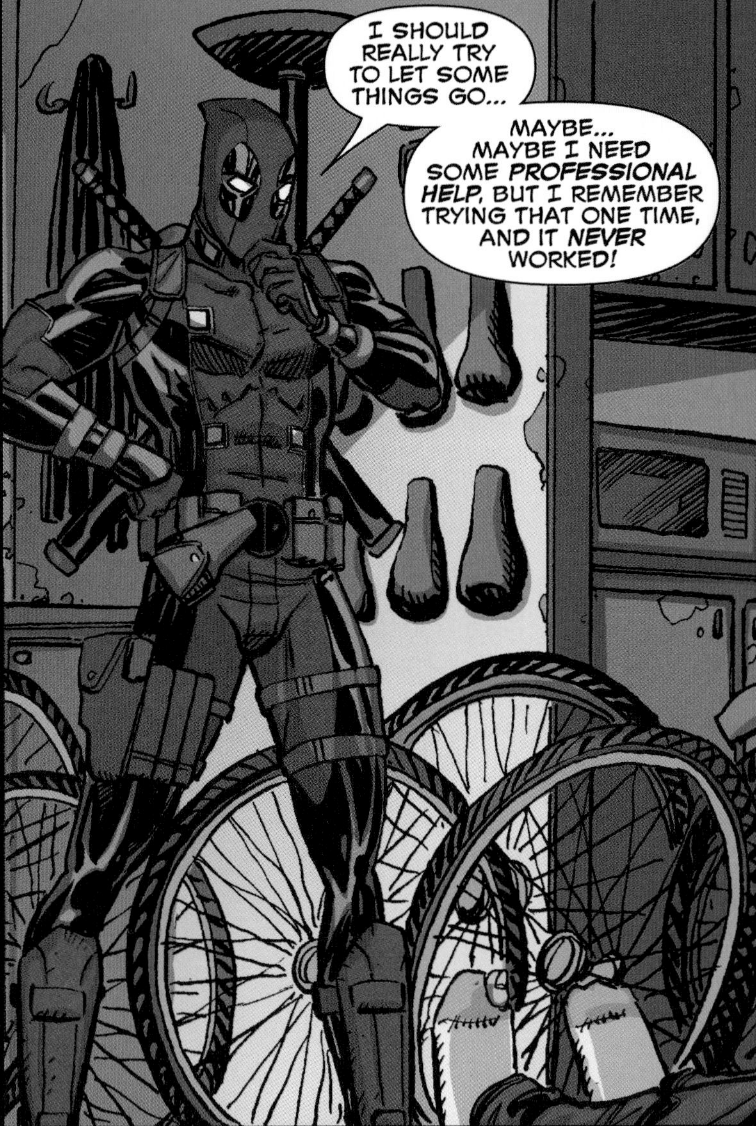
I SHOULD REALLY TRY TO LET SOME THINGS GO...
MAYBE... MAYBE I NEED SOME *PROFESSIONAL HELP*, BUT I REMEMBER TRYING THAT ONE TIME, AND IT *NEVER* WORKED!

08: THE ABILITY TO MONOLOGUE.

"THERE YOU ARE, SINISTER VOICES AND EVIL IMPULSES...

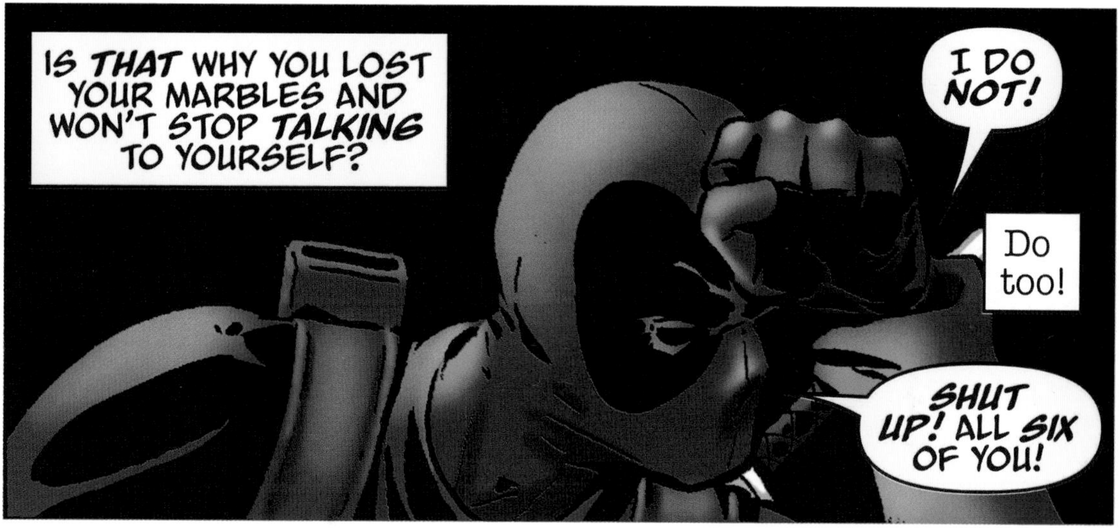
IS *THAT* WHY YOU LOST YOUR MARBLES AND WON'T STOP *TALKING* TO YOURSELF?
I DO *NOT!*
Do too!
SHUT UP! ALL *SIX* OF YOU!

...I MISSED YOU."

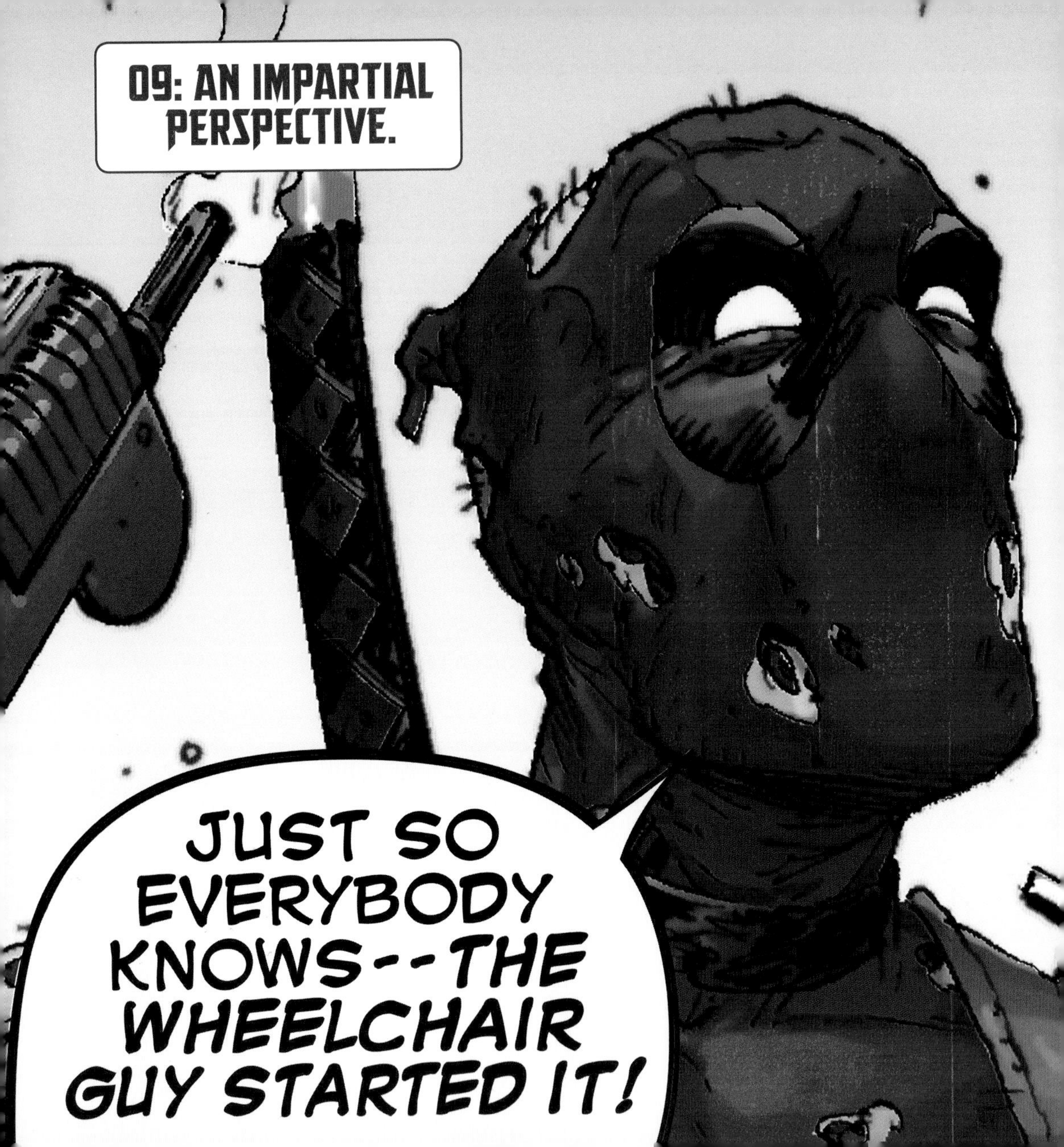
09: AN IMPARTIAL PERSPECTIVE.
JUST SO EVERYBODY KNOWS--THE WHEELCHAIR GUY STARTED IT!

10: BE CERTIFIED SANE.

"I AM THE DR. PHIL OF THE SUPER-POWERED LUNATIC WORLD."

CHAPTER TWO

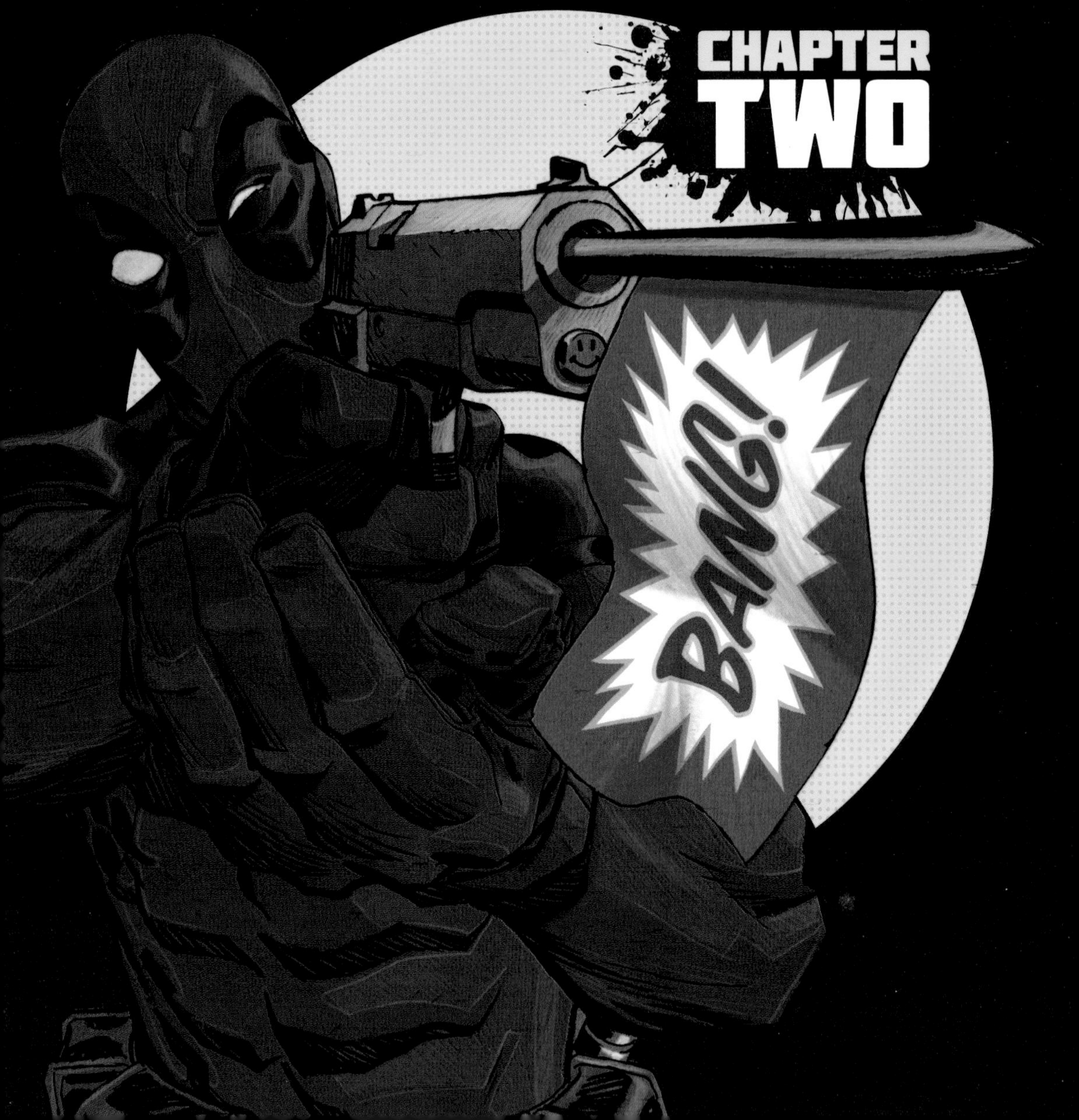
BANG!

DEADPOOL'S EPIC ASS KICKING SHOWOWN COUNTDOWN

I'VE FOUGHT EVERYONE FROM THE AVENGERS TO DEAD
PRESIDENTS... SPOILER ALERT - I WIN (MOSTLY)!

"THIS IS THE WORST SHOW THAT ABE LINCOLN'S EVER HAD TO SIT THROUGH."

#9

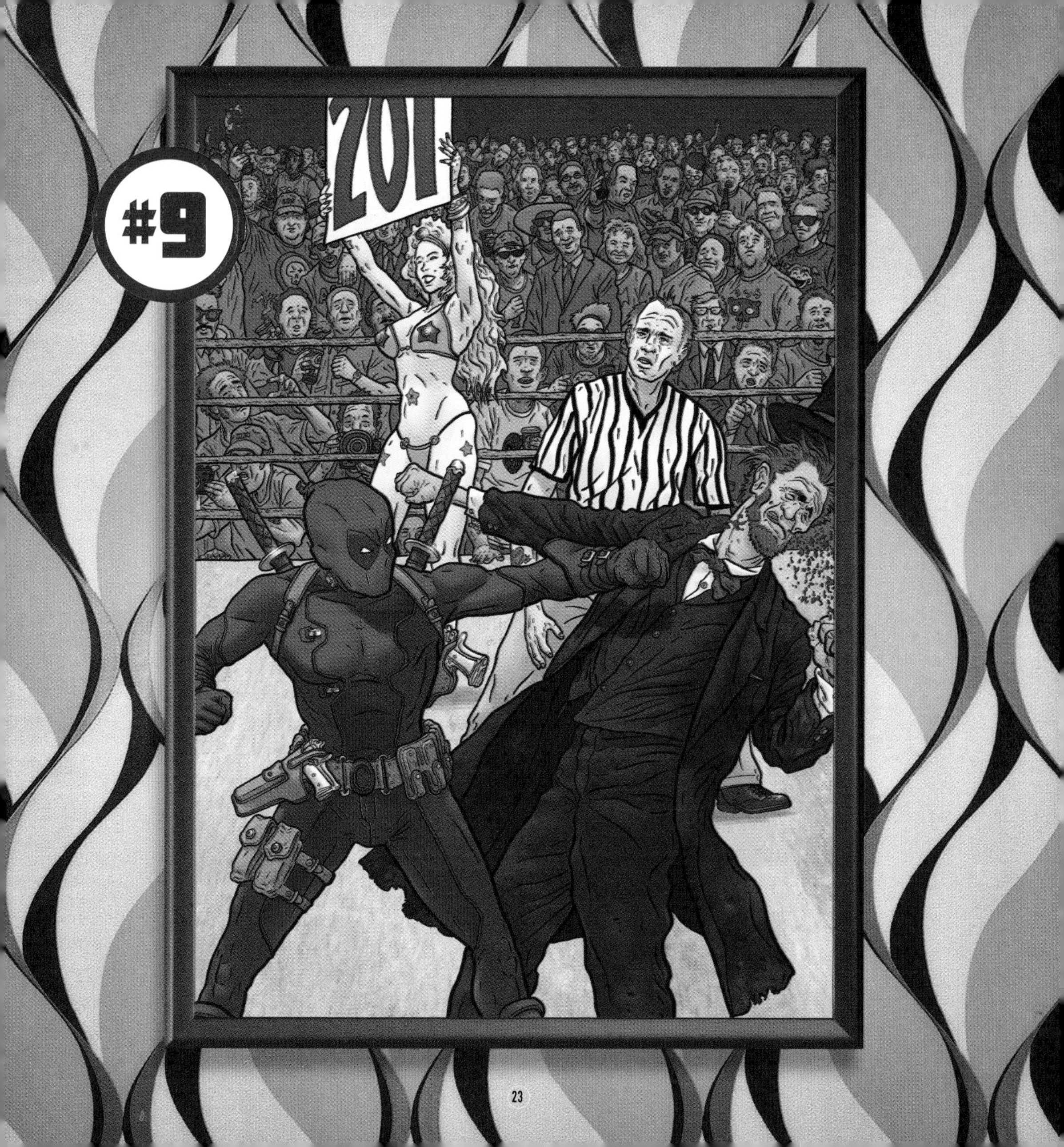

#8

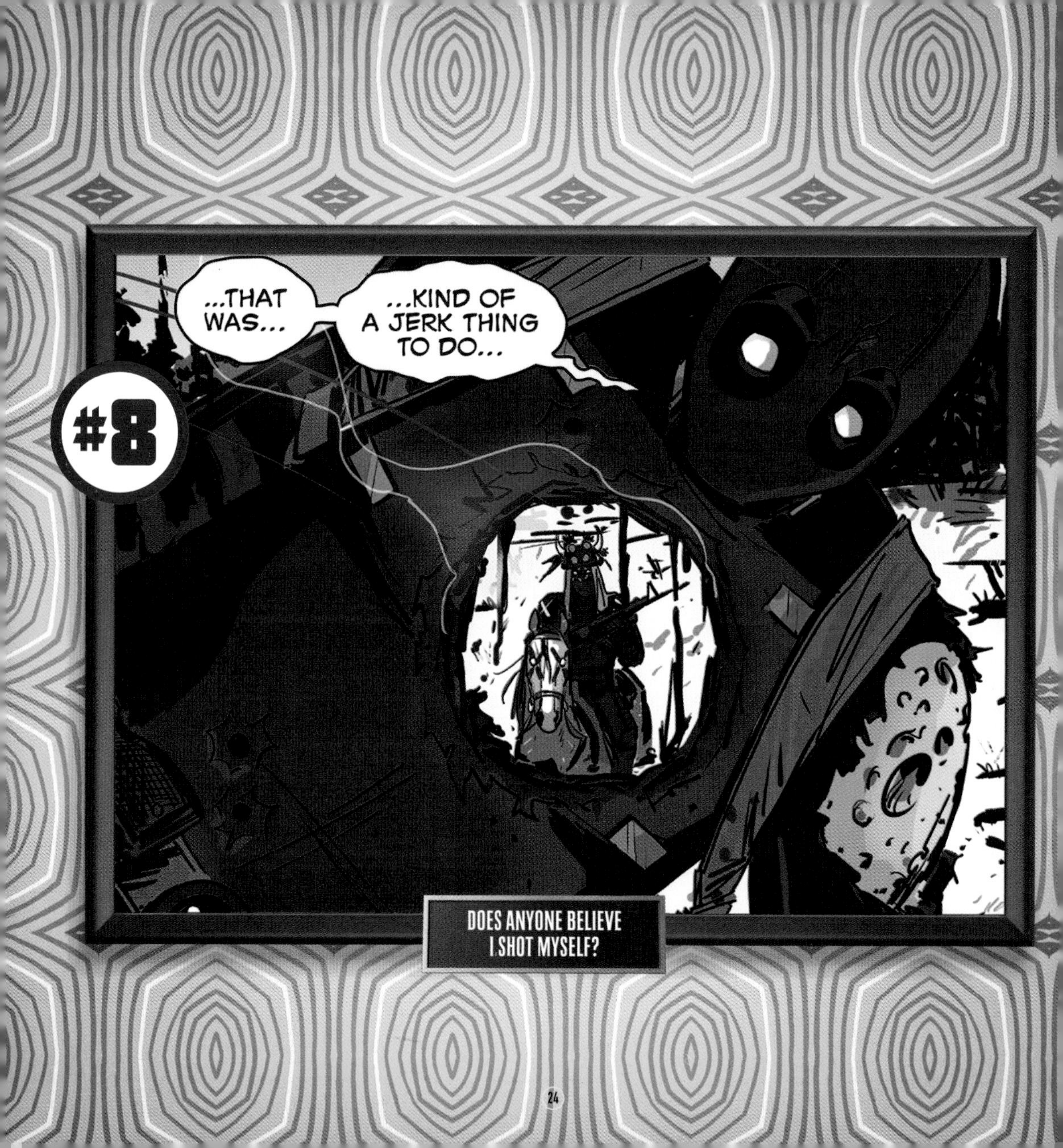
...THAT WAS...
...KIND OF A JERK THING TO DO...

DOES ANYONE BELIEVE I SHOT MYSELF?

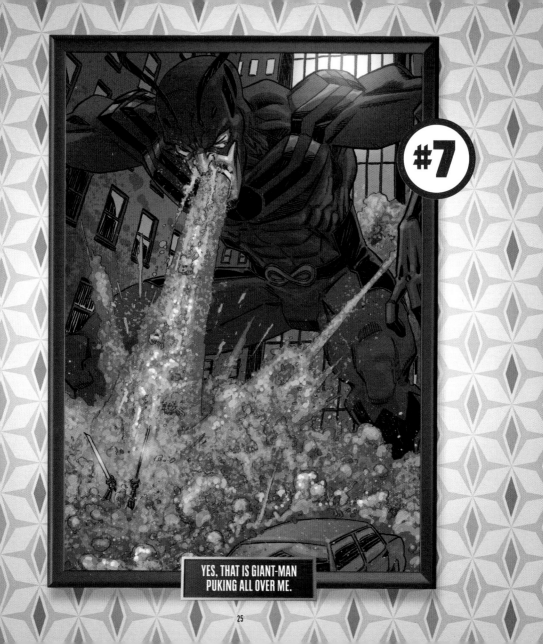

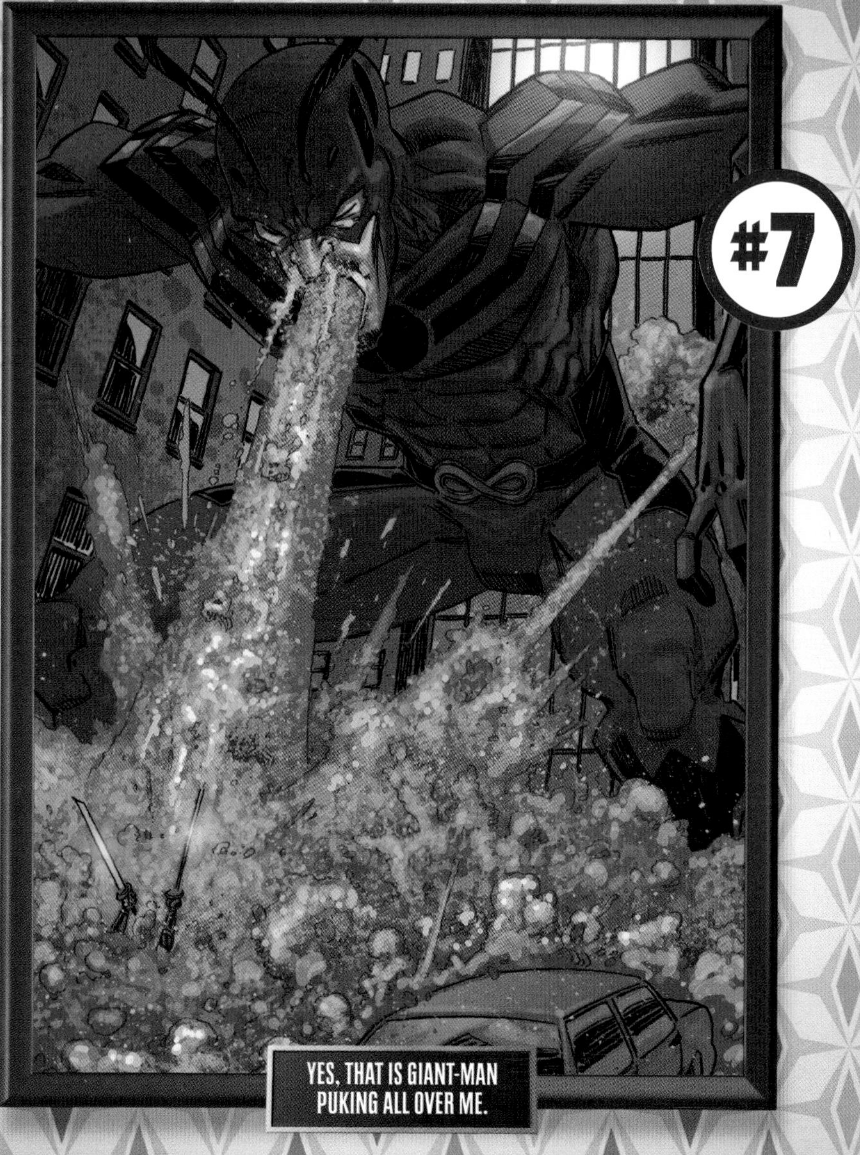
#7
YES, THAT IS GIANT-MAN PUKING ALL OVER ME.

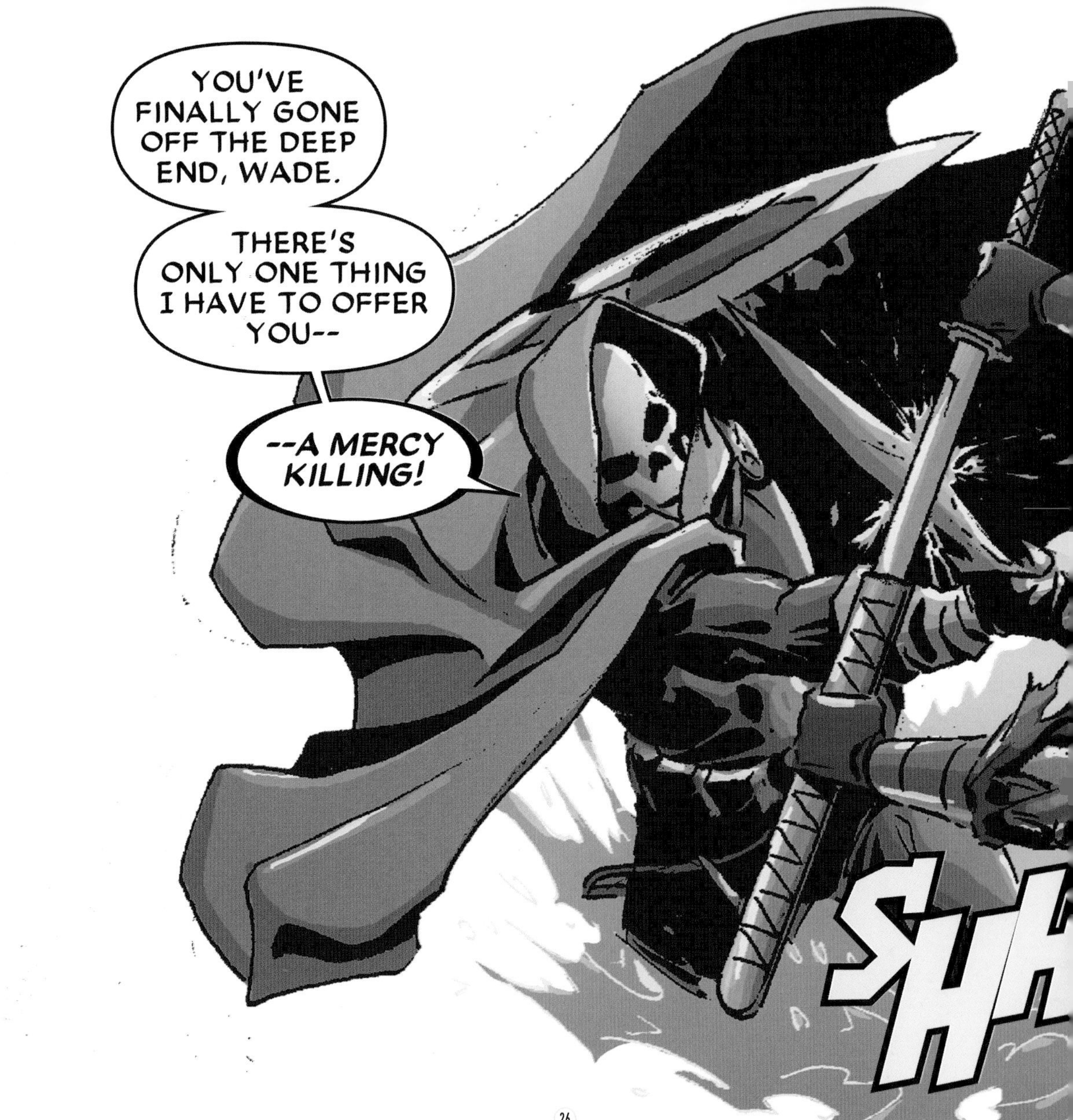
YOU'VE FINALLY GONE OFF THE DEEP END, WADE.
THERE'S ONLY ONE THING I HAVE TO OFFER YOU--
--A MERCY KILLING!

#6

"NOTE TO SELF: FOR FUTURE BATTLES, STEAL IRON MAN'S ARMOR."

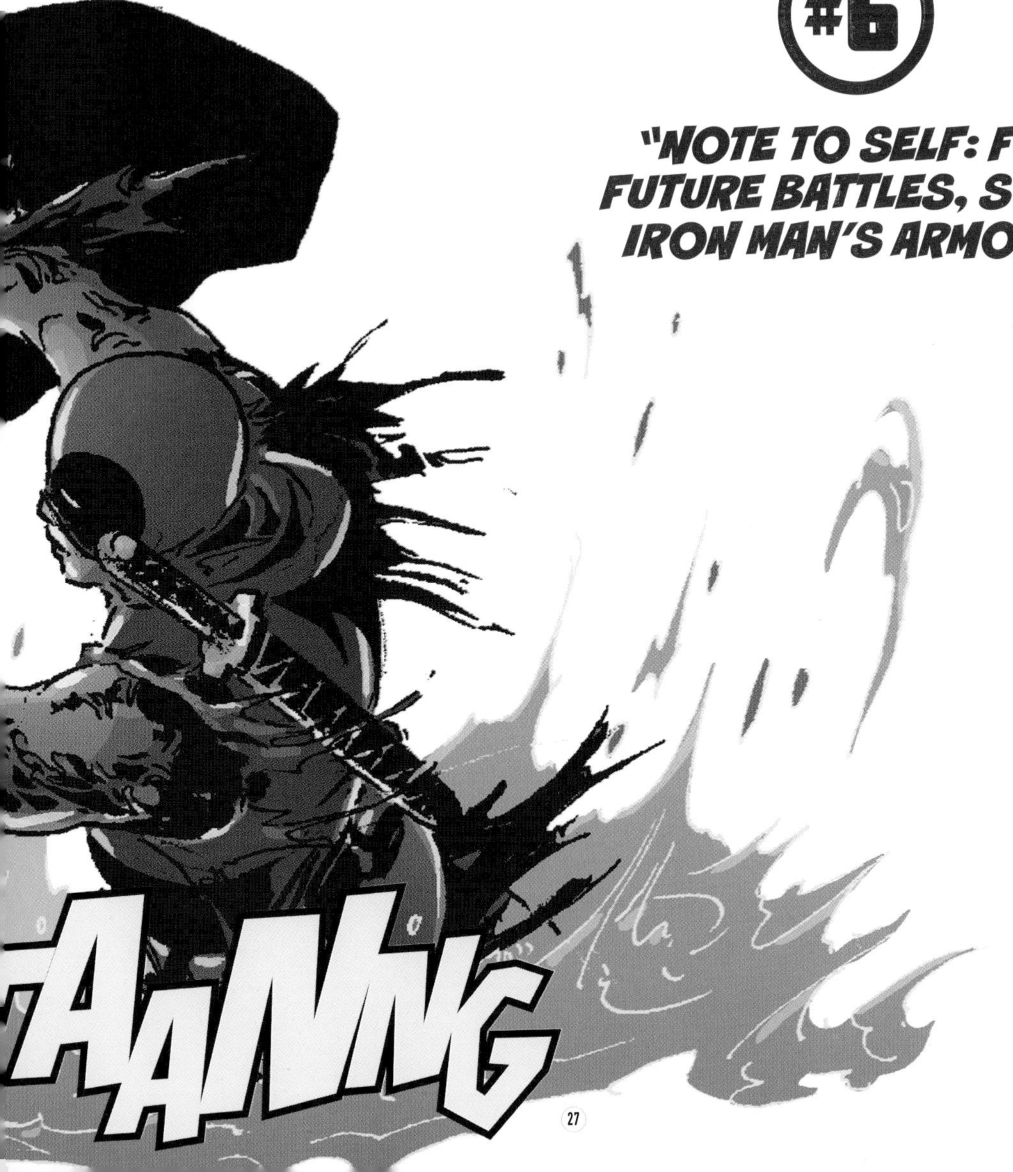
AANNG

#5

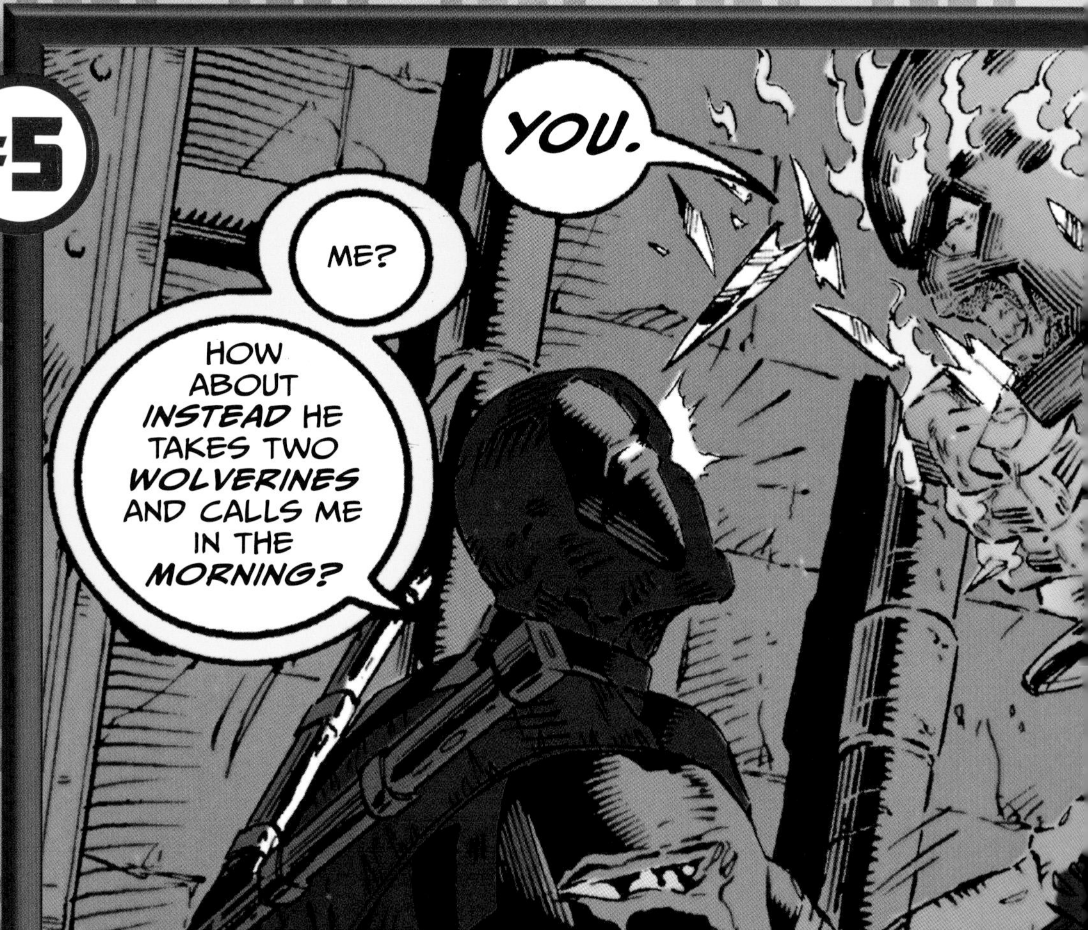
YOU.
ME?
HOW ABOUT INSTEAD HE TAKES TWO WOLVERINES AND CALLS ME IN THE MORNING?

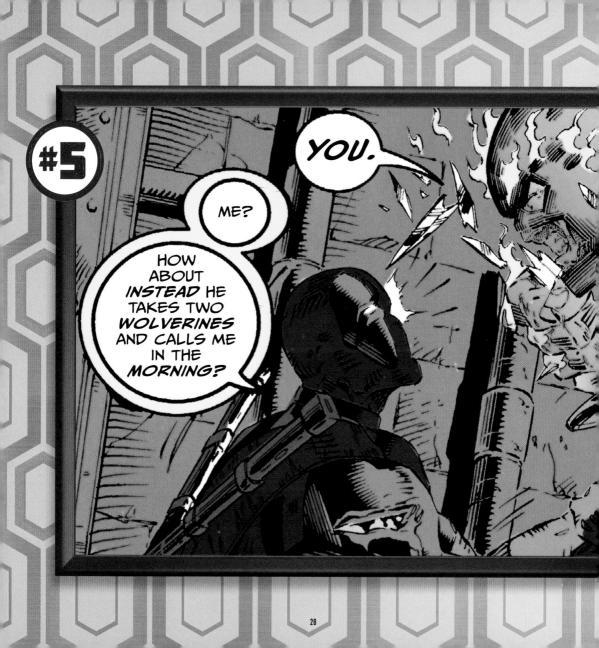

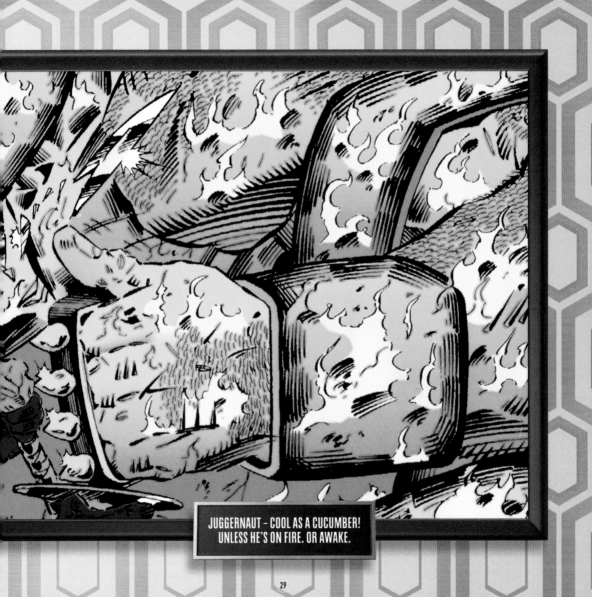

JUGGERNAUT – COOL AS A CUCUMBER!
UNLESS HE'S ON FIRE. OR AWAKE.

#4

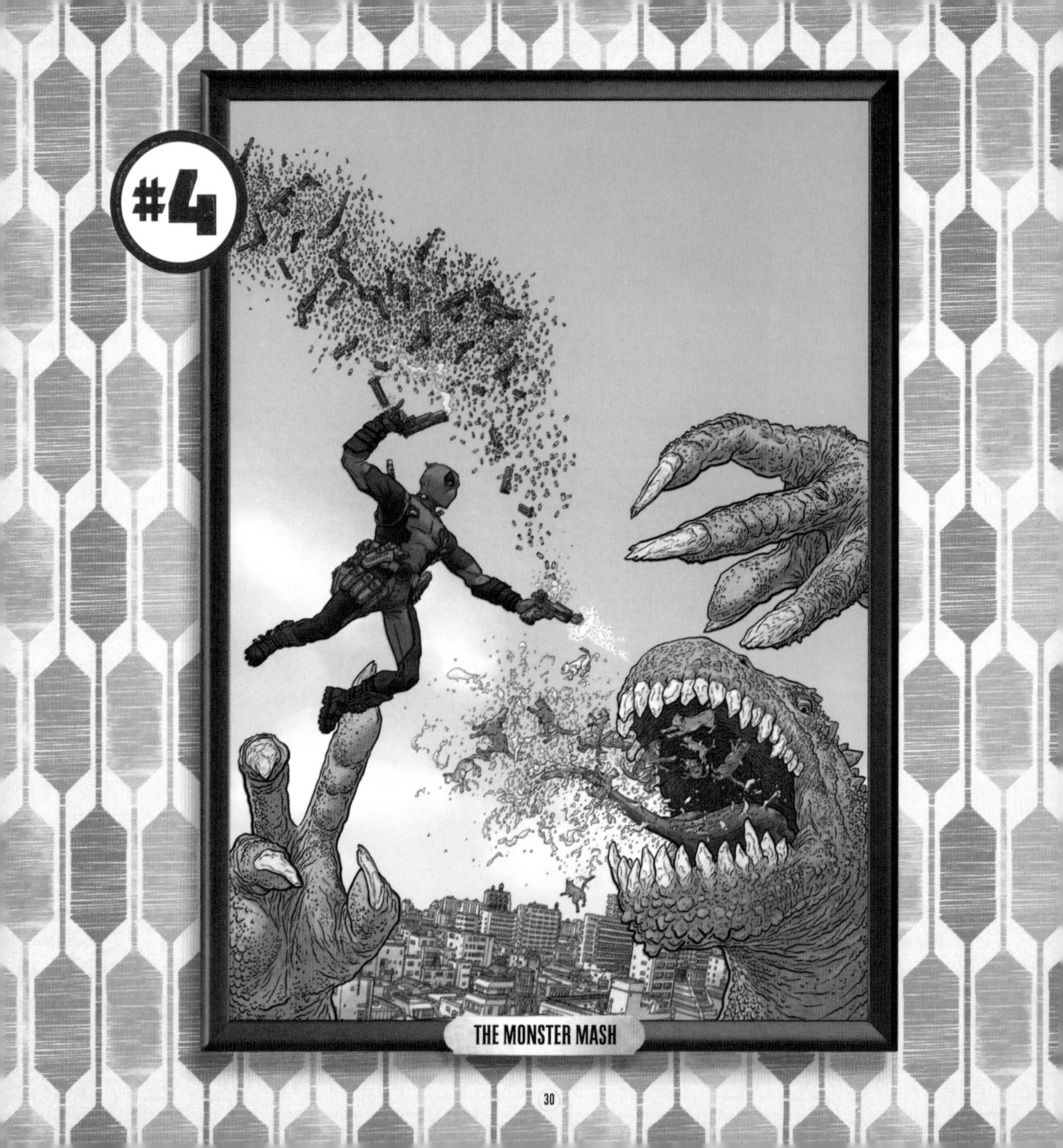

THE MONSTER MASH

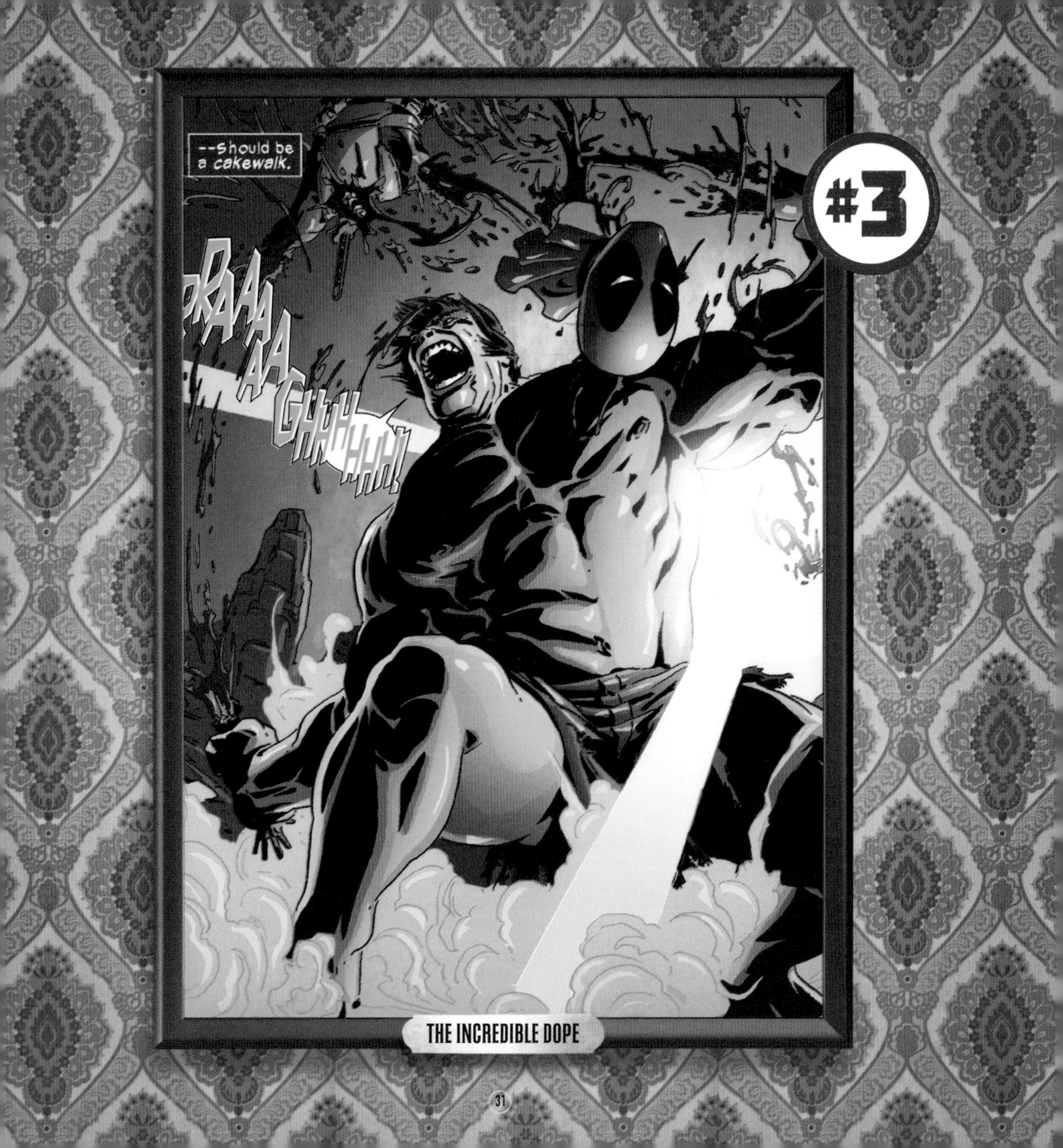
--Should be a cakewalk.
RRAAAAAAGHHHHHHH!

#3

THE INCREDIBLE DOPE

#2

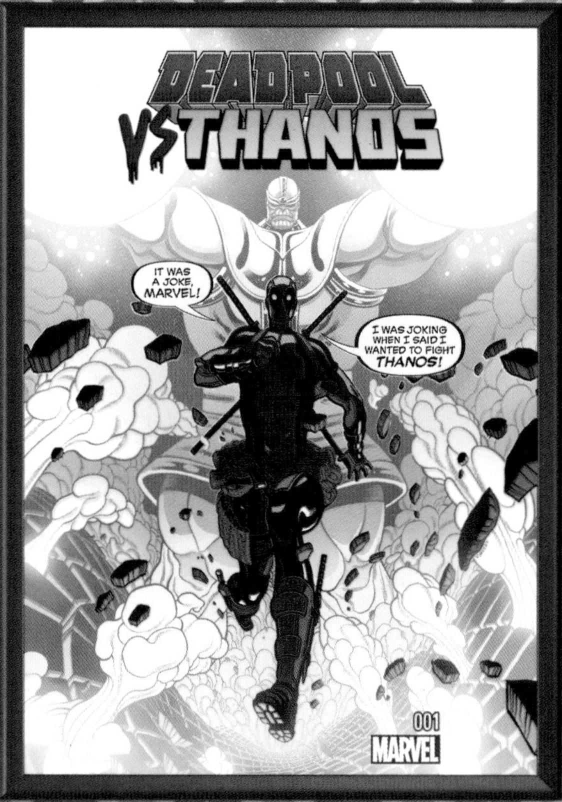

DEADPOOL VS THANOS
IT WAS A JOKE, MARVEL!
I WAS JOKING WHEN I SAID I WANTED TO FIGHT THANOS!
001
MARVEL

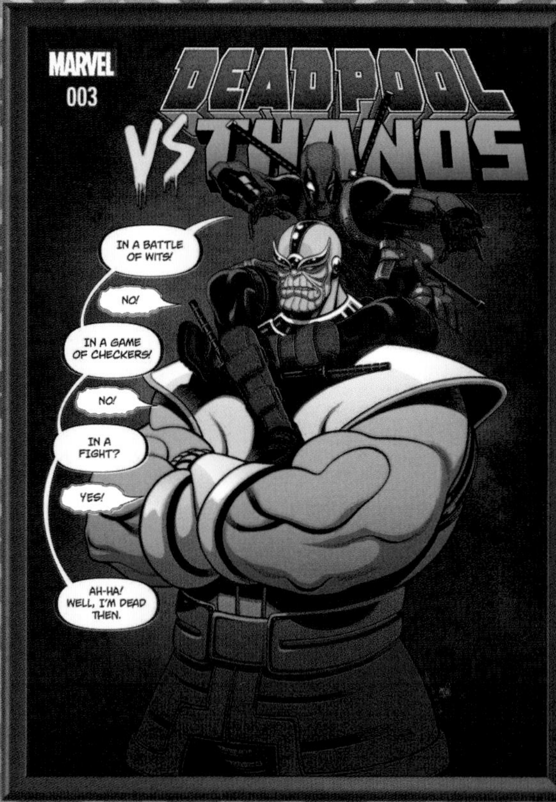

MARVEL
003
DEADPOOL VS THANOS
IN A BATTLE OF WITS!
NO!
IN A GAME OF CHECKERS!
NO!
IN A FIGHT?
YES!
AH-HA! WELL, I'M DEAD THEN.

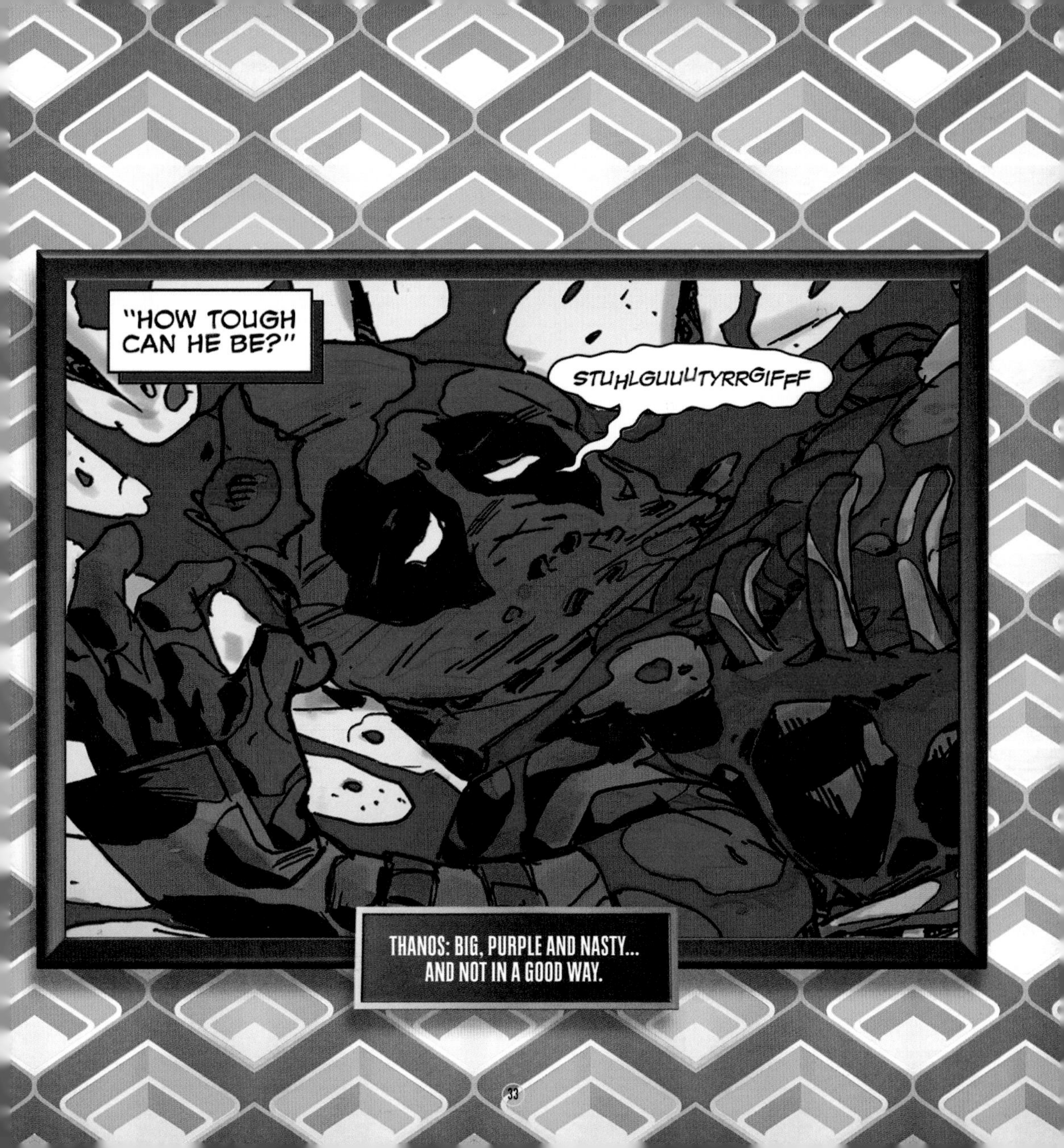
"HOW TOUGH
CAN HE BE?"
STUHLGUUUTYRRGIFFF

THANOS: BIG, PURPLE AND NASTY...
AND NOT IN A GOOD WAY.

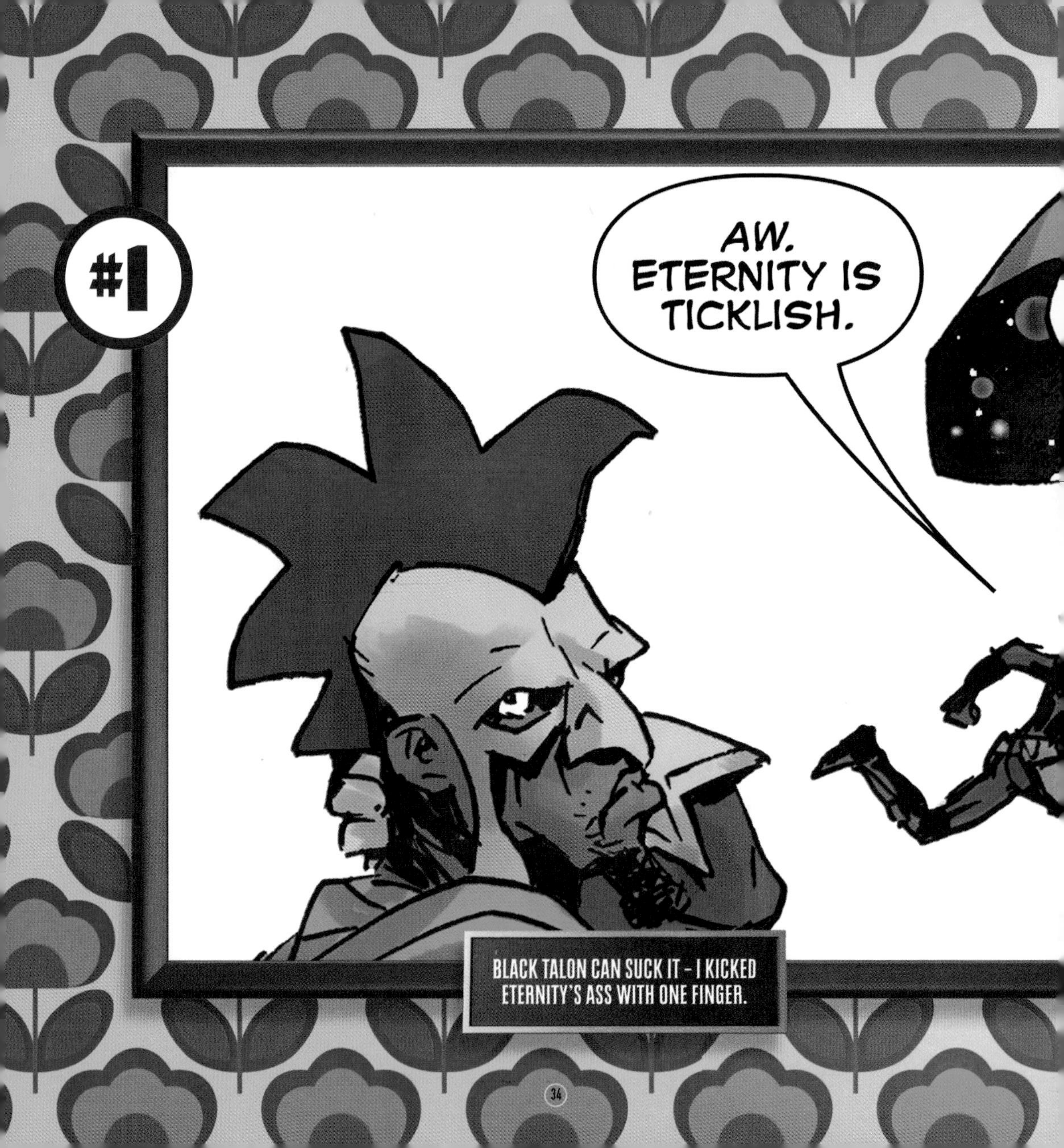
#1
AW. ETERNITY IS TICKLISH.
BLACK TALON CAN SUCK IT - I KICKED ETERNITY'S ASS WITH ONE FINGER.

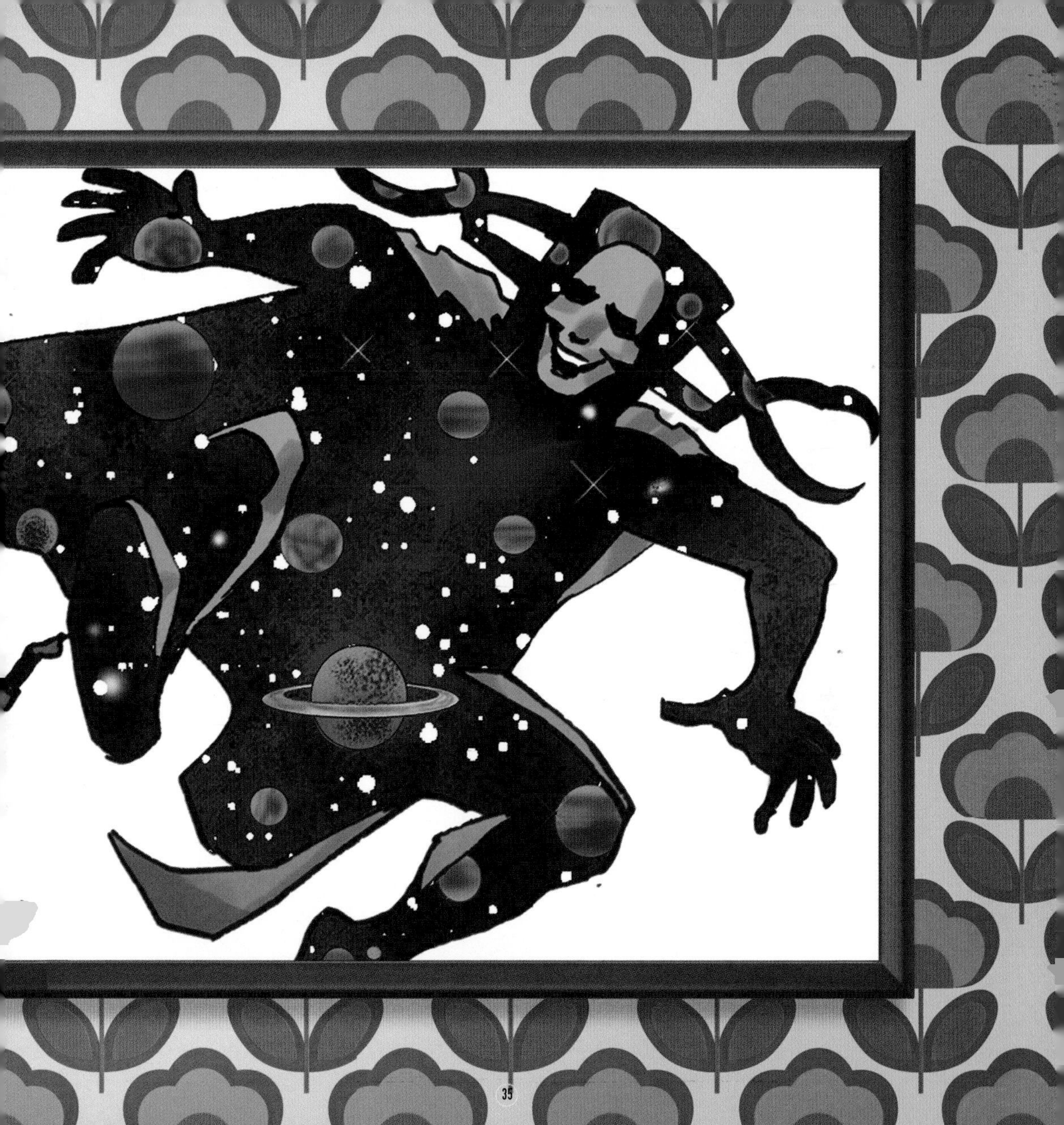

CHAPTER THREE

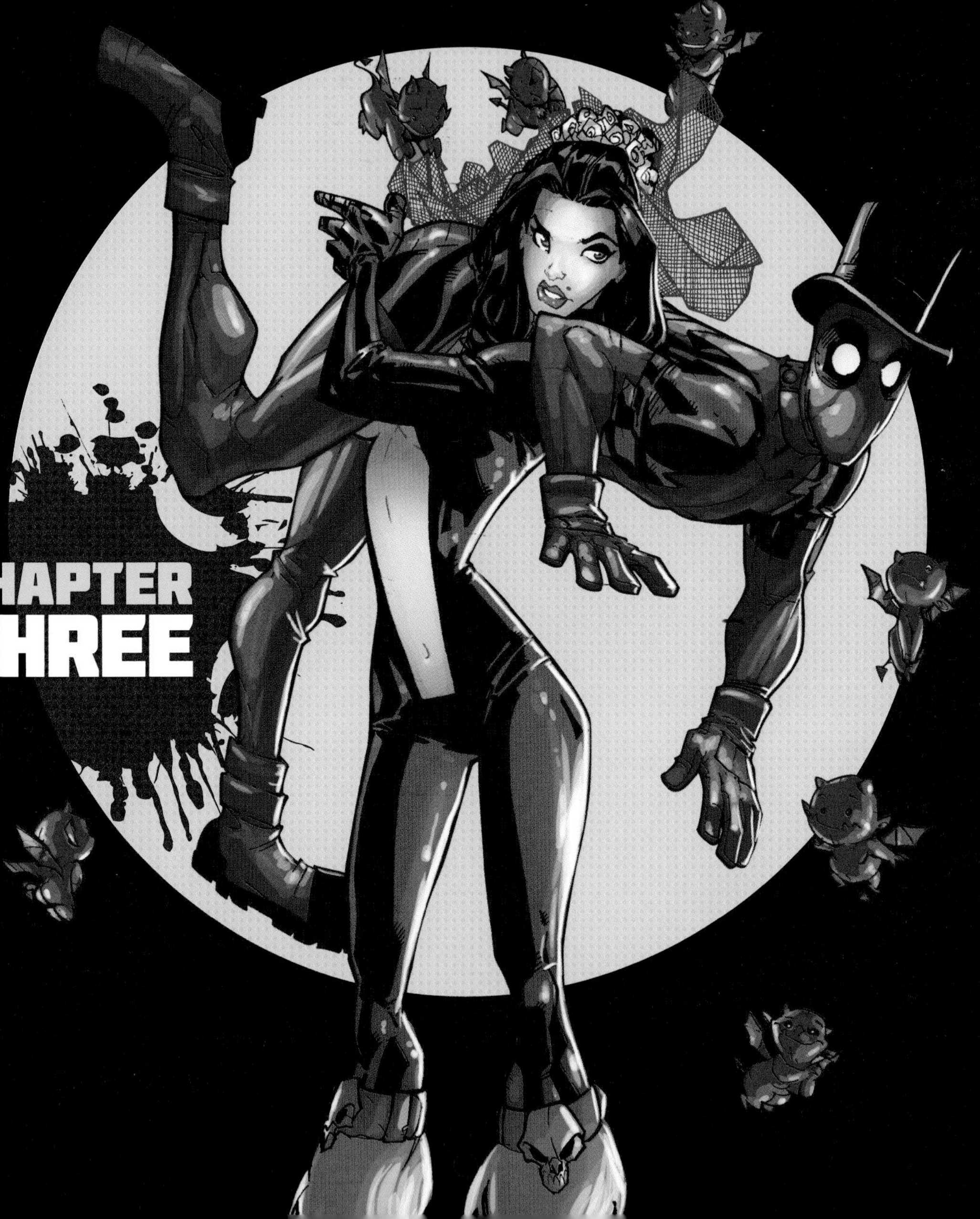

DEADPOOL'S RULES ON DATING

(OR AS I LIKE TO CALL IT: HOW TO GAIN THEIR HEART WITHOUT USING A KATANA!)

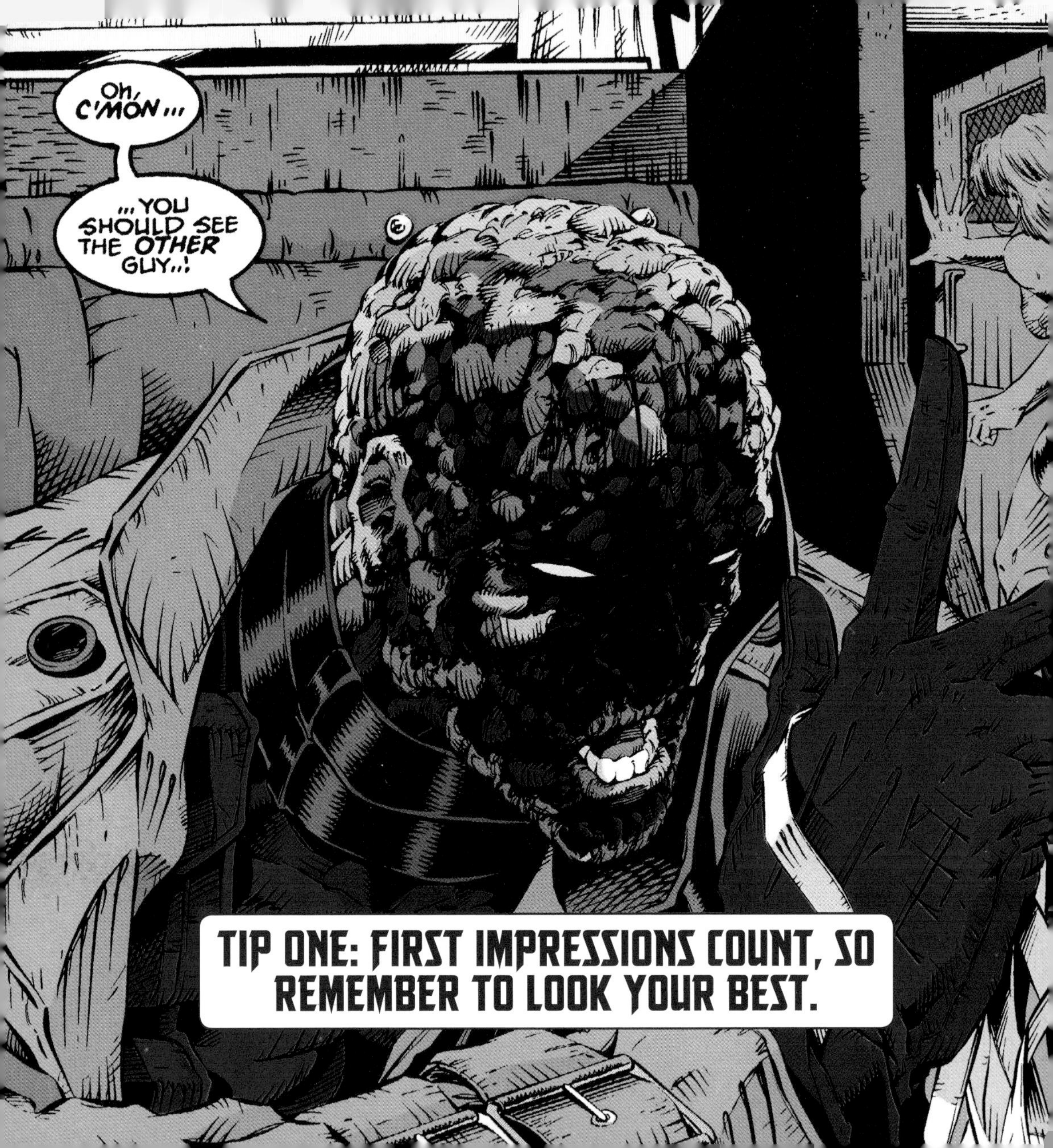
Oh, C'MON...
...YOU SHOULD SEE THE OTHER GUY...!
TIP ONE: FIRST IMPRESSIONS COUNT, SO REMEMBER TO LOOK YOUR BEST.

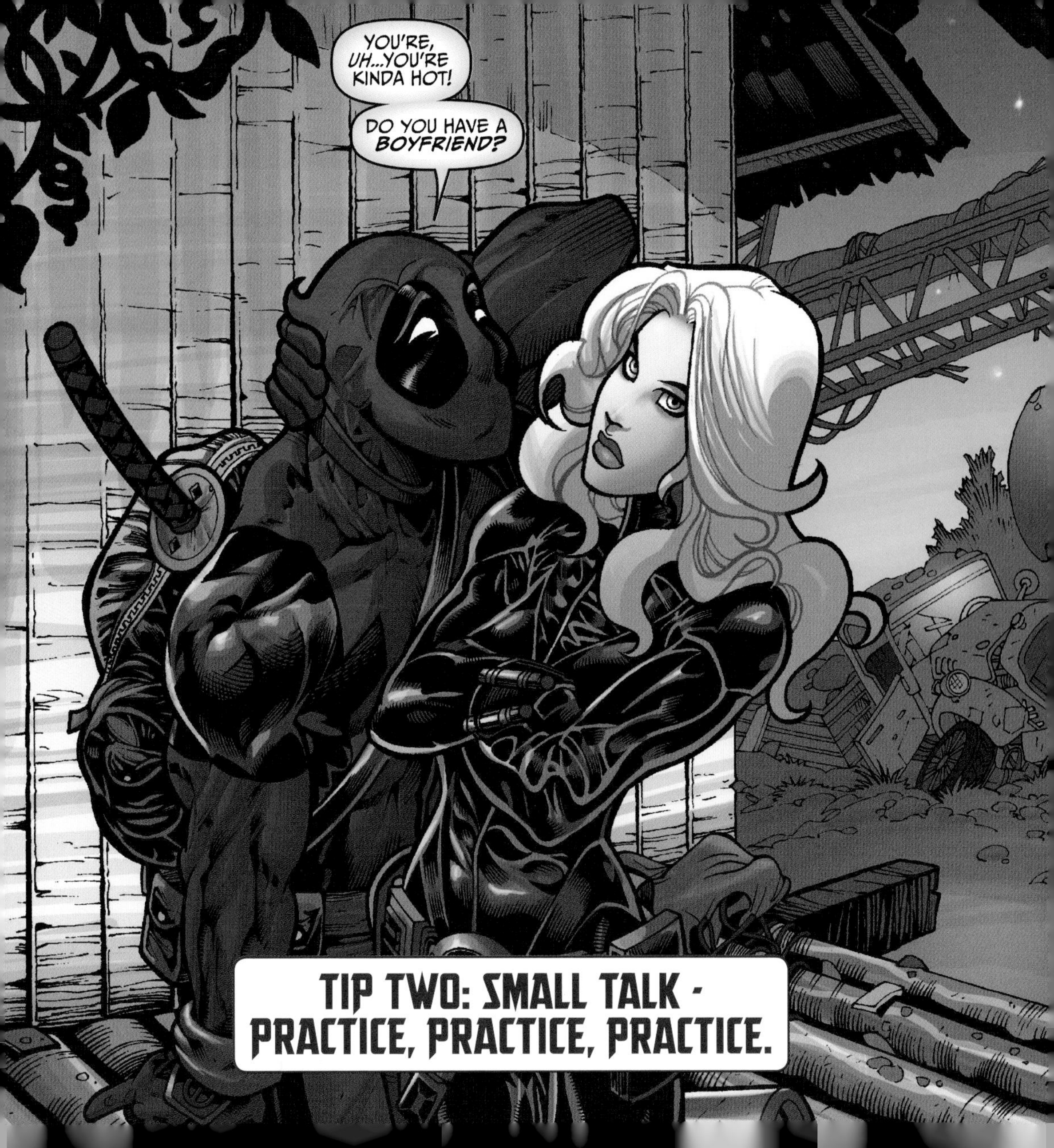
YOU'RE, UH...YOU'RE KINDA HOT!
DO YOU HAVE A BOYFRIEND?
TIP TWO: SMALL TALK - PRACTICE, PRACTICE, PRACTICE.

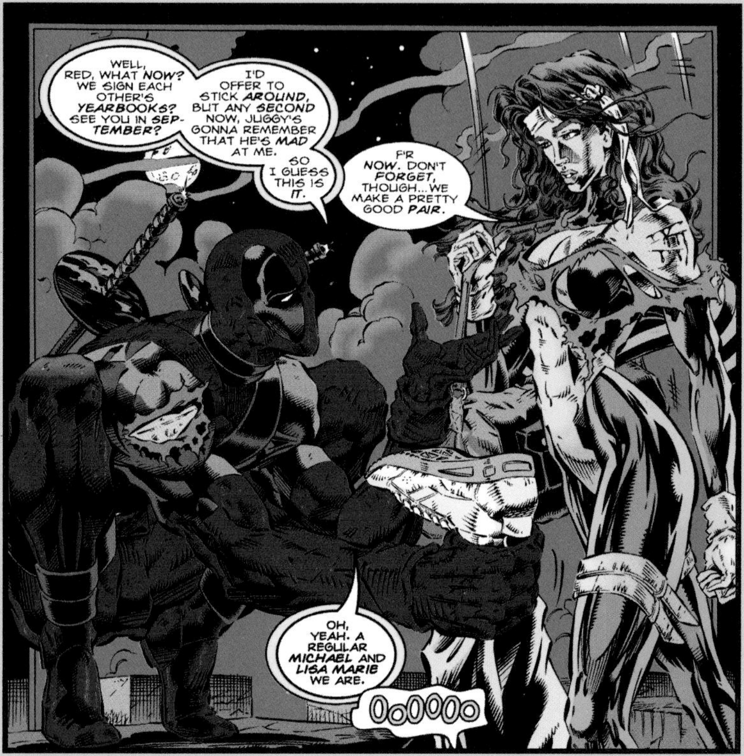
WELL, RED, WHAT NOW? WE SIGN EACH OTHER'S YEARBOOKS? SEE YOU IN SEP-TEMBER?
I'D OFFER TO STICK AROUND, BUT ANY SECOND NOW, JUGGY'S GONNA REMEMBER THAT HE'S MAD AT ME.
SO I GUESS THIS IS IT.
F'R NOW. DON'T FORGET, THOUGH... WE MAKE A PRETTY GOOD PAIR.
OH, YEAH. A REGULAR MICHAEL AND LISA MARIE WE ARE.
OoOOOo

TIP THREE: RESPECT BOUNDARIES.

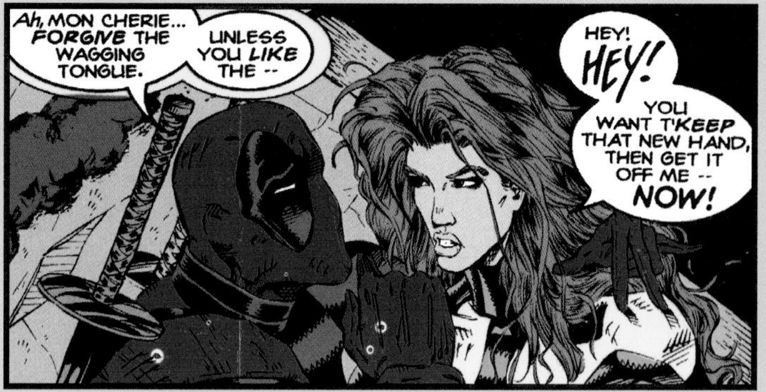
Ah, MON CHERIE... FORGIVE THE WAGGING TONGUE.
UNLESS YOU LIKE THE --
HEY! HEY!
YOU WANT T'KEEP THAT NEW HAND, THEN GET IT OFF ME -- NOW!

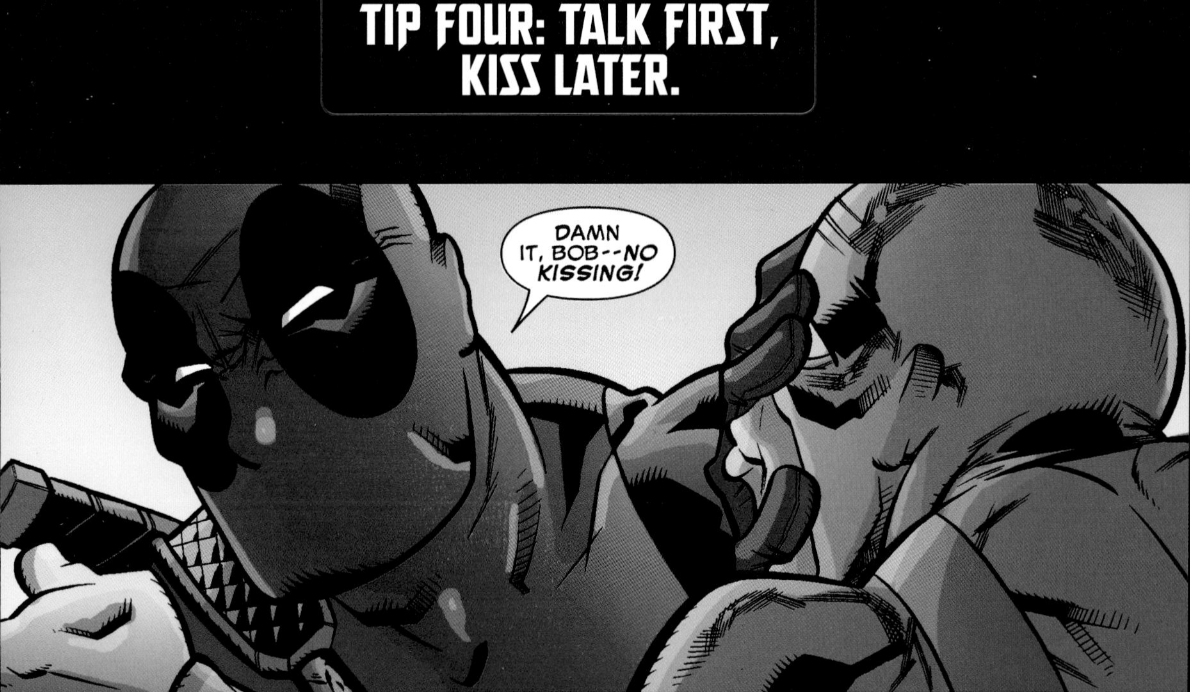
TIP FOUR: TALK FIRST, KISS LATER.
DAMN IT, BOB--NO KISSING!

PROMISES MEAN EVERYTHING TO ME, WADE...I AM A PROMISE.
A PROMISE THAT IS KEPT BY EVERYONE BUT YOU.
BABY, I'M... I'M GONNA CHANGE. FOR YOU. SO WE CAN BE TOGETHER.
I GOT A PLAN.
IT'S REALLY BIG, THOUGH...
...AN' IT'S GONNA BE REALLY $#%&#% HARD TO PULL OFF.
THAT'S WHAT SHE SAID.

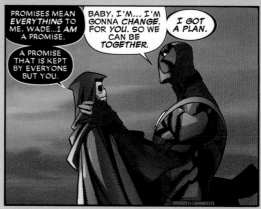

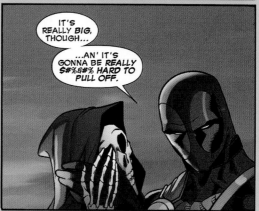

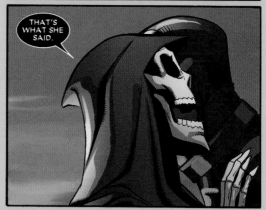

TIP FIVE: A SENSE OF HUMOR IS EVERYTHING.

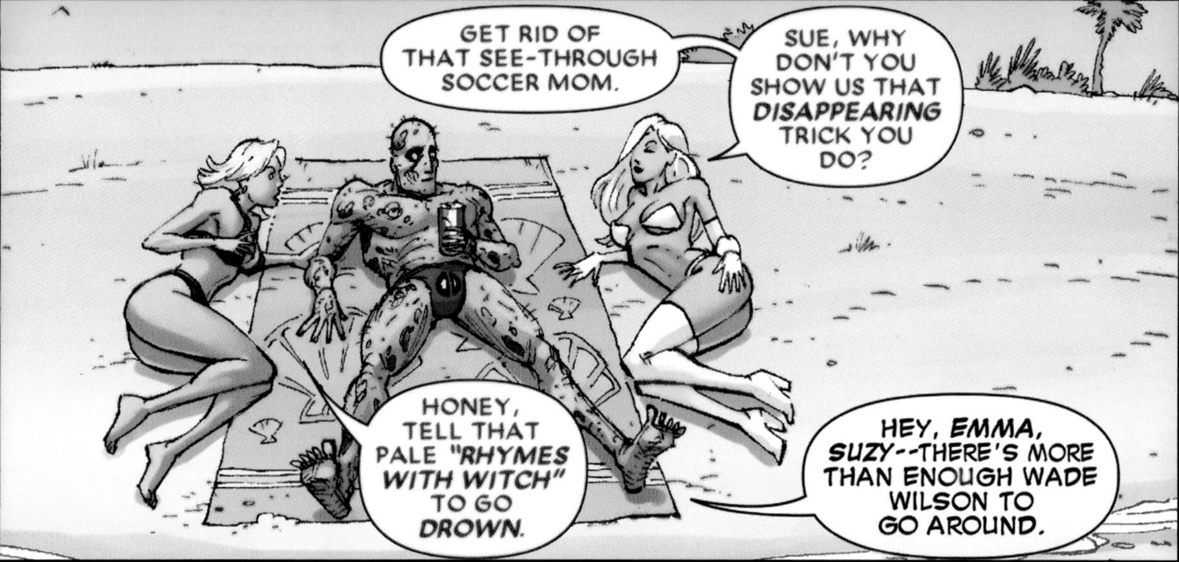
GET RID OF THAT SEE-THROUGH SOCCER MOM.
SUE, WHY DON'T YOU SHOW US THAT *DISAPPEARING* TRICK YOU DO?
HONEY, TELL THAT PALE *"RHYMES WITH WITCH"* TO GO *DROWN.*
HEY, *EMMA, SUZY*--THERE'S MORE THAN ENOUGH WADE WILSON TO GO AROUND.

TIP SIX: DOUBLE DATE MEANS FOUR, NOT THREE.

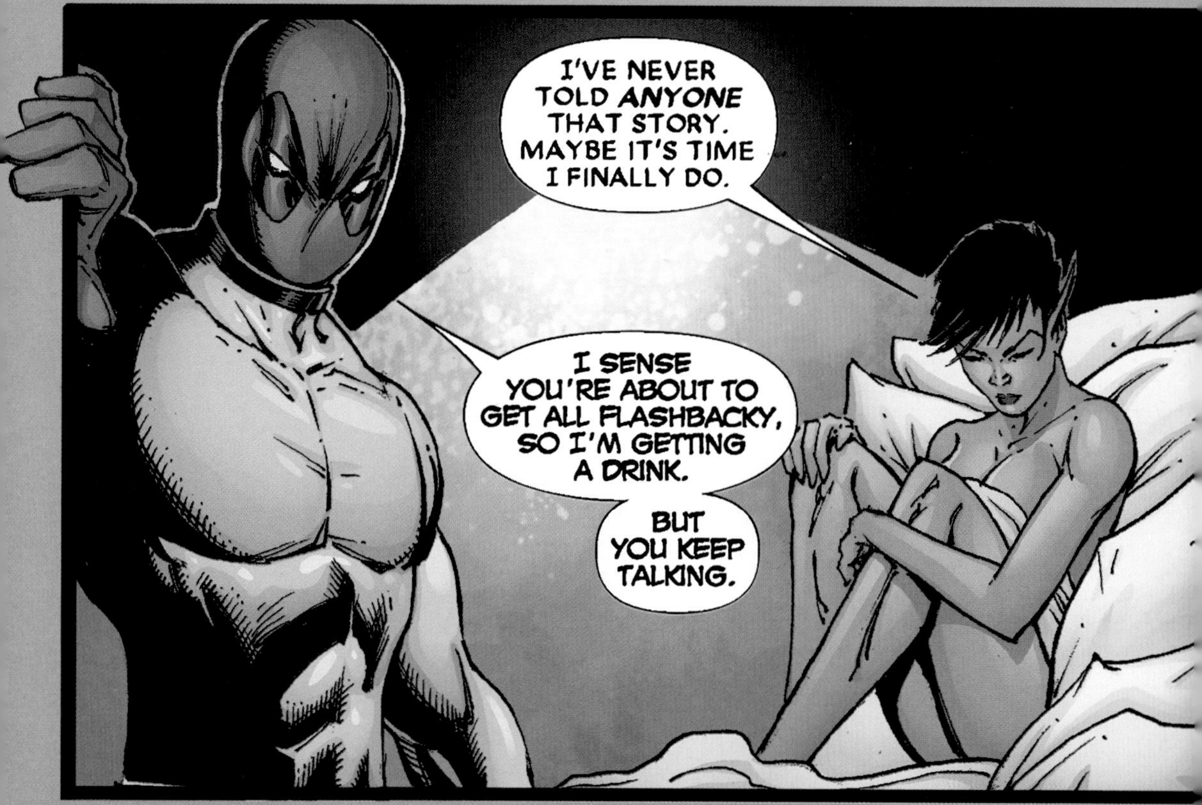
I'VE NEVER TOLD ANYONE THAT STORY. MAYBE IT'S TIME I FINALLY DO.
I SENSE YOU'RE ABOUT TO GET ALL FLASHBACKY, SO I'M GETTING A DRINK.
BUT YOU KEEP TALKING.

TIP SEVEN: LISTENING IS KEY - OR JUST NODDING OCCASSIONALLY.

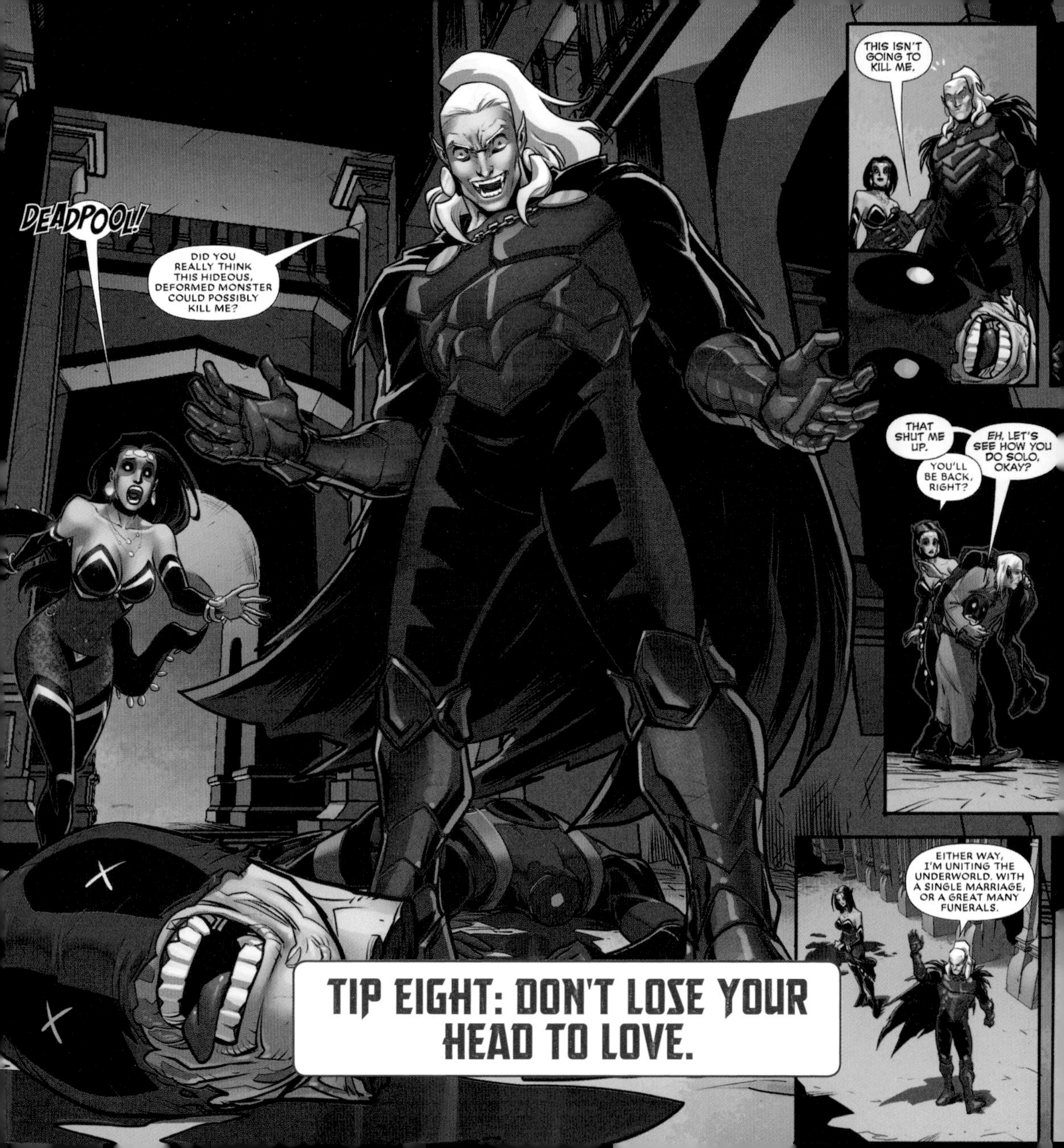
DEADPOOL!!
DID YOU REALLY THINK THIS HIDEOUS, DEFORMED MONSTER COULD POSSIBLY KILL ME?
THIS ISN'T GOING TO KILL ME.
THAT SHUT ME UP.
YOU'LL BE BACK, RIGHT?
EH, LET'S SEE HOW YOU DO SOLO, OKAY?
EITHER WAY, I'M UNITING THE UNDERWORLD. WITH A SINGLE MARRIAGE, OR A GREAT MANY FUNERALS.
TIP EIGHT: DON'T LOSE YOUR HEAD TO LOVE.

CHAPTER FOUR

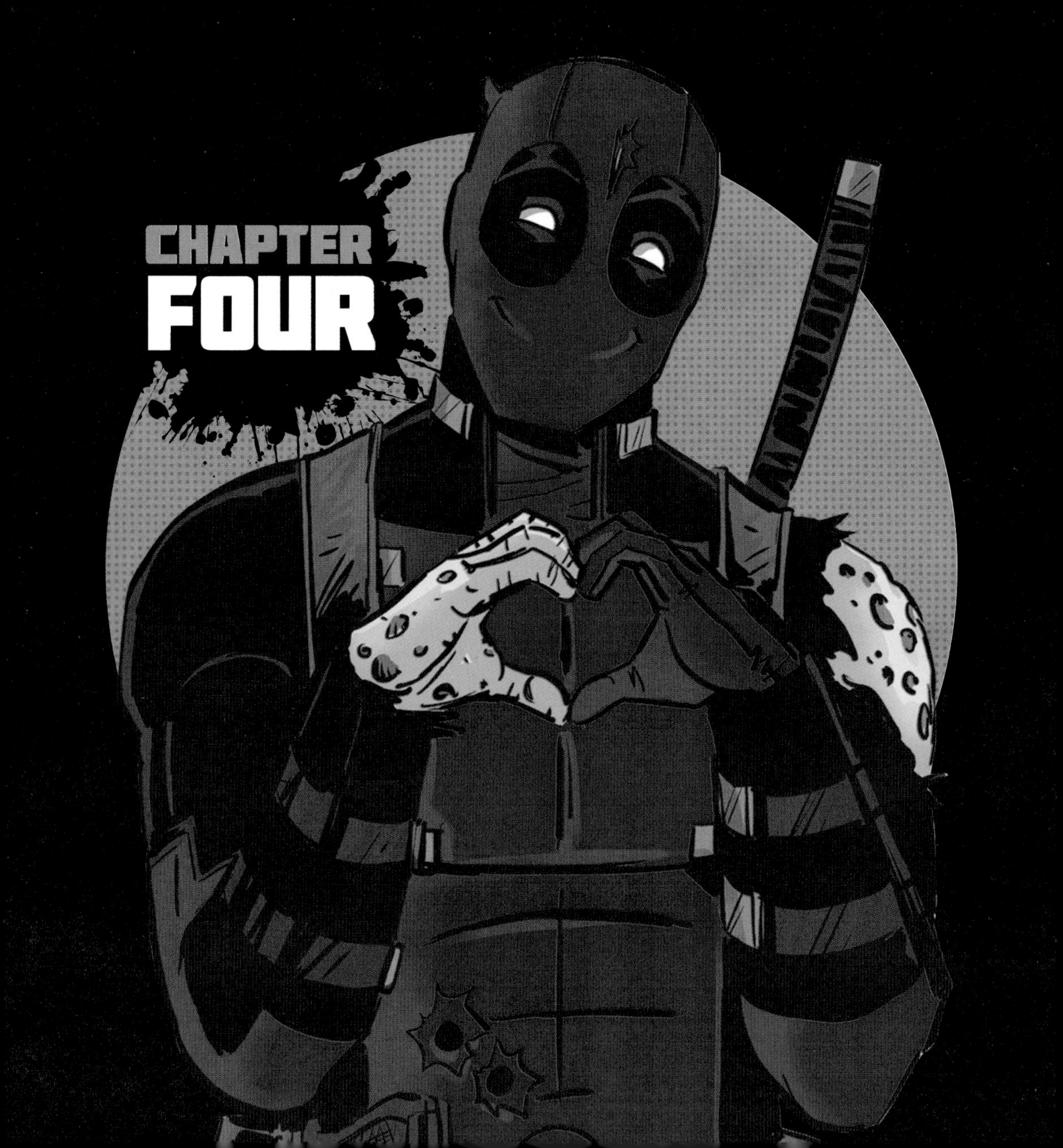

DEADPOOL LOVES...

EVERYBODY LOOKS AT ME AND THNKS I'M JUST ANOTHER HEARTLESS MERC. IT'S NOT ENOUGH I OCCASIONALLY MAKE THE HEROIC CHOICE, I GOTTA HAVE A HEART TOO! SO LET ME SHARE WITH YOU A FEW OF MY NOT-SO-SECRET PASSIONS IN LIFE.

"TIME TO MAKE THE
CHIMICHANGAS!"

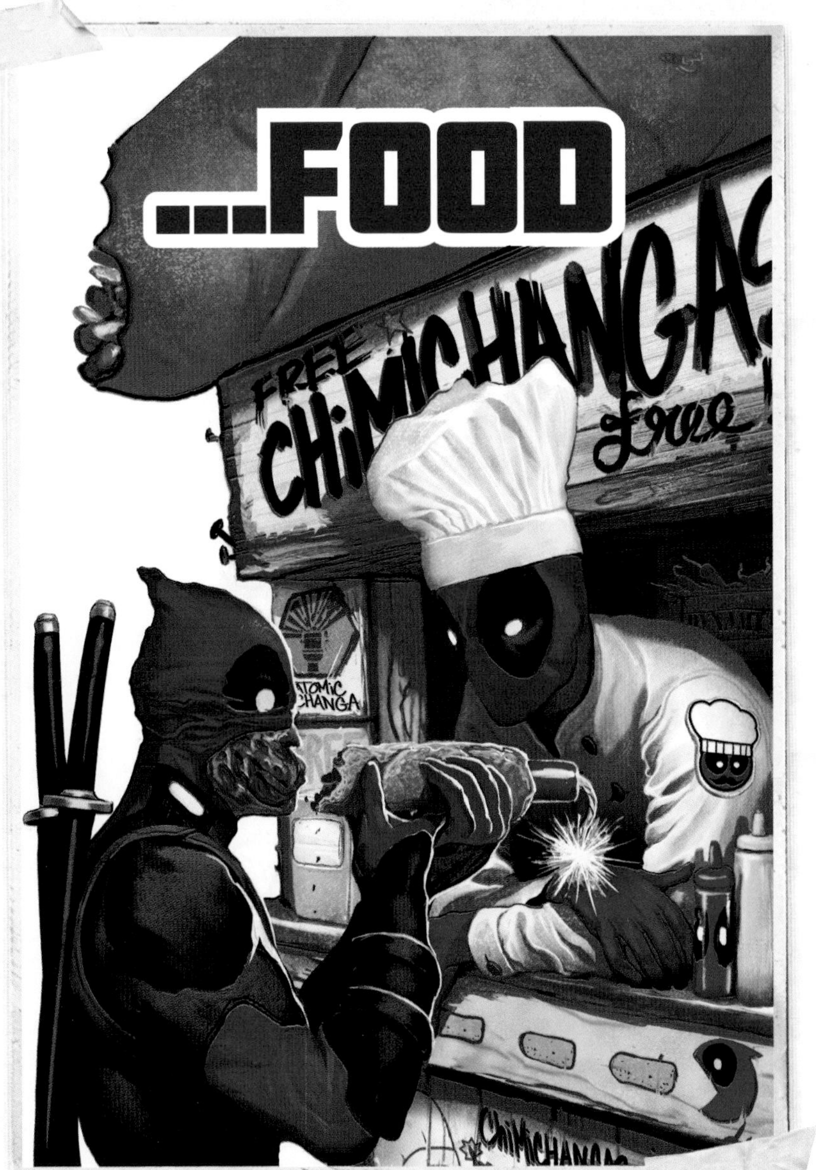
...FOOD
FREE
CHiMiCHANGA
Free
TOMiC
CHANGA

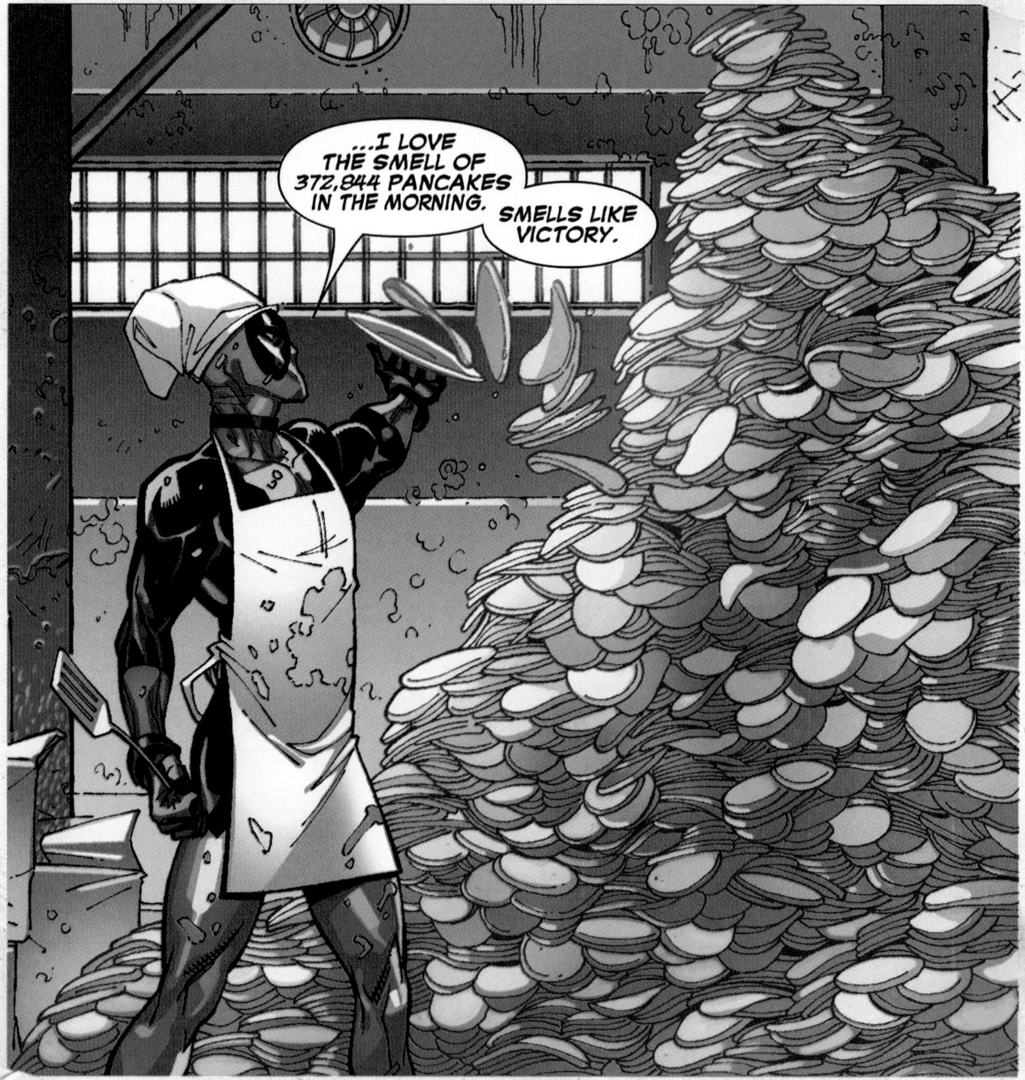
...I LOVE THE SMELL OF 372,844 PANCAKES IN THE MORNING.
SMELLS LIKE VICTORY.

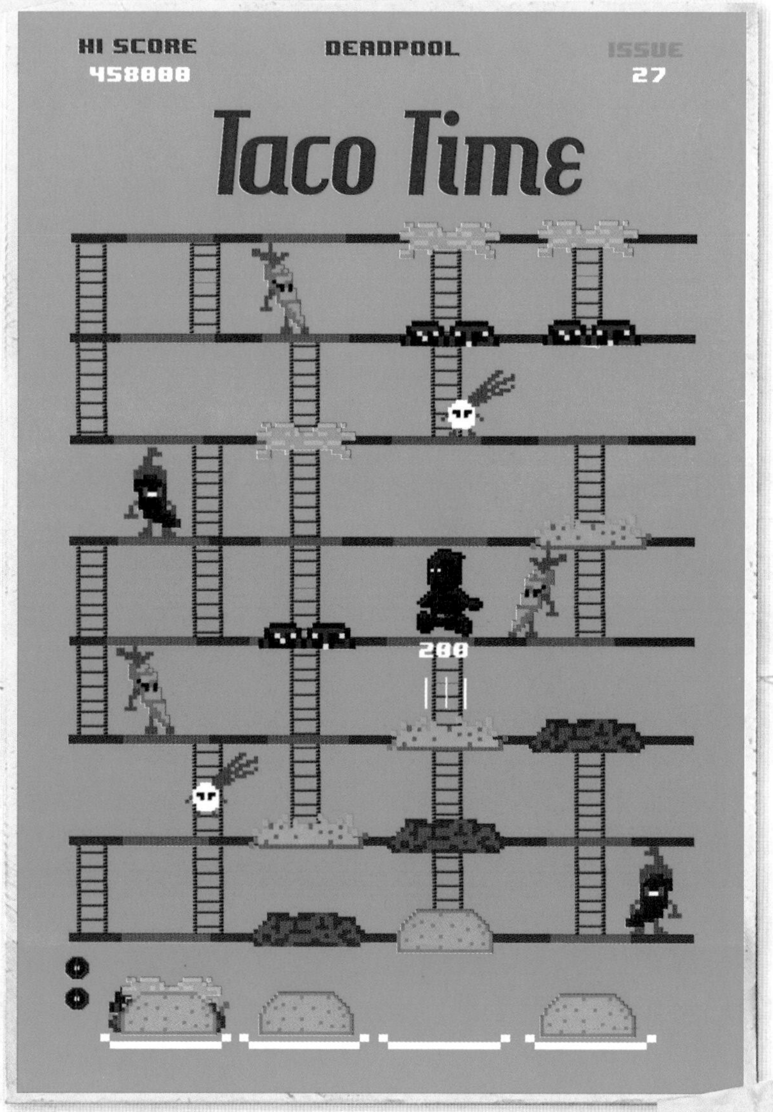
HI SCORE
458000
DEADPOOL
ISSUE
27
Taco Time
200

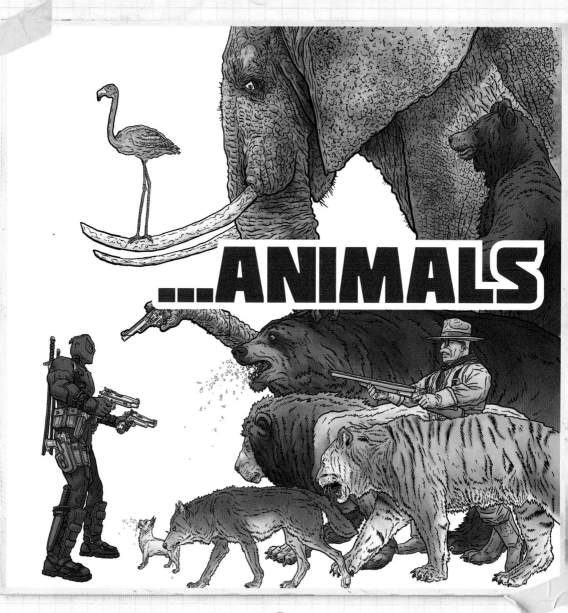

...ANIMALS

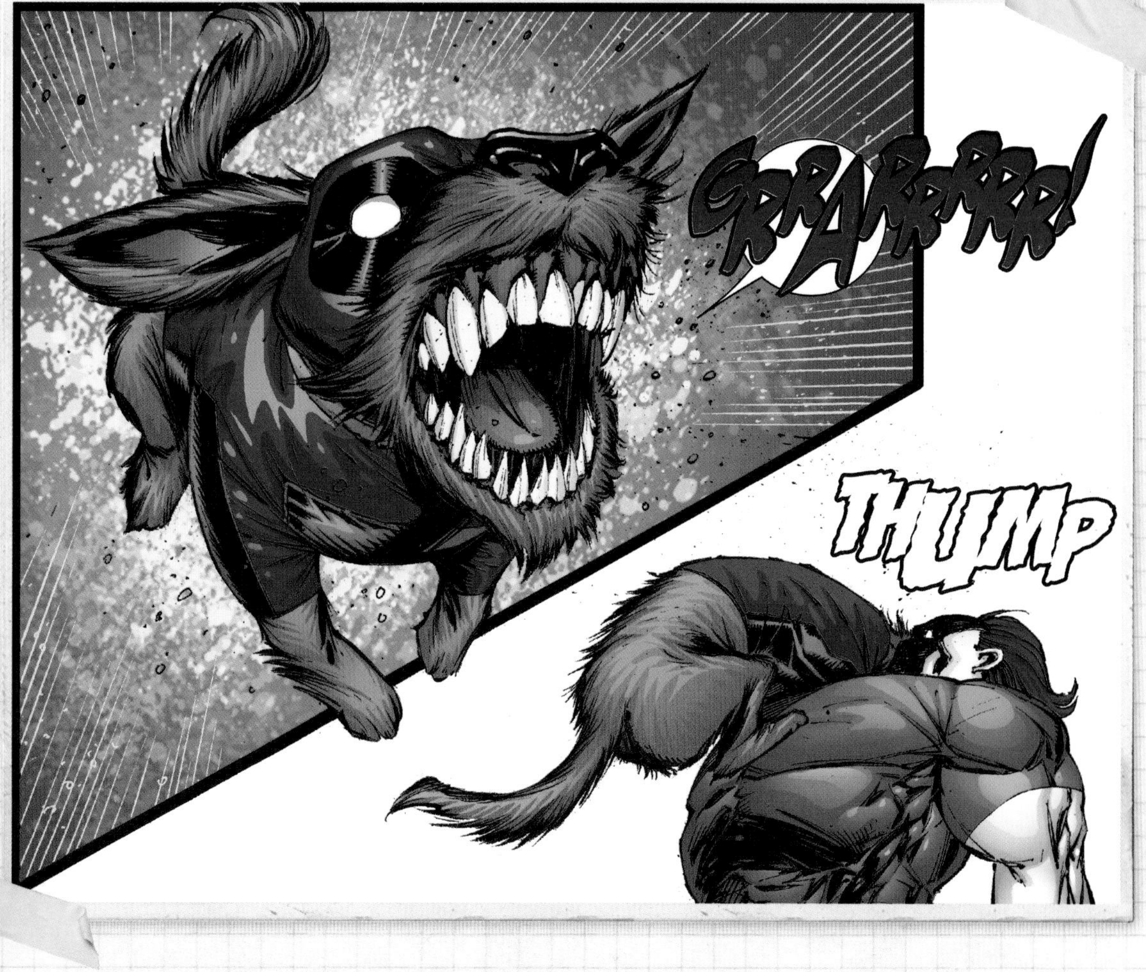
GRRARRRRRR!
THUMP

"THE DOG ATE MY AMMUNITION!"

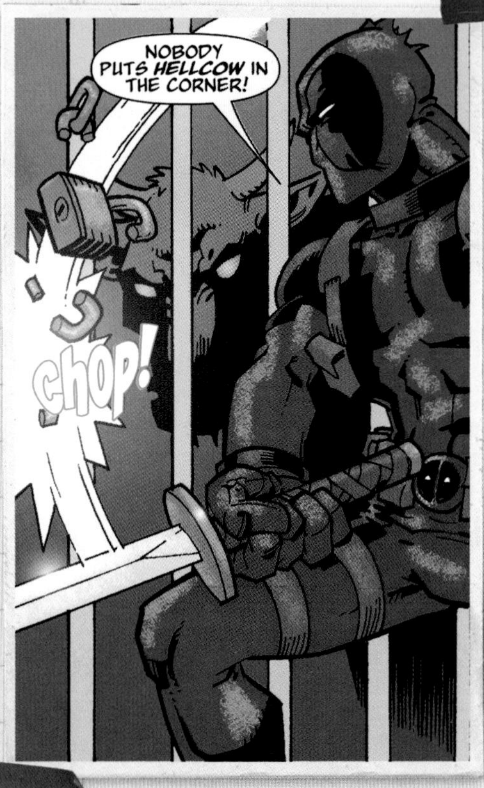
NOBODY PUTS HELLCOW IN THE CORNER!
CHOP!

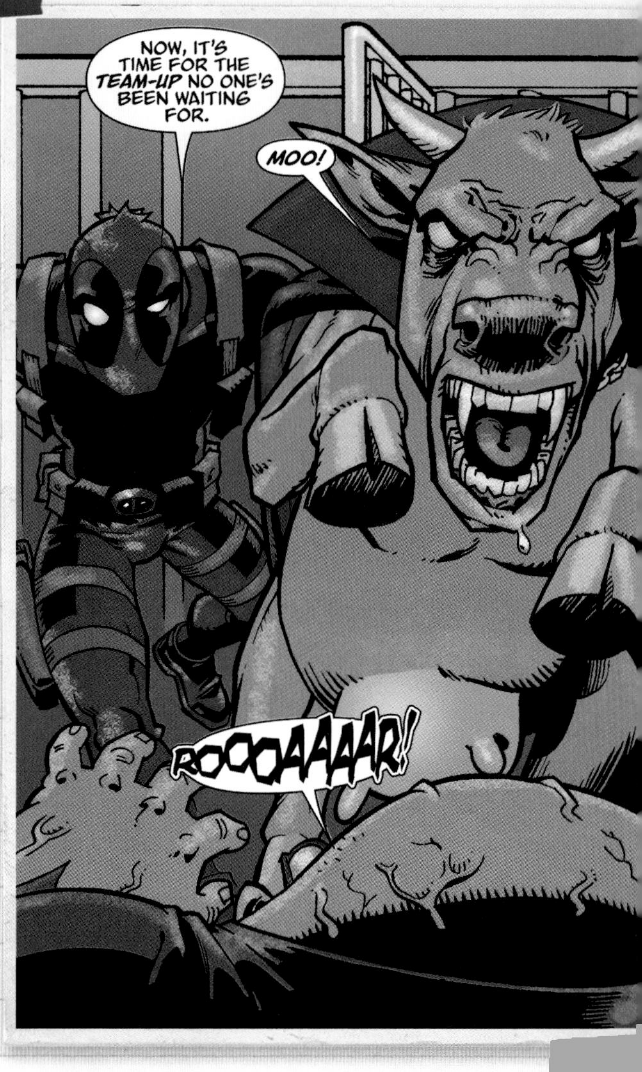
NOW, IT'S TIME FOR THE TEAM-UP NO ONE'S BEEN WAITING FOR.
MOO!
ROOOAAAAR!

FREEING COWS FROM CAGES - I SHOULD JOIN PETA!

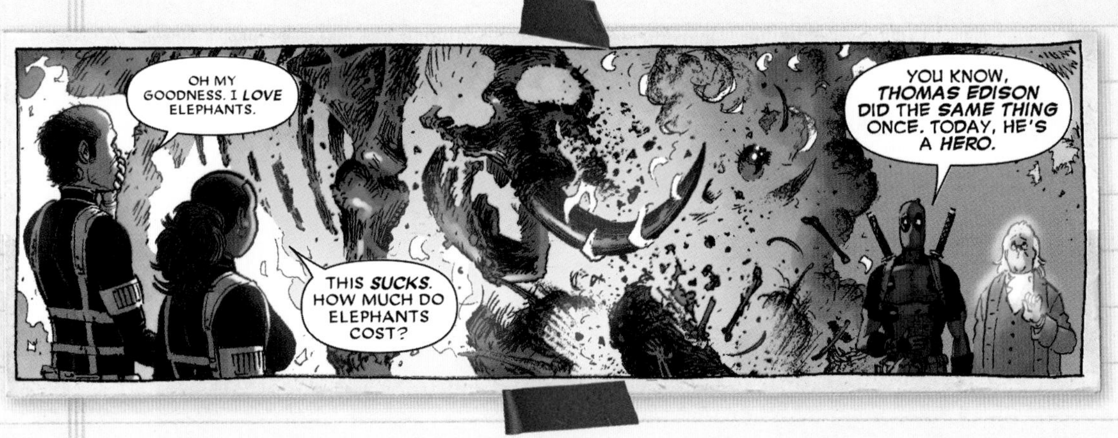
OH MY GOODNESS. I LOVE ELEPHANTS.
THIS SUCKS. HOW MUCH DO ELEPHANTS COST?
YOU KNOW, THOMAS EDISON DID THE SAME THING ONCE. TODAY, HE'S A HERO.

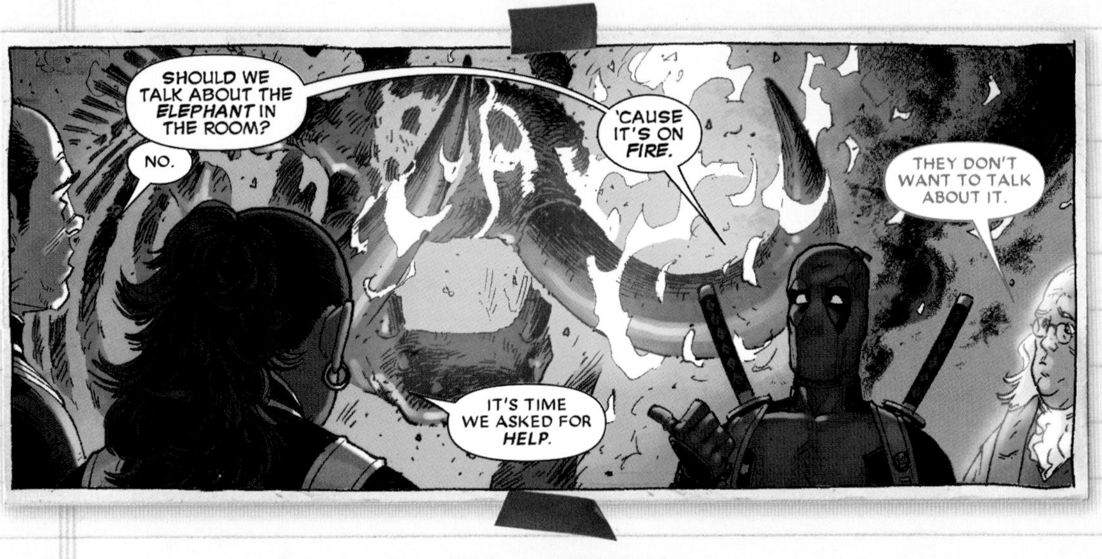
SHOULD WE TALK ABOUT THE ELEPHANT IN THE ROOM?
'CAUSE IT'S ON FIRE.
NO.
THEY DON'T WANT TO TALK ABOUT IT.
IT'S TIME WE ASKED FOR HELP.

MMM... ROAST ELEPHANTS

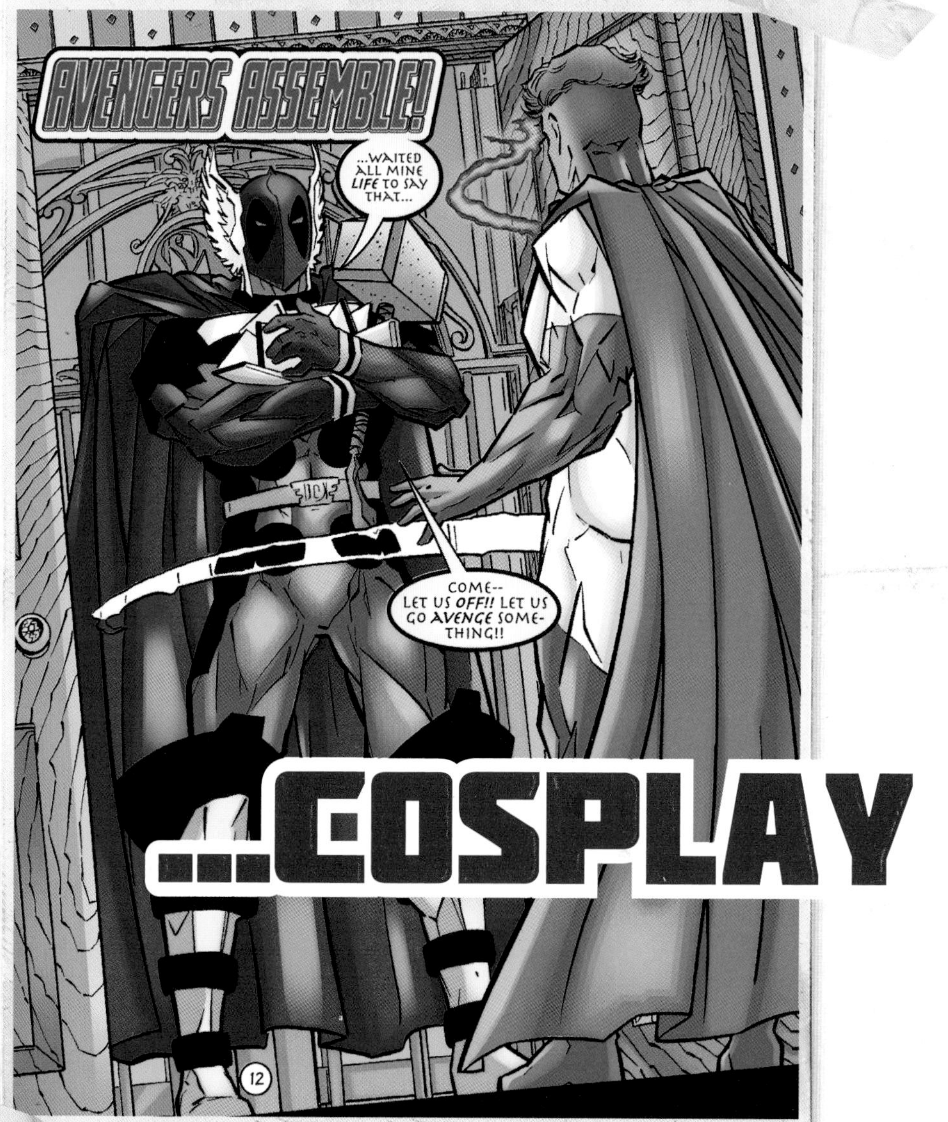
AVENGERS ASSEMBLE!
...WAITED ALL MINE LIFE TO SAY THAT...
COME-- LET US OFF!! LET US GO AVENGE SOME-THING!!
12
...COSPLAY

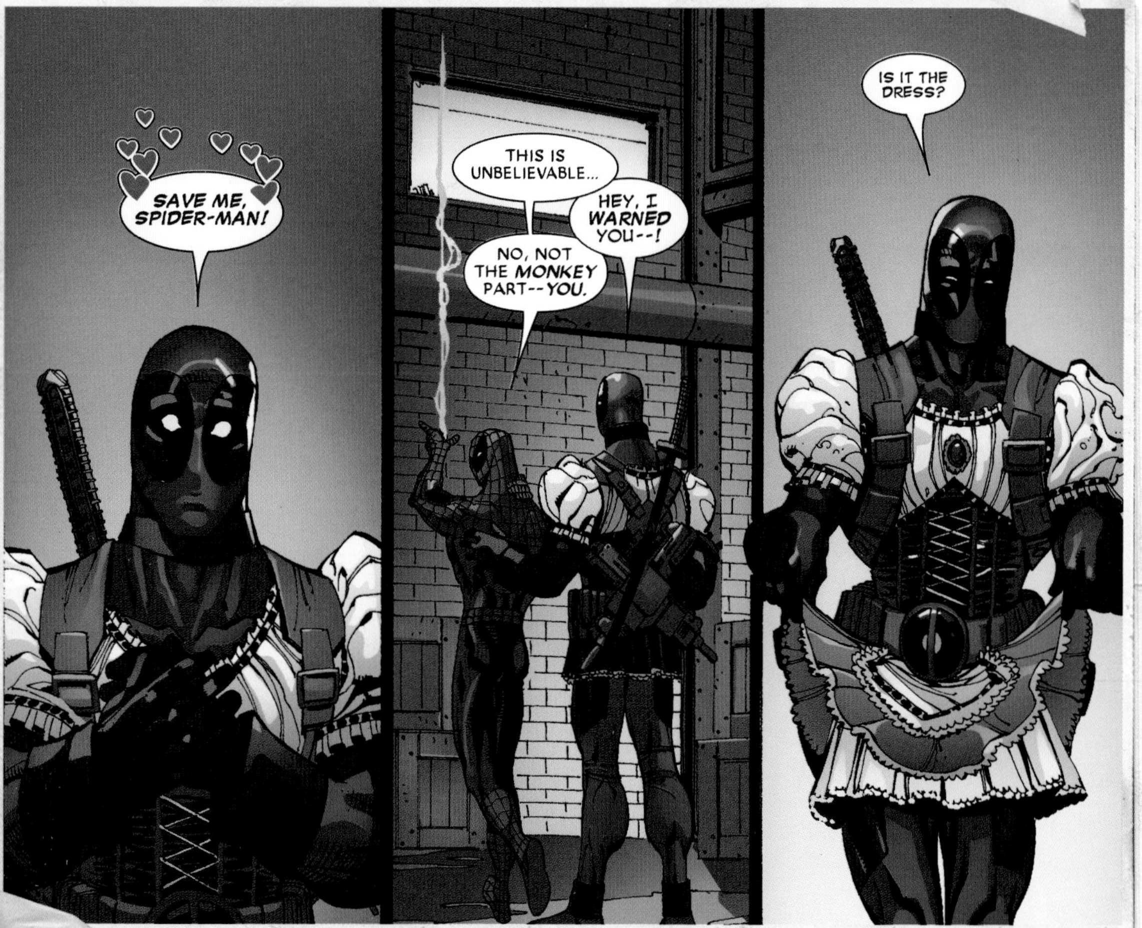
SAVE ME, SPIDER-MAN!
THIS IS UNBELIEVABLE...
HEY, I WARNED YOU--!
NO, NOT THE MONKEY PART--YOU.
IS IT THE DRESS?

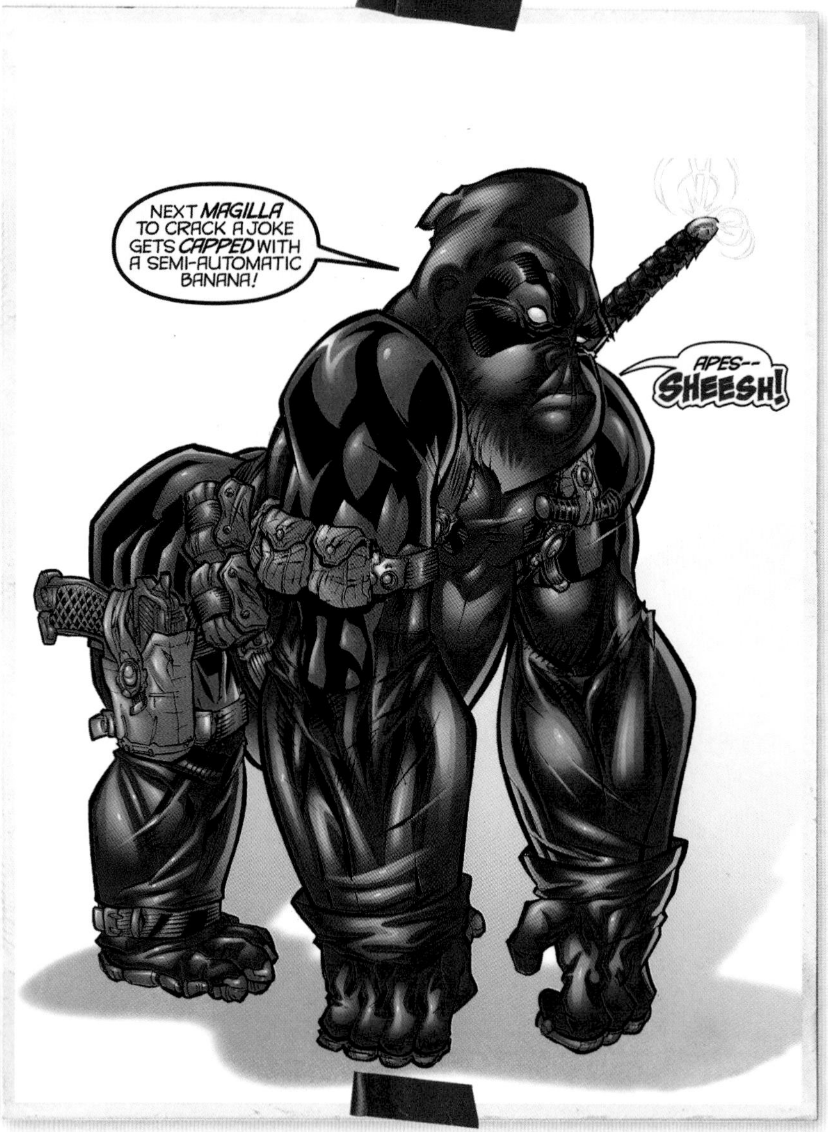
NEXT MAGILLA TO CRACK A JOKE GETS CAPPED WITH A SEMI-AUTOMATIC BANANA!
APES-- SHEESH!

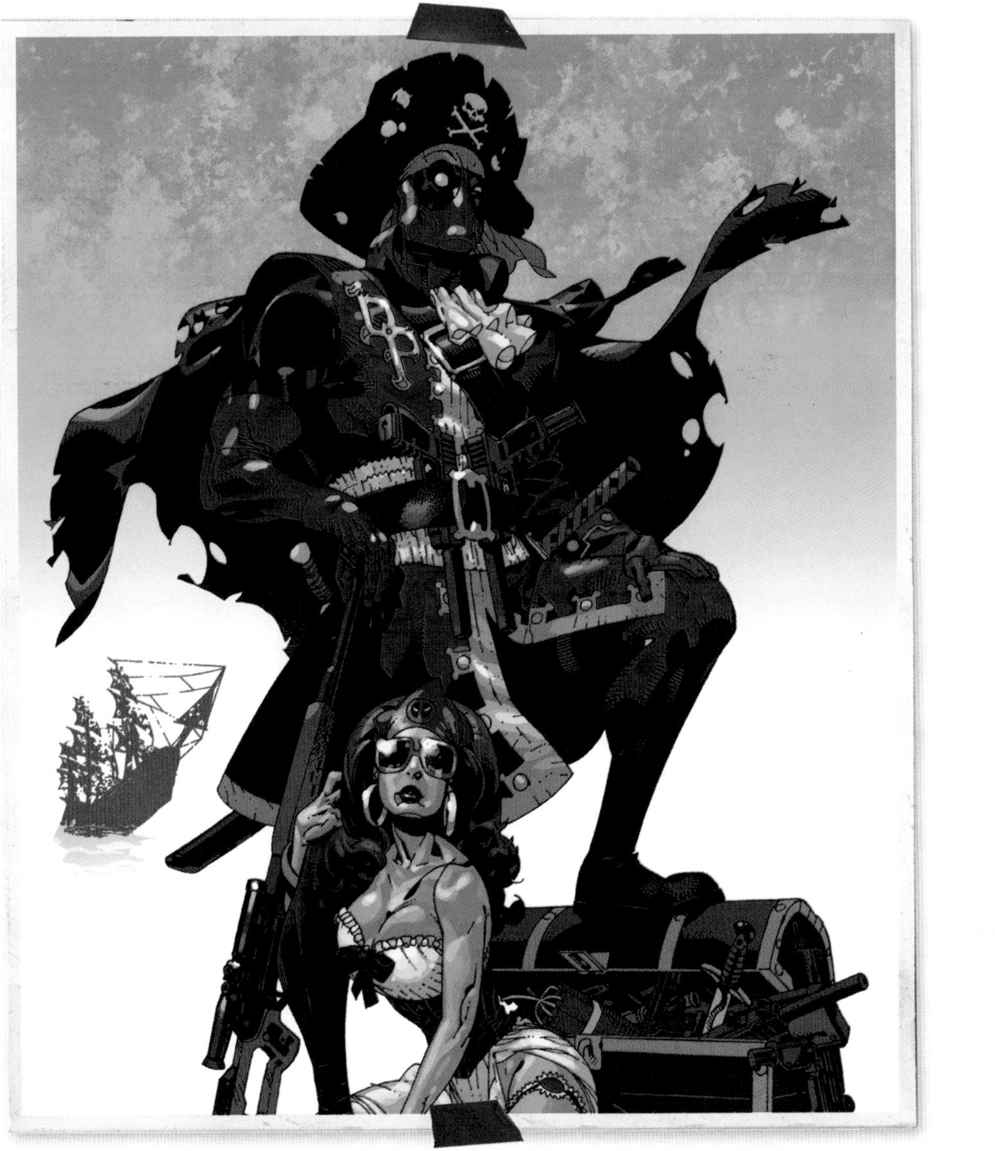

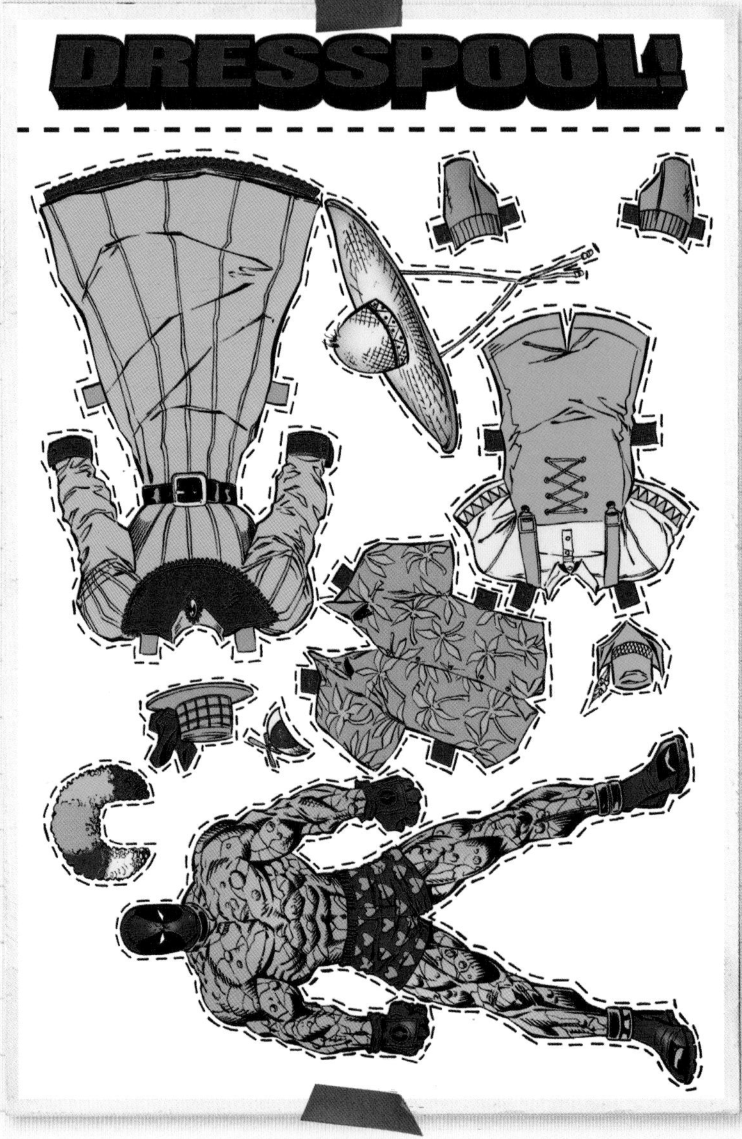
DRESSPOOL!

hey, Kids! get some scissors
and tape and dress deadpool
up the way you like him!

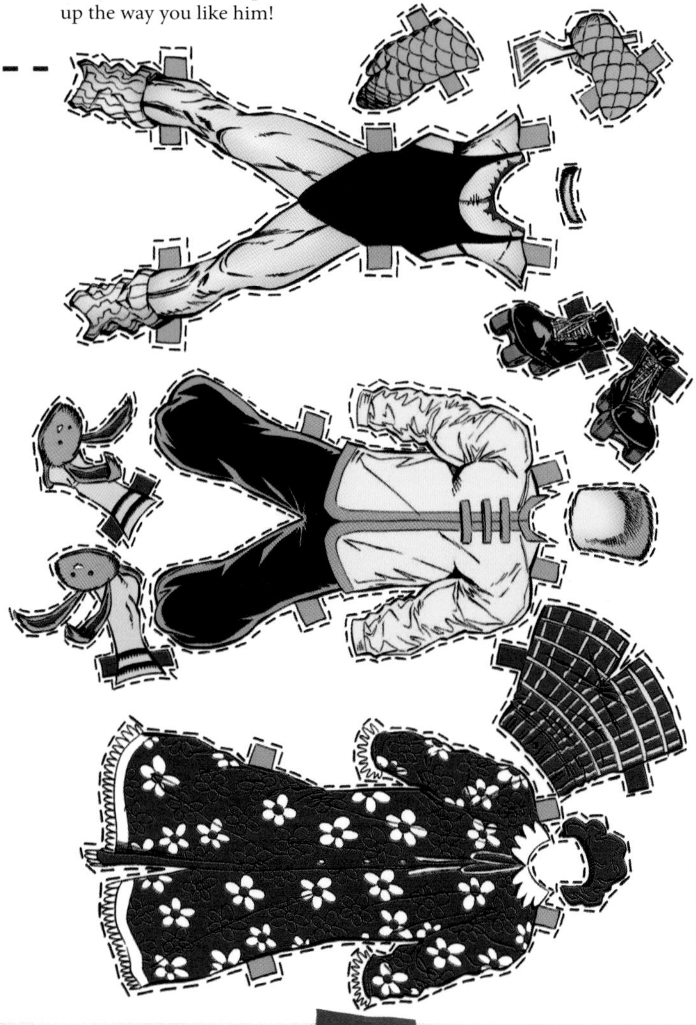

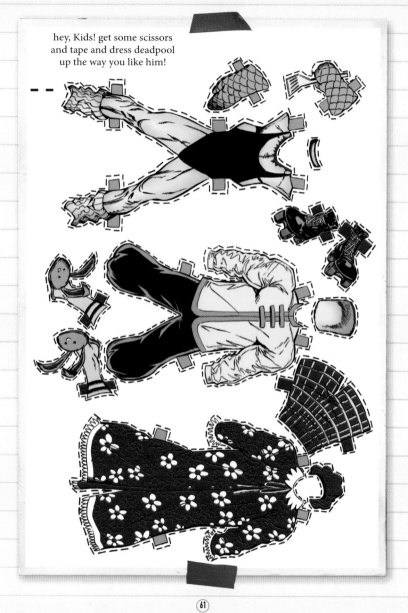

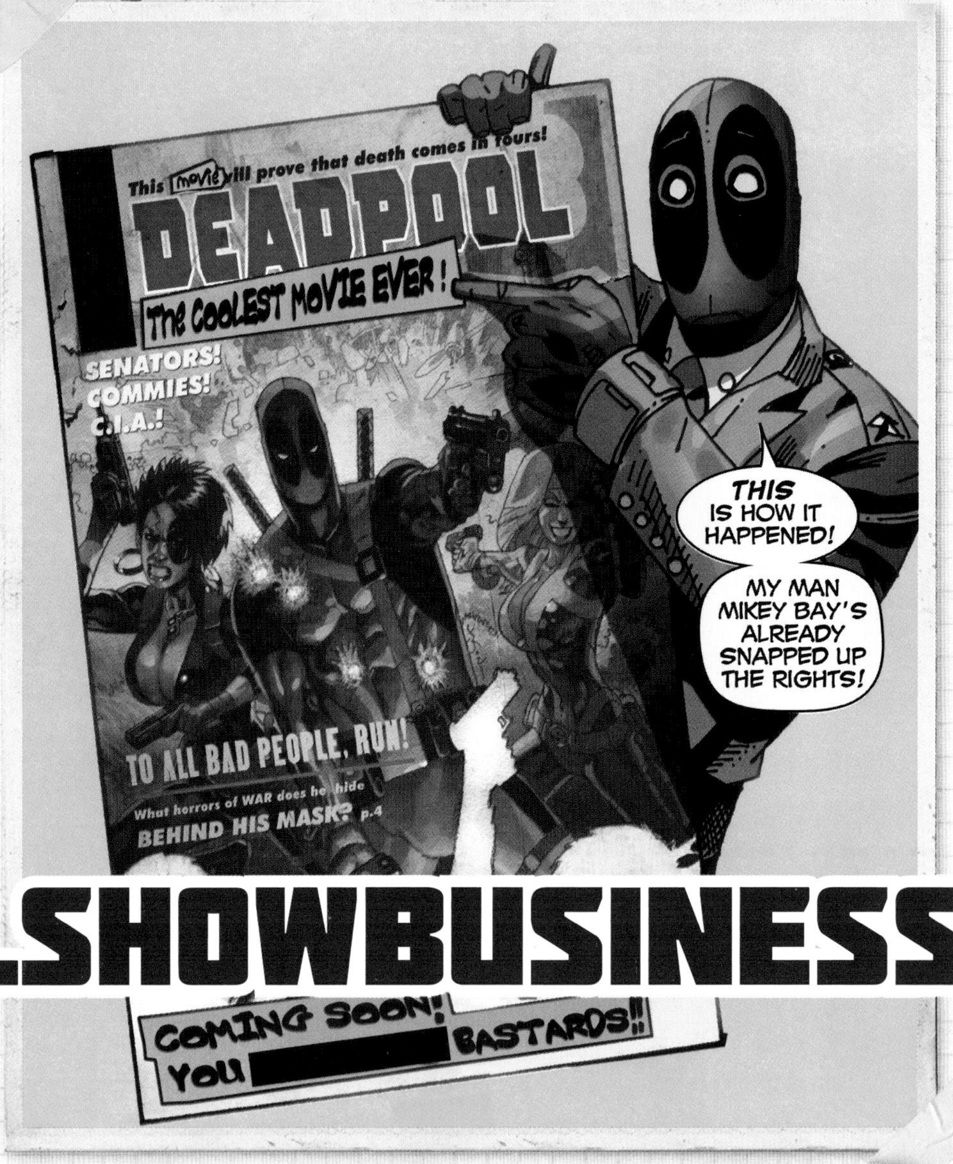
This movie will prove that death comes in fours!
DEADPOOL 3
The COOLEST MOVIE EVER!
SENATORS!
COMMIES!
C.I.A.!
TO ALL BAD PEOPLE, RUN!
What horrors of WAR does he hide
BEHIND HIS MASK? p.4
THIS IS HOW IT HAPPENED!
MY MAN MIKEY BAY'S ALREADY SNAPPED UP THE RIGHTS!
COMING SOON!
YOU [redacted] BASTARDS!!

...SHOWBUSINESS

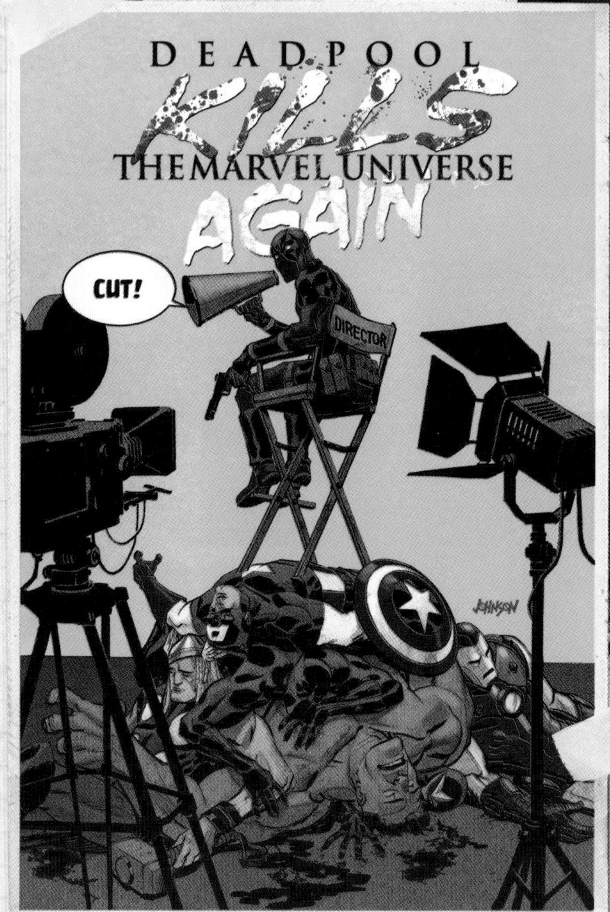
DEADPOOL
KILLS
THE MARVEL UNIVERSE
AGAIN
CUT!
DIRECTOR
JOHNSON

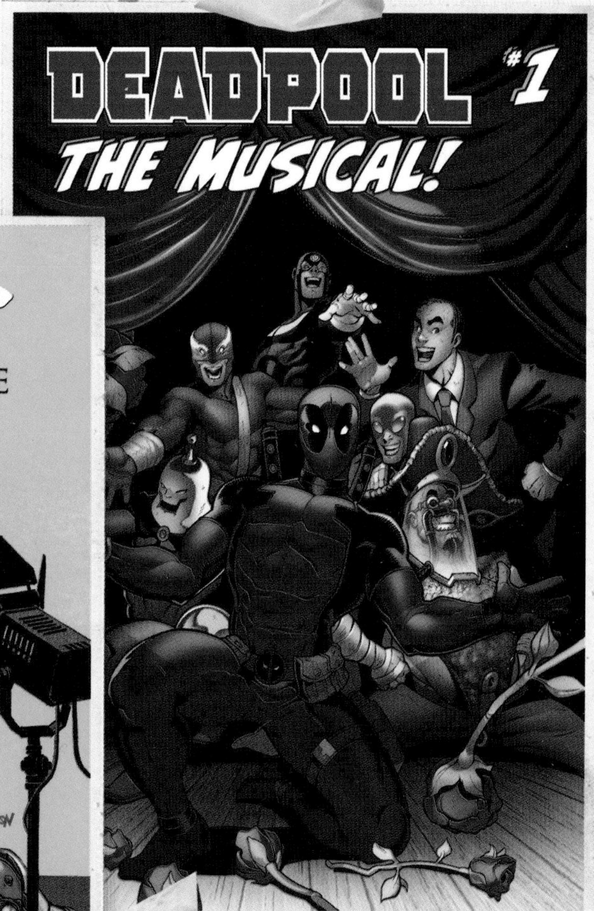
DEADPOOL #1
THE MUSICAL!

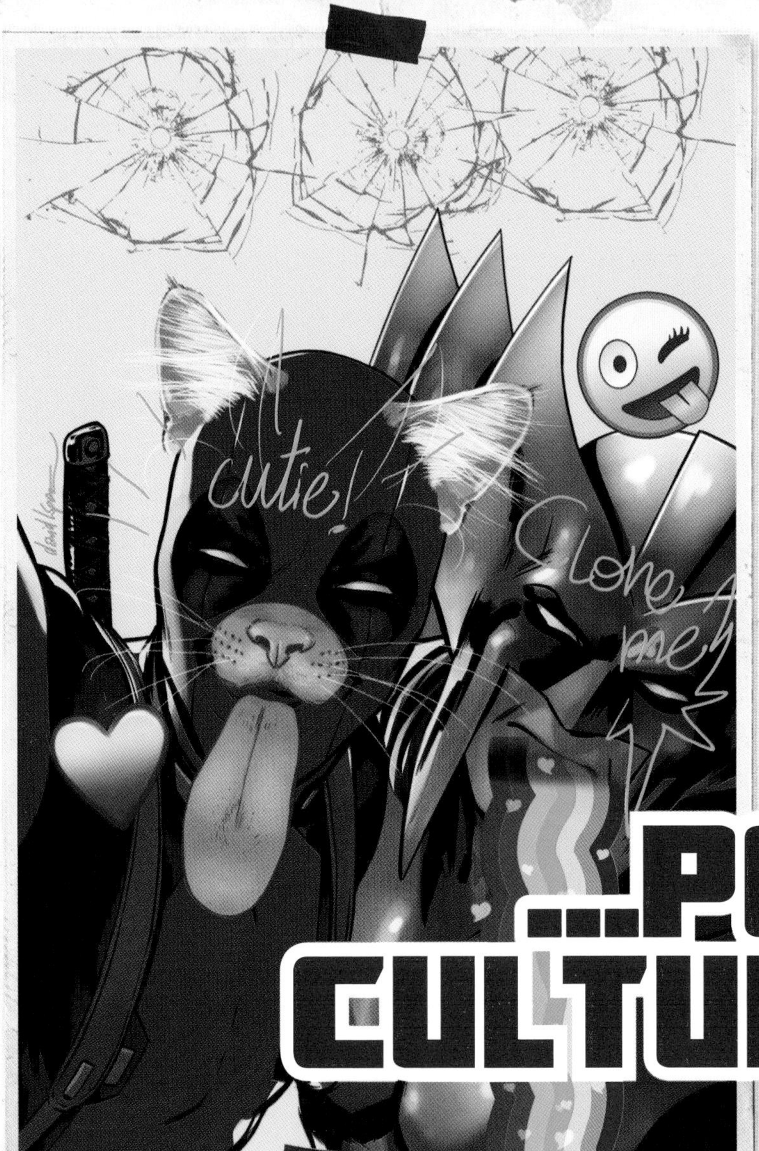
cutie!
Clone me

....POP CULTURE

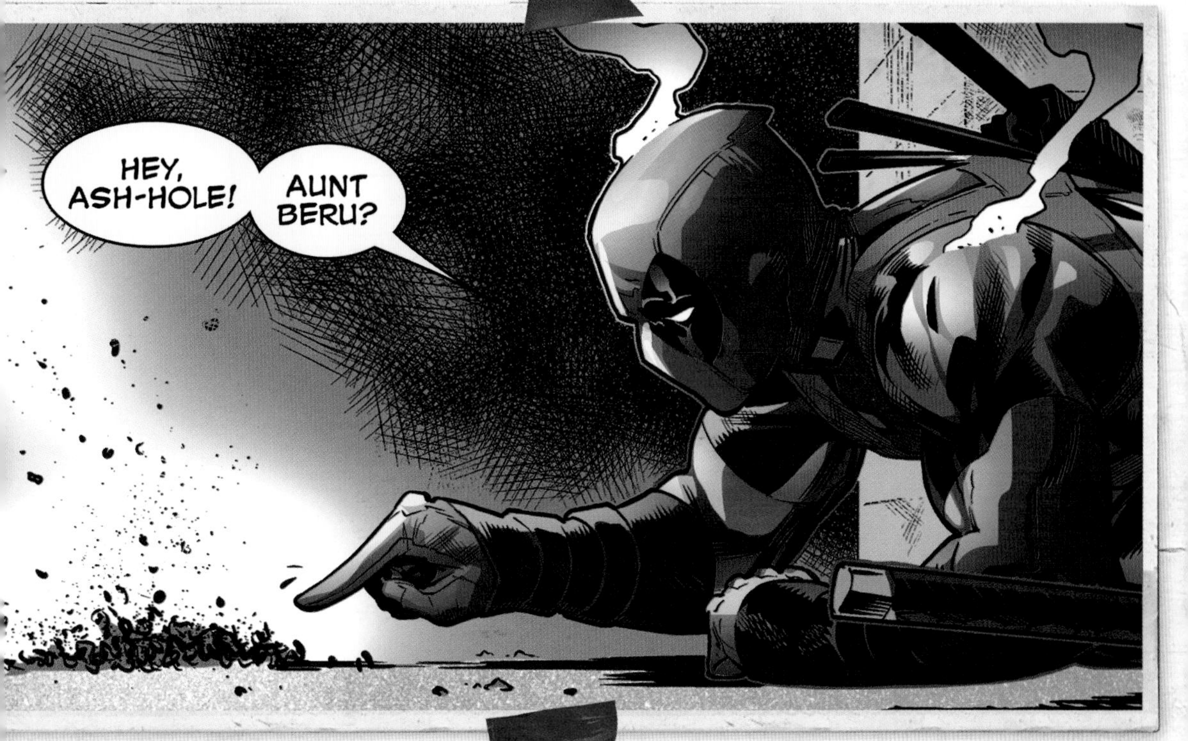
HEY, ASH-HOLE!
AUNT BERU?

"OBLIQUE, OBSCURE, IRREVERENT AND IRRELEVANT REFERENCES ARE MY TRADEMARK SHTICK!"

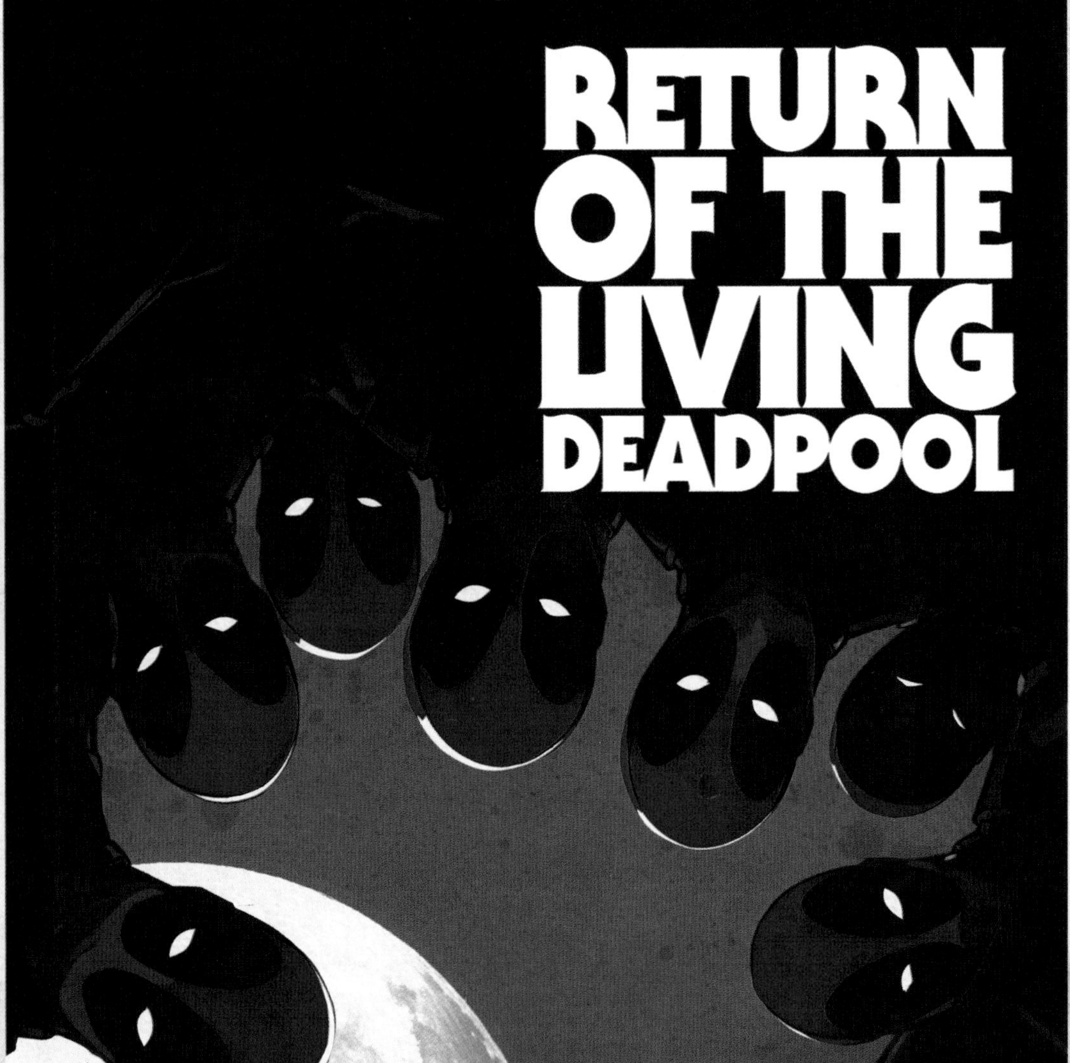
RETURN OF THE LIVING DEADPOOL

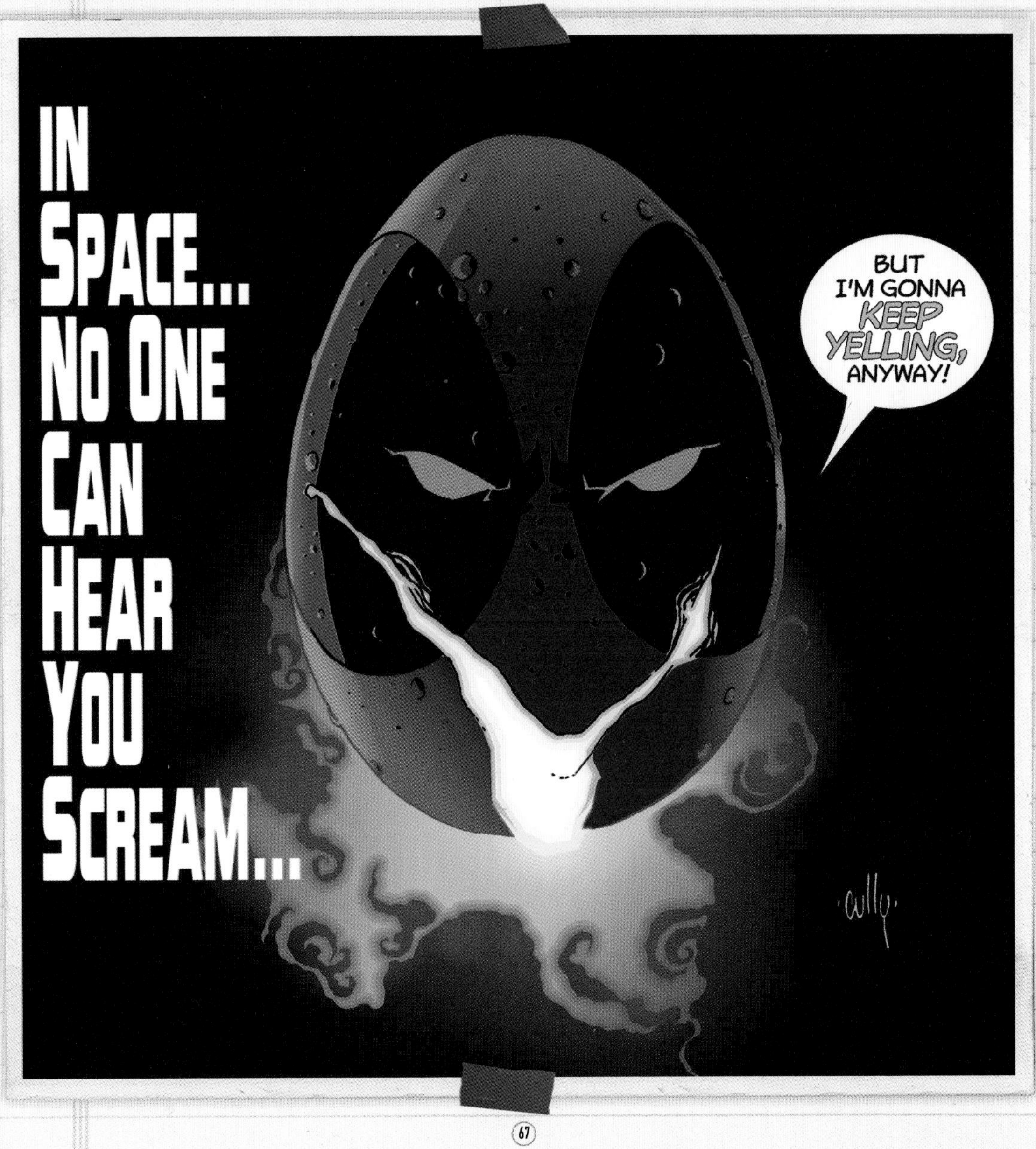
IN SPACE... NO ONE CAN HEAR YOU SCREAM...
BUT I'M GONNA KEEP YELLING, ANYWAY!
·cully·

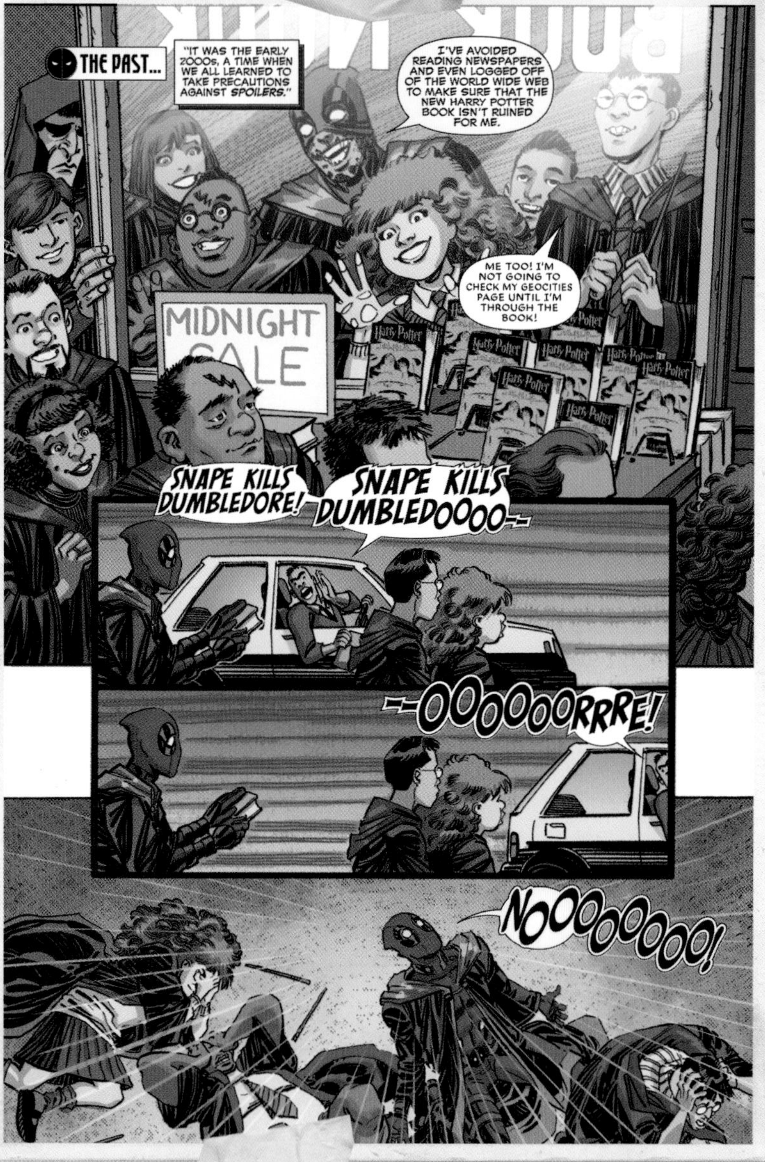
THE PAST...
"IT WAS THE EARLY 2000s, A TIME WHEN WE ALL LEARNED TO TAKE PRECAUTIONS AGAINST SPOILERS."
I'VE AVOIDED READING NEWSPAPERS AND EVEN LOGGED OFF OF THE WORLD WIDE WEB TO MAKE SURE THAT THE NEW HARRY POTTER BOOK ISN'T RUINED FOR ME.
ME TOO! I'M NOT GOING TO CHECK MY GEOCITIES PAGE UNTIL I'M THROUGH THE BOOK!
MIDNIGHT SALE
Harry Potter
SNAPE KILLS DUMBLEDORE!
SNAPE KILLS DUMBLEDOOOO--
--OOOOOOORRRE!
NOOOOOOOO!

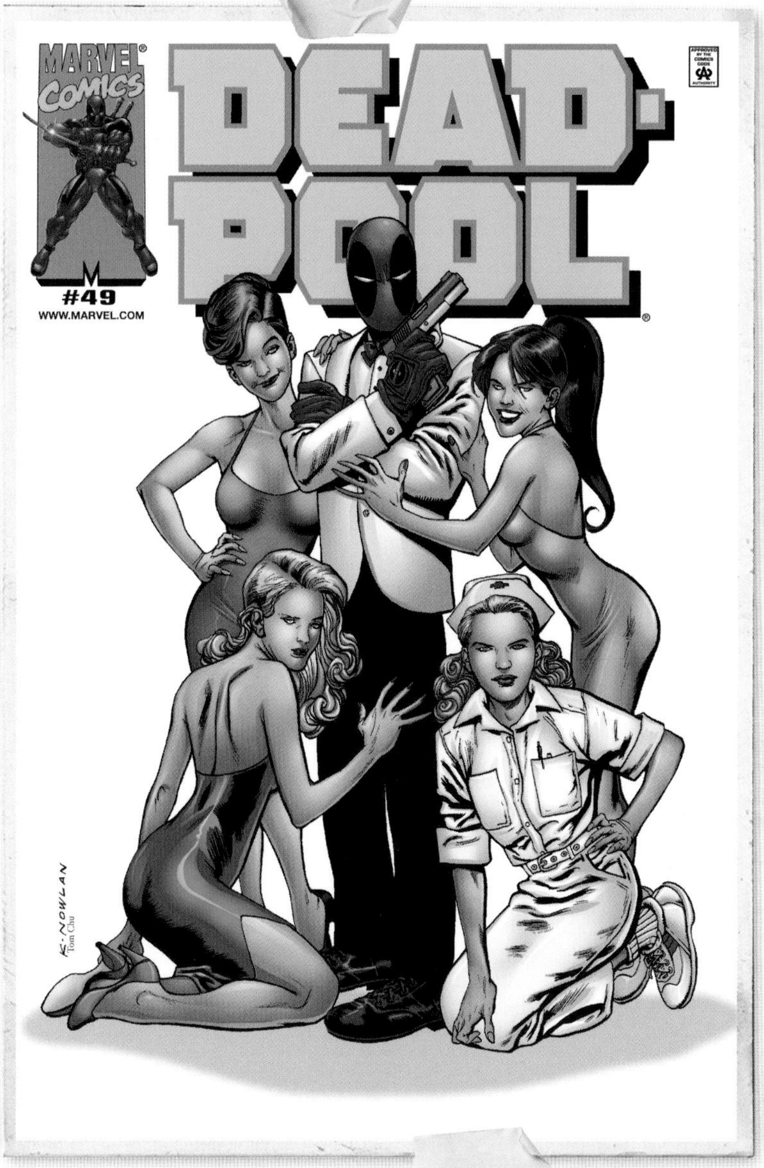
MARVEL COMICS
DEAD-POOL
#49
WWW.MARVEL.COM
APPROVED BY THE COMICS CODE AUTHORITY
K. NOWLAN
Tom Chu

CHAPTER FIVE

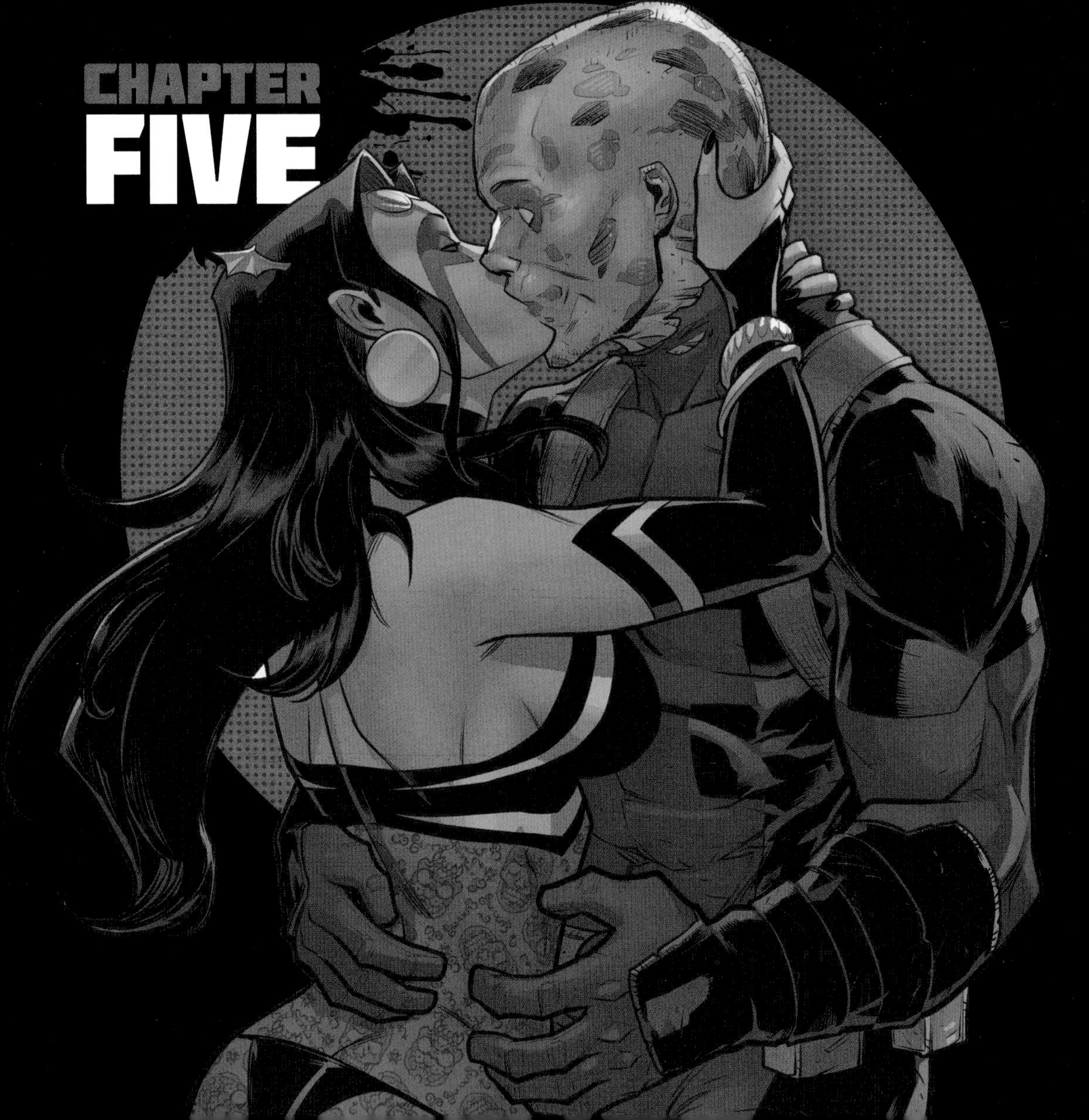

DEADPOOL'S TOP ROMANTIC MOMENTS

IT'S ALMOST IMPOSSIBLE TO KEEP THIS WISE-CRACKING MODERN-DAY CASANOVA FROM WAGGING HIS TONGUE ONE WAY OR ANOTHER. WHAT CAN I SAY? THE LADIES/FELLAS/OTHER-WORDLY BEINGS CAN'T GET ENOUGH OF THE OL' DP...

"OH, BELIEVE ME, I LOVE MYSELF AT LEAST ONCE A DAY."

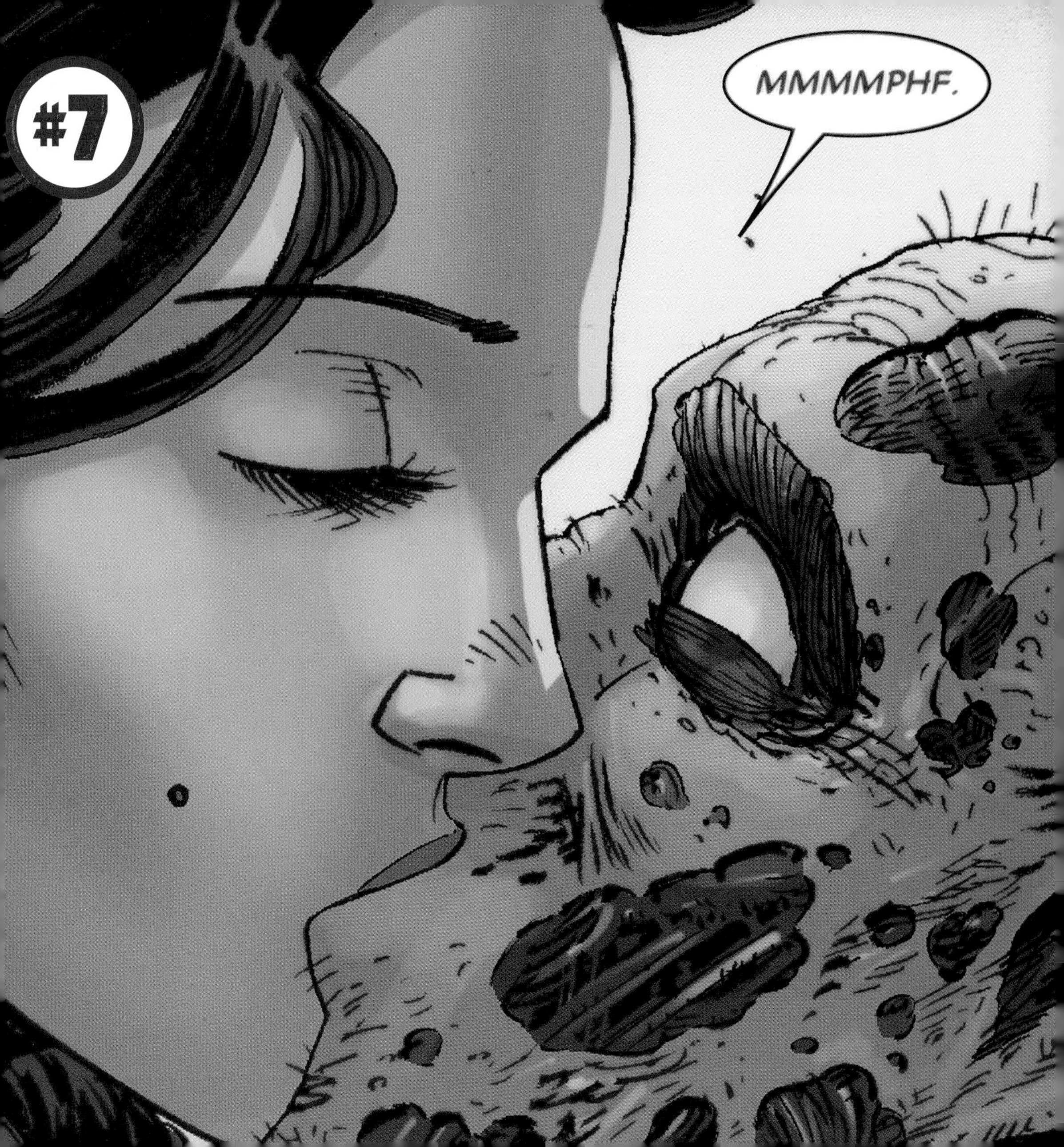
#7
MMMMPHF.

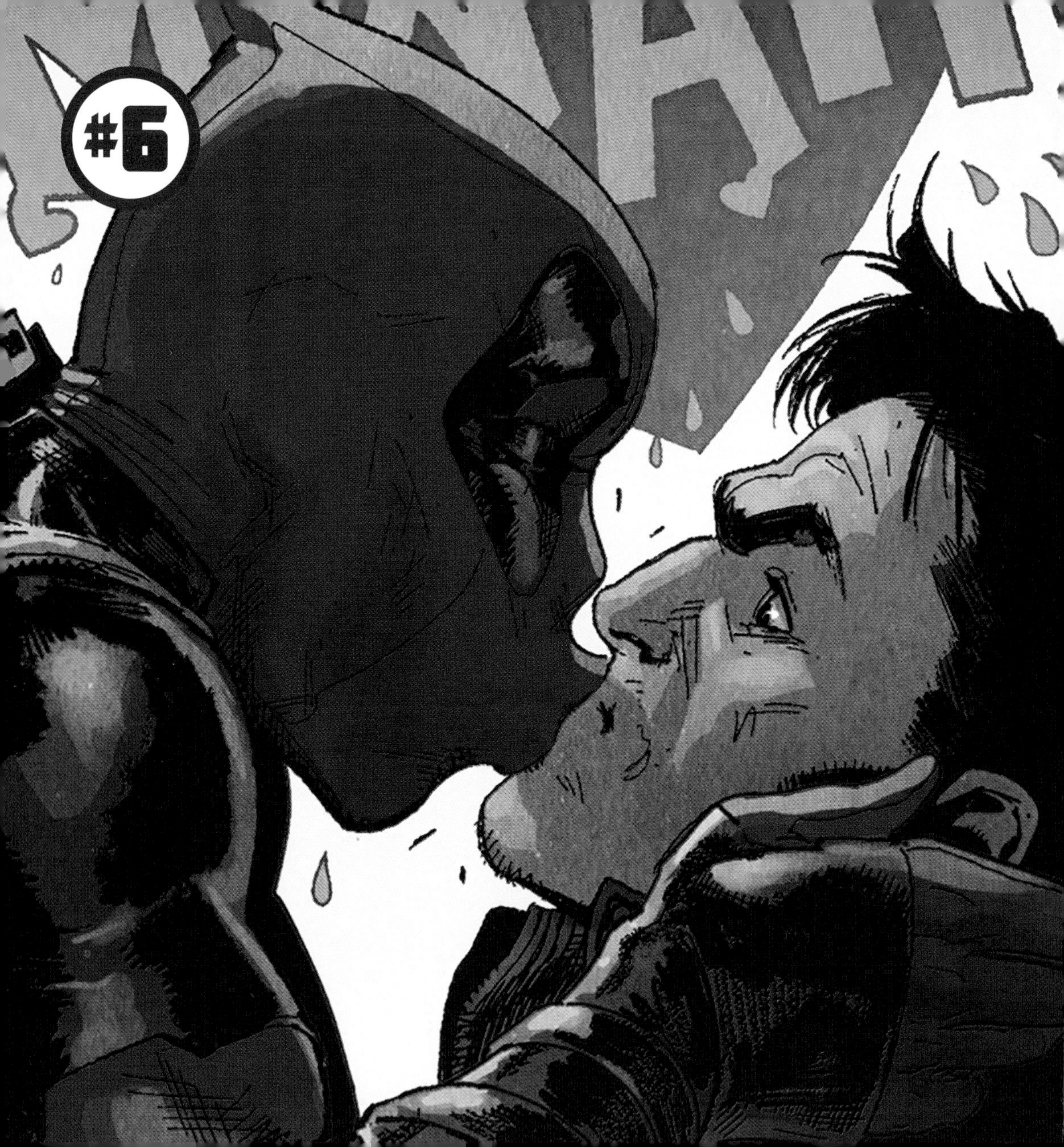
#6

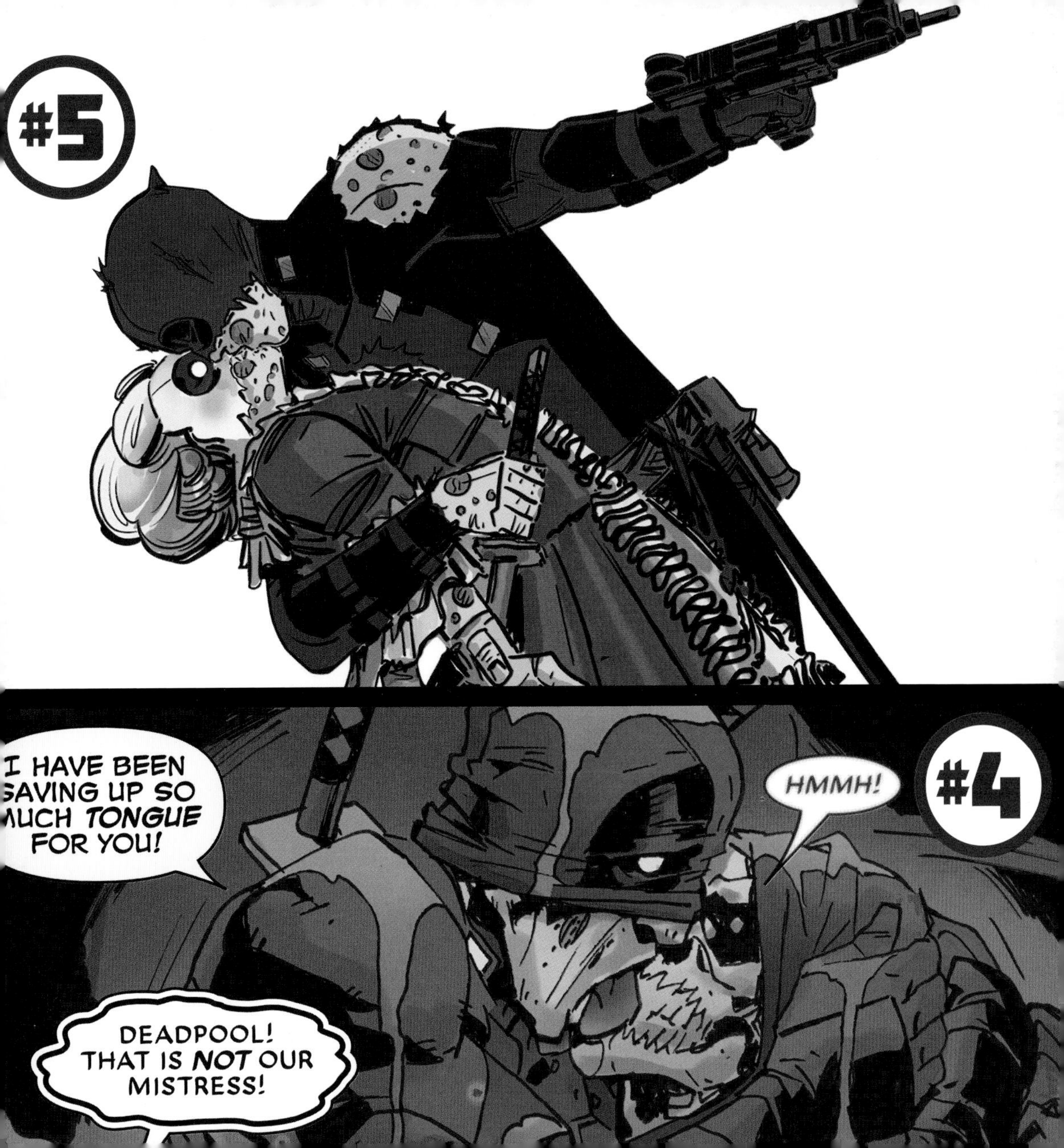
#5
#4
I HAVE BEEN SAVING UP SO MUCH TONGUE FOR YOU!
HMMH!
DEADPOOL! THAT IS NOT OUR MISTRESS!

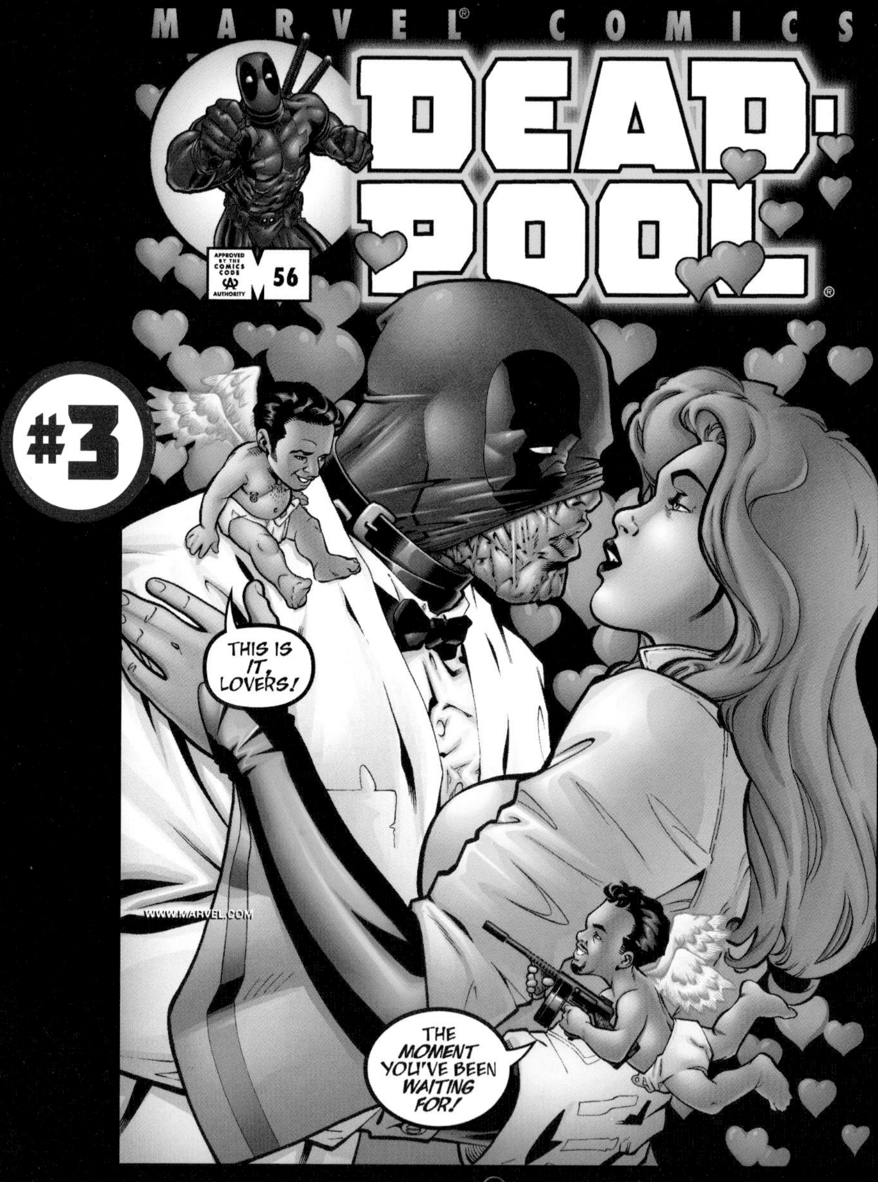
MARVEL COMICS
DEAD-POOL
APPROVED BY THE COMICS CODE AUTHORITY
56
#3
THIS IS IT, LOVERS!
WWW.MARVEL.COM
THE MOMENT YOU'VE BEEN WAITING FOR!

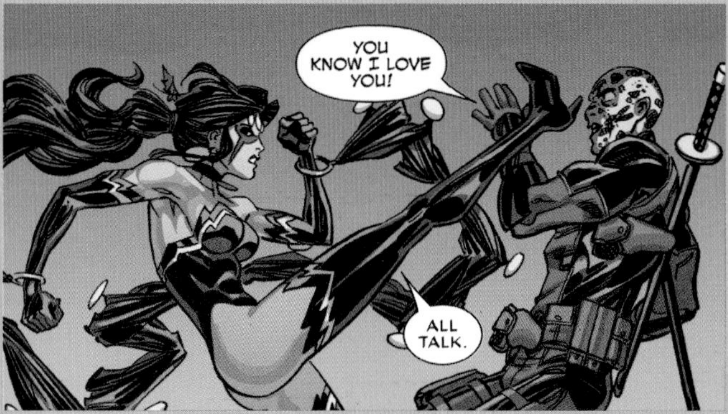
YOU KNOW I LOVE YOU!
ALL TALK.

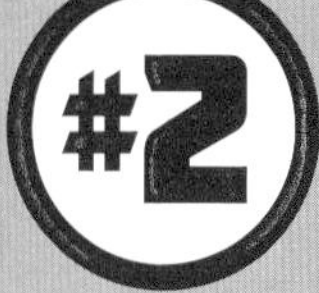
#2

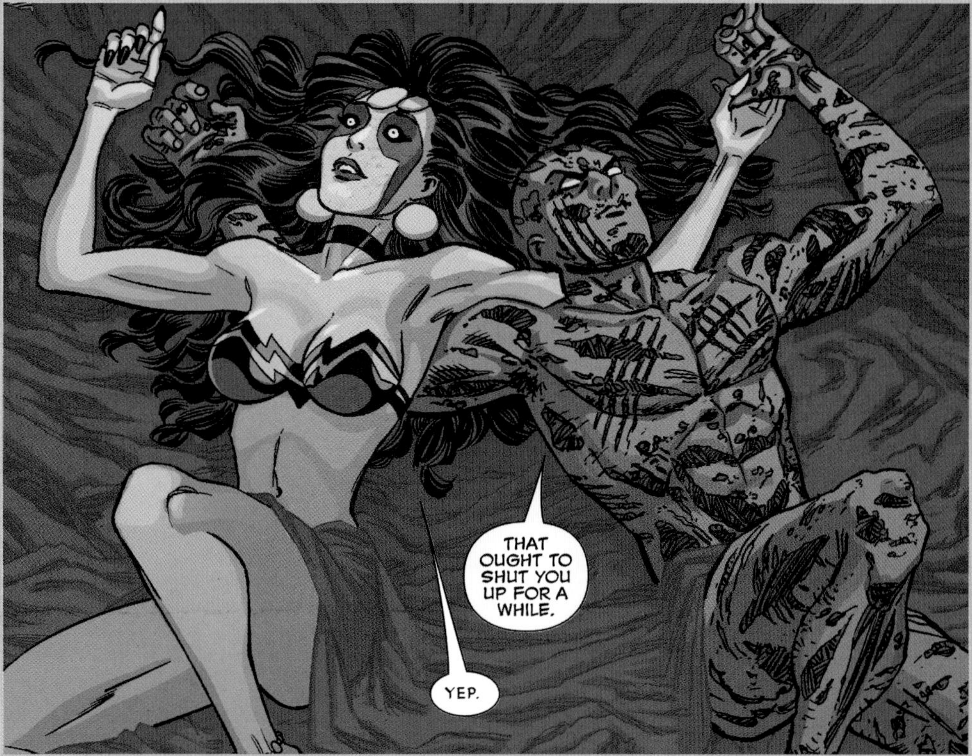
THAT OUGHT TO SHUT YOU UP FOR A WHILE.
YEP.

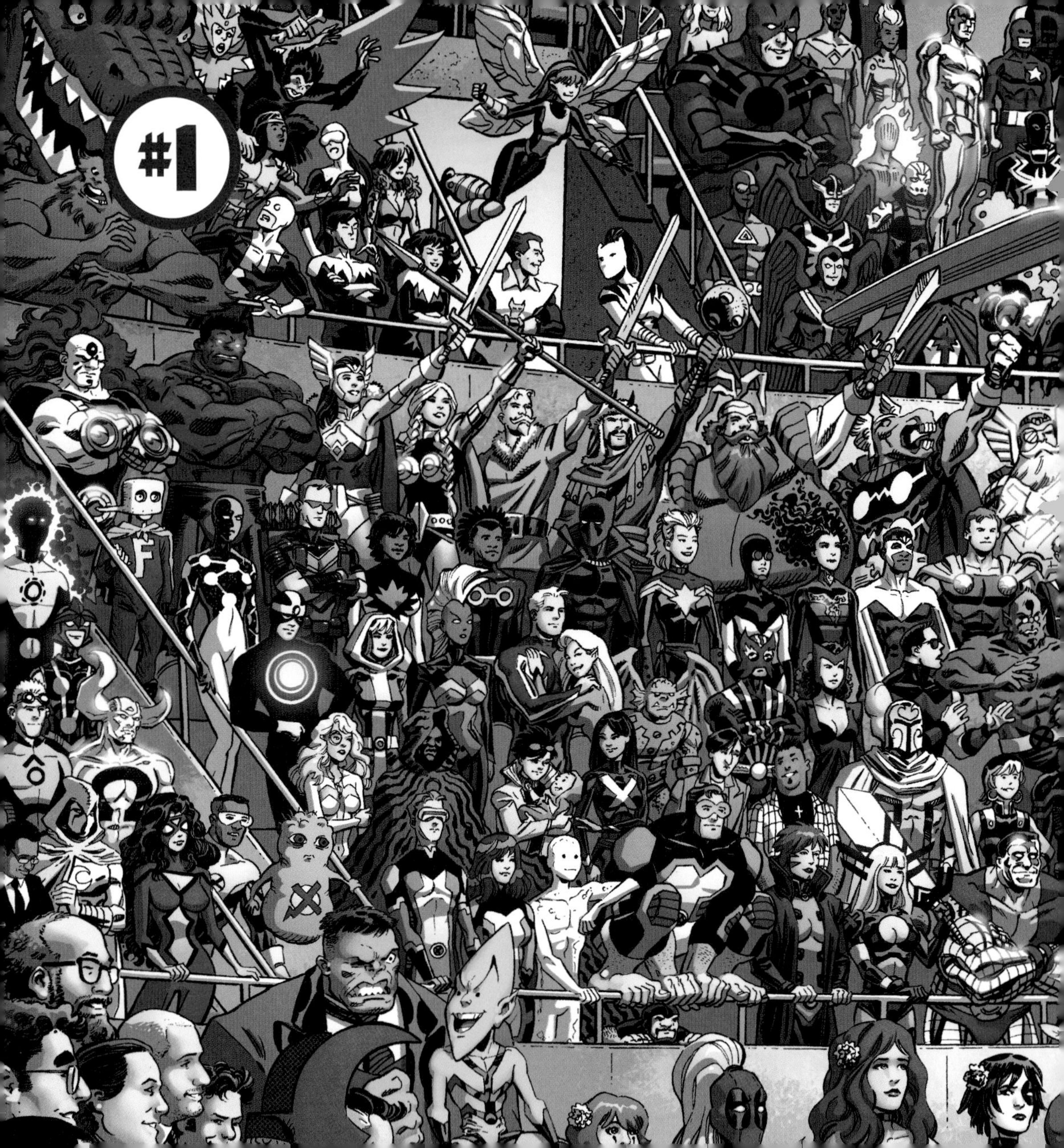

#1

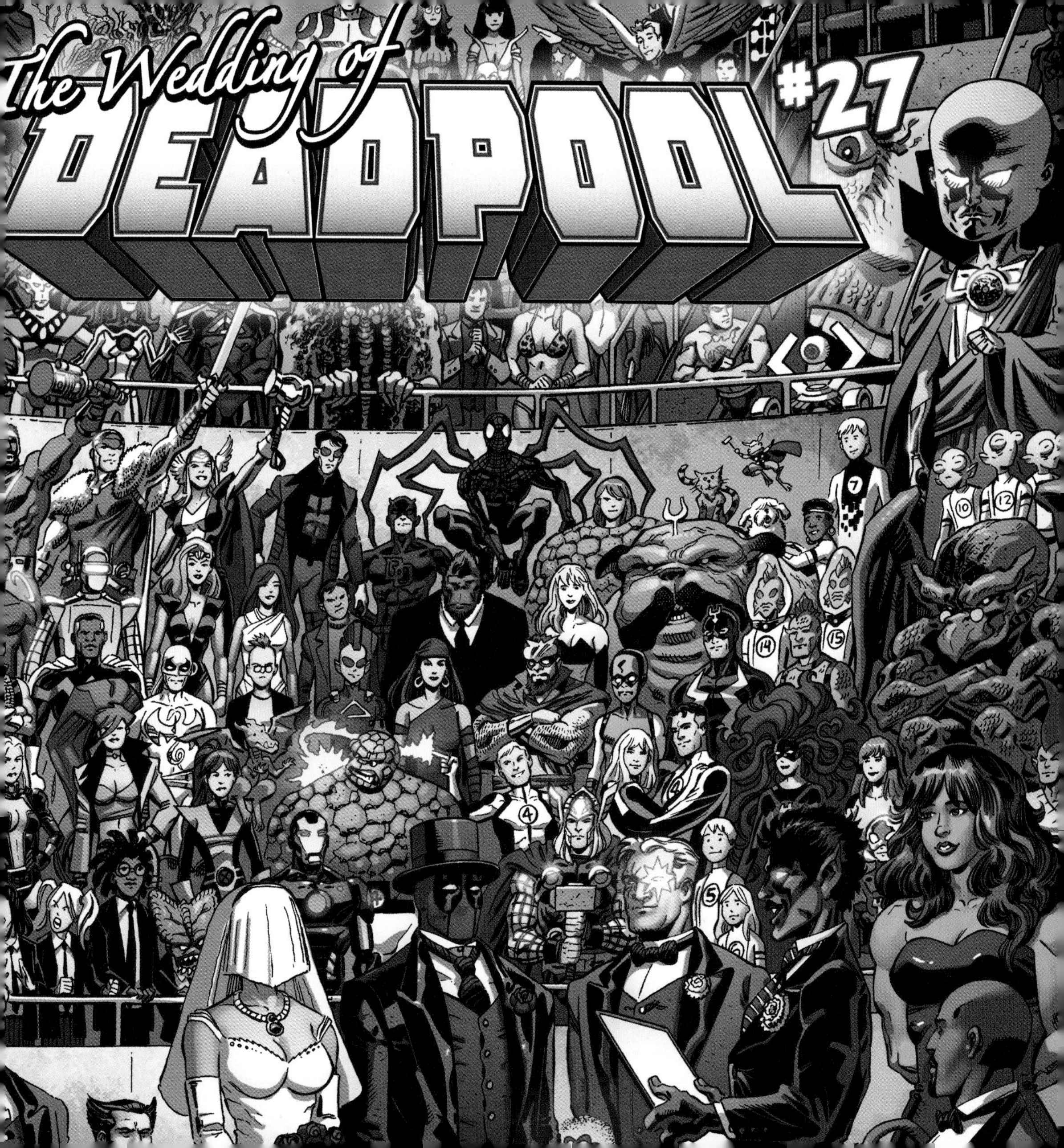
The Wedding of
DEADPOOL
#27

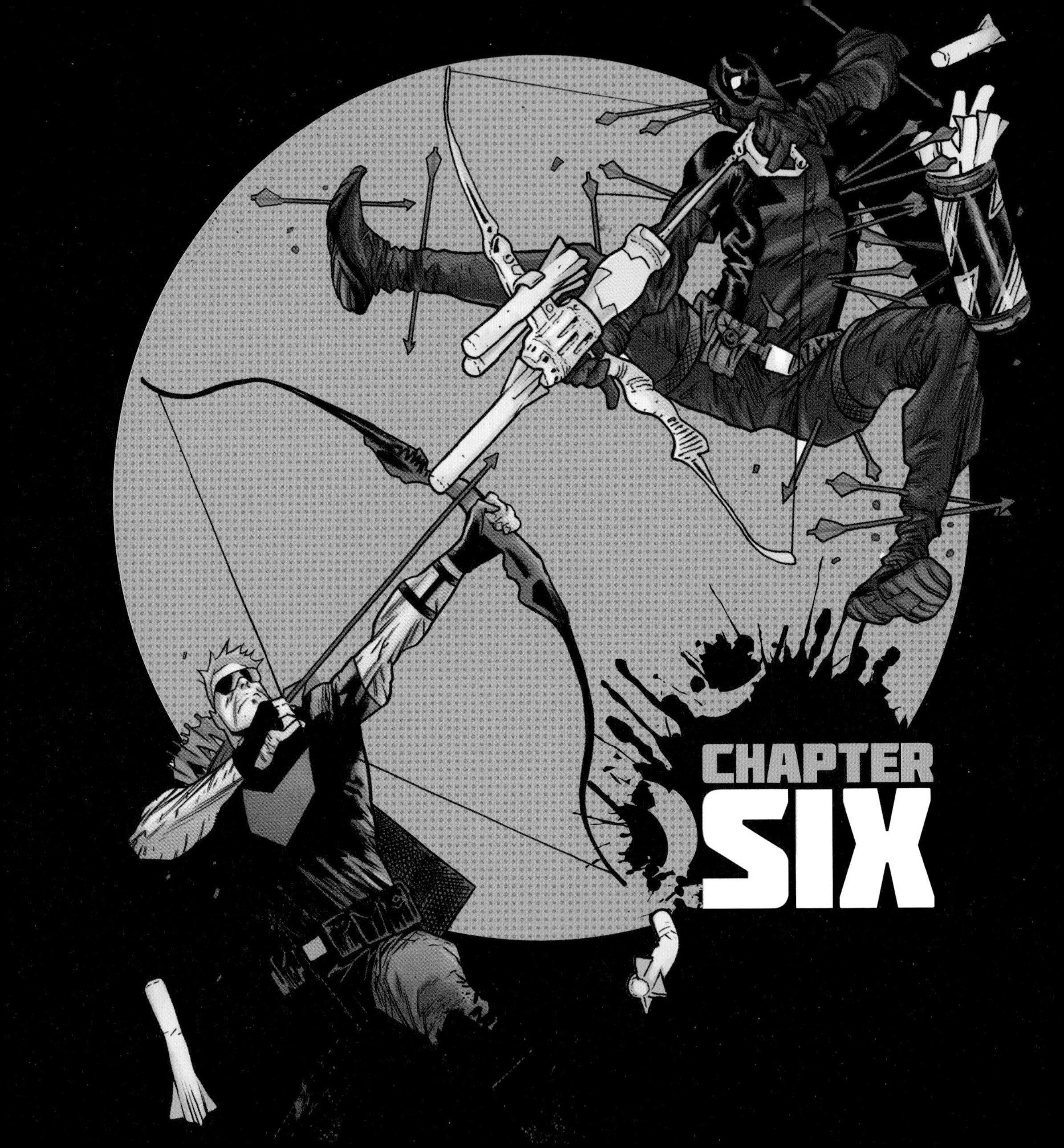
CHAPTER
SIX

DEADPOOL'S TEAM UP SPECTACULAR

SHAGGY & SCOOBY, SONNY & CHER, BONNIE & CLYDE...
EVERY DEADPOOL NEEDS A BUDDY TO TEAM-UP WITH
WHEN MARVEL CANCELS HIS OWN COMIC!

LADIES, GENTLEMEN, MUTANTS AND
MISCREANTS: MY FRENEMIES...

"WHEN EVERYONE THINKS YOU'RE WRONG, IT'S HARD TO DO THE RIGHT THING. KNOWWHATI'MSAYIN'?"

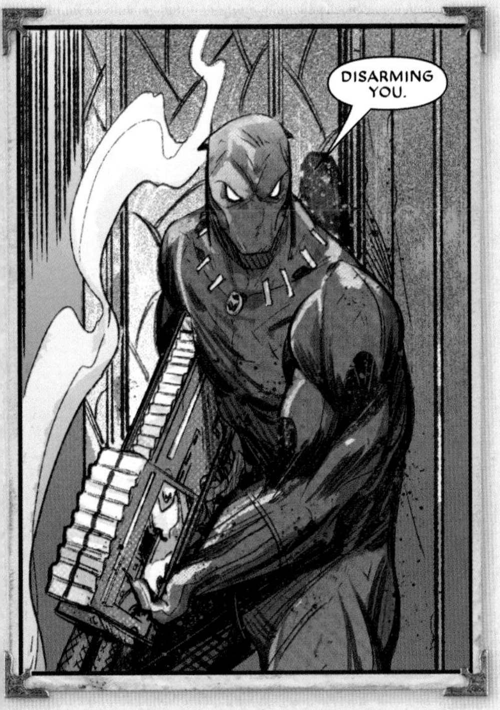
DISARMING YOU.

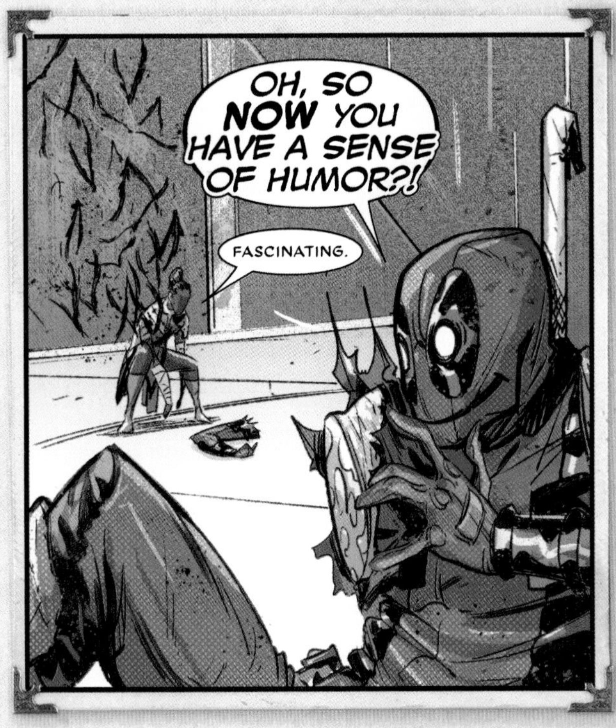
OH, SO NOW YOU HAVE A SENSE OF HUMOR?!
FASCINATING.

BLACK PANTHER - NOT A FUNNY GUY!

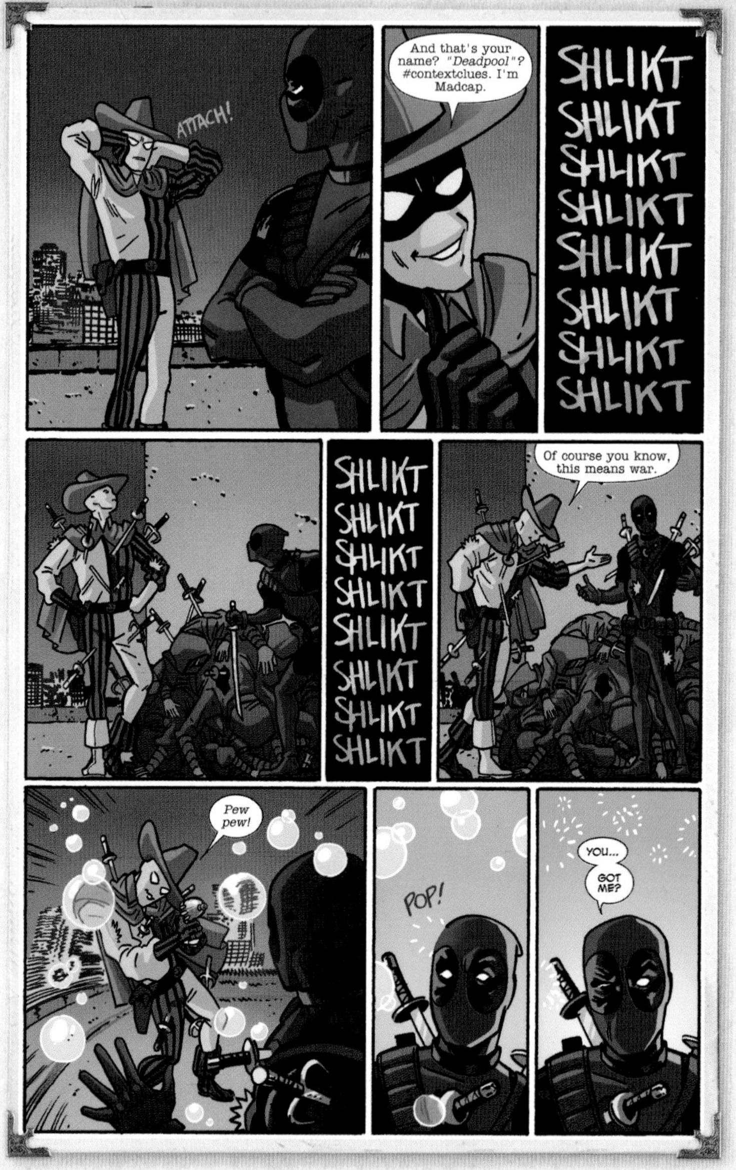
ATTACH!
And that's your name? "Deadpool"? #contextclues. I'm Madcap.
SHLIKT SHLIKT SHLIKT SHLIKT SHLIKT SHLIKT SHLIKT SHLIKT
SHLIKT SHLIKT SHLIKT SHLIKT SHLIKT SHLIKT SHLIKT SHLIKT
Of course you know, this means war.
Pew pew!
POP!
YOU...
GOT ME?

IT'S ALL IN THE NAME... MAD - ABSOLUTELY! CAP - HE WEARS ONE, DUH!

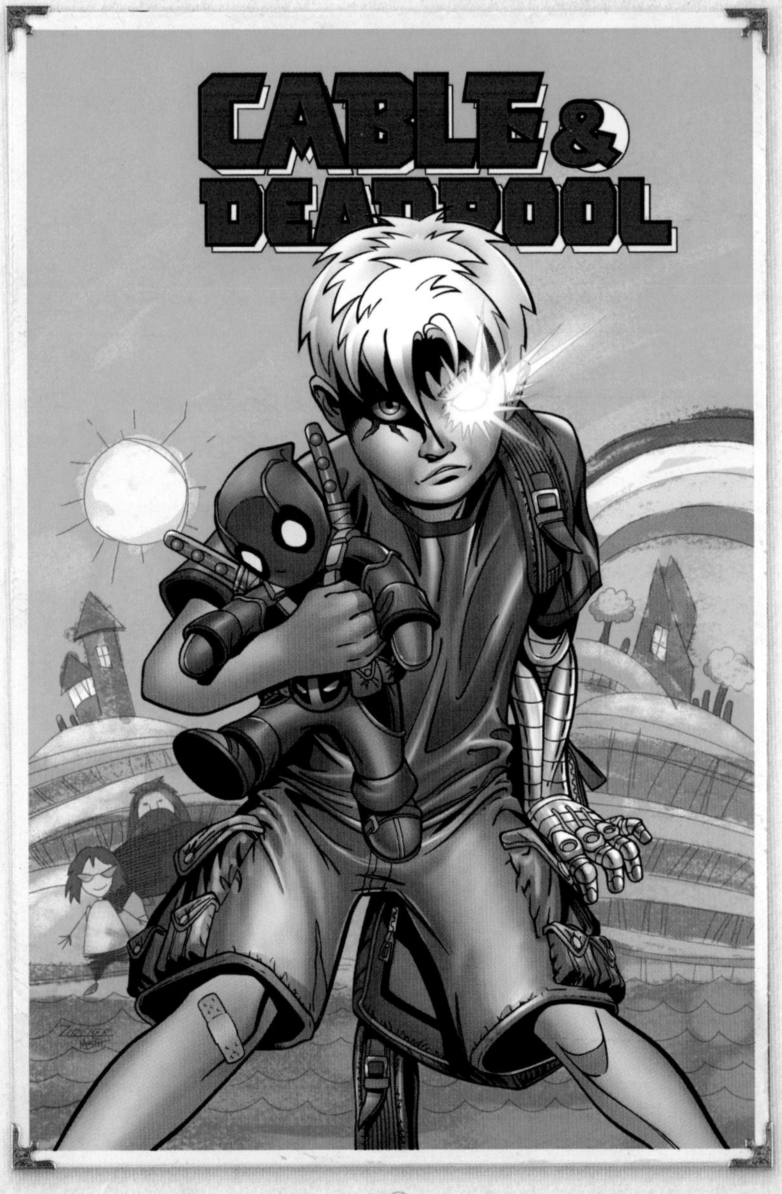
CABLE & DEADPOOL

BESTIES
XXX

WRAPPED IN
SPIDEY'S WEBS...
AM I DREAMING?

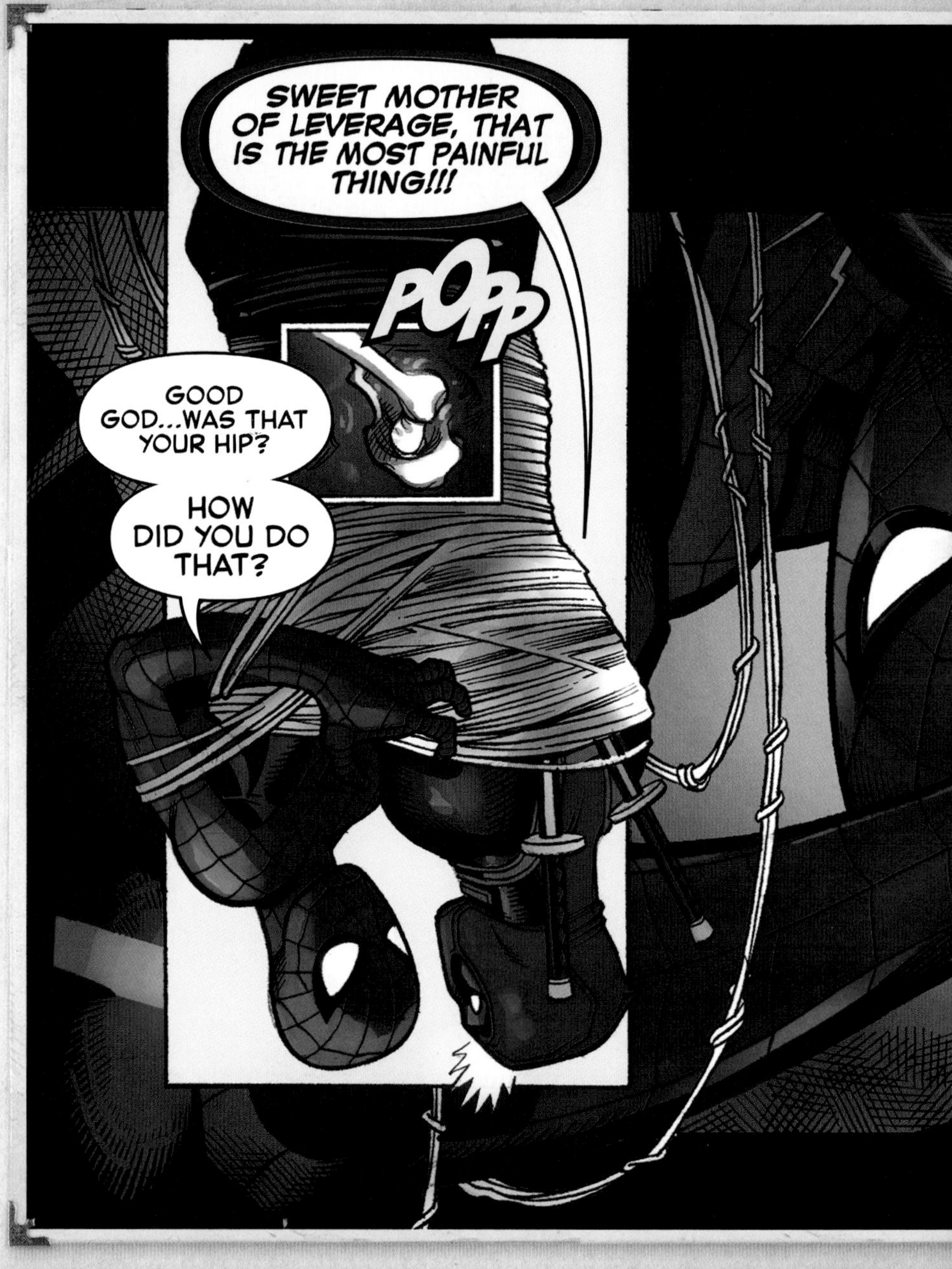
SWEET MOTHER OF LEVERAGE, THAT IS THE MOST PAINFUL THING!!!
POPP
GOOD GOD...WAS THAT YOUR HIP?
HOW DID YOU DO THAT?

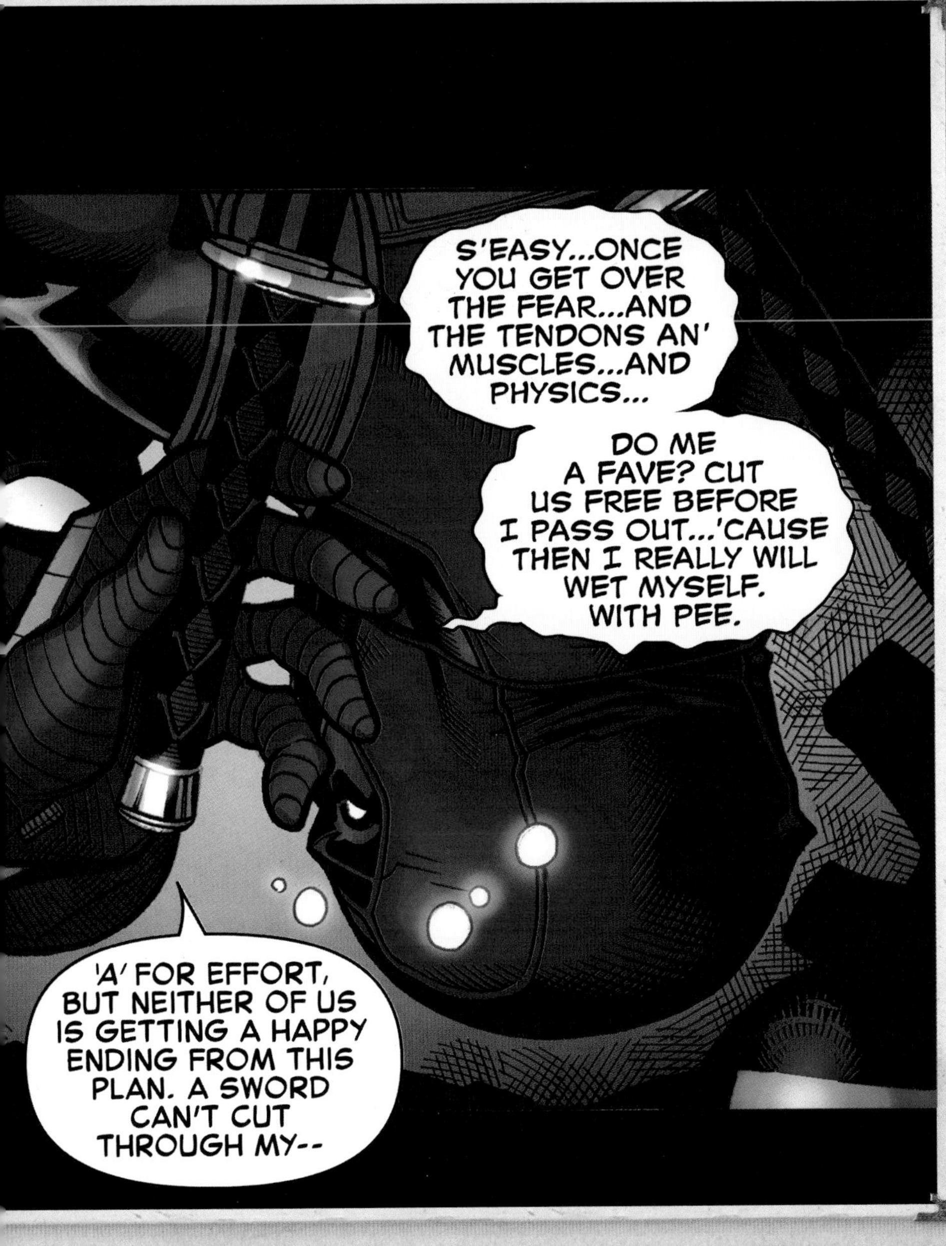
S'EASY...ONCE YOU GET OVER THE FEAR...AND THE TENDONS AN' MUSCLES...AND PHYSICS...
DO ME A FAVE? CUT US FREE BEFORE I PASS OUT...'CAUSE THEN I REALLY WILL WET MYSELF. WITH PEE.
'A' FOR EFFORT, BUT NEITHER OF US IS GETTING A HAPPY ENDING FROM THIS PLAN. A SWORD CAN'T CUT THROUGH MY--

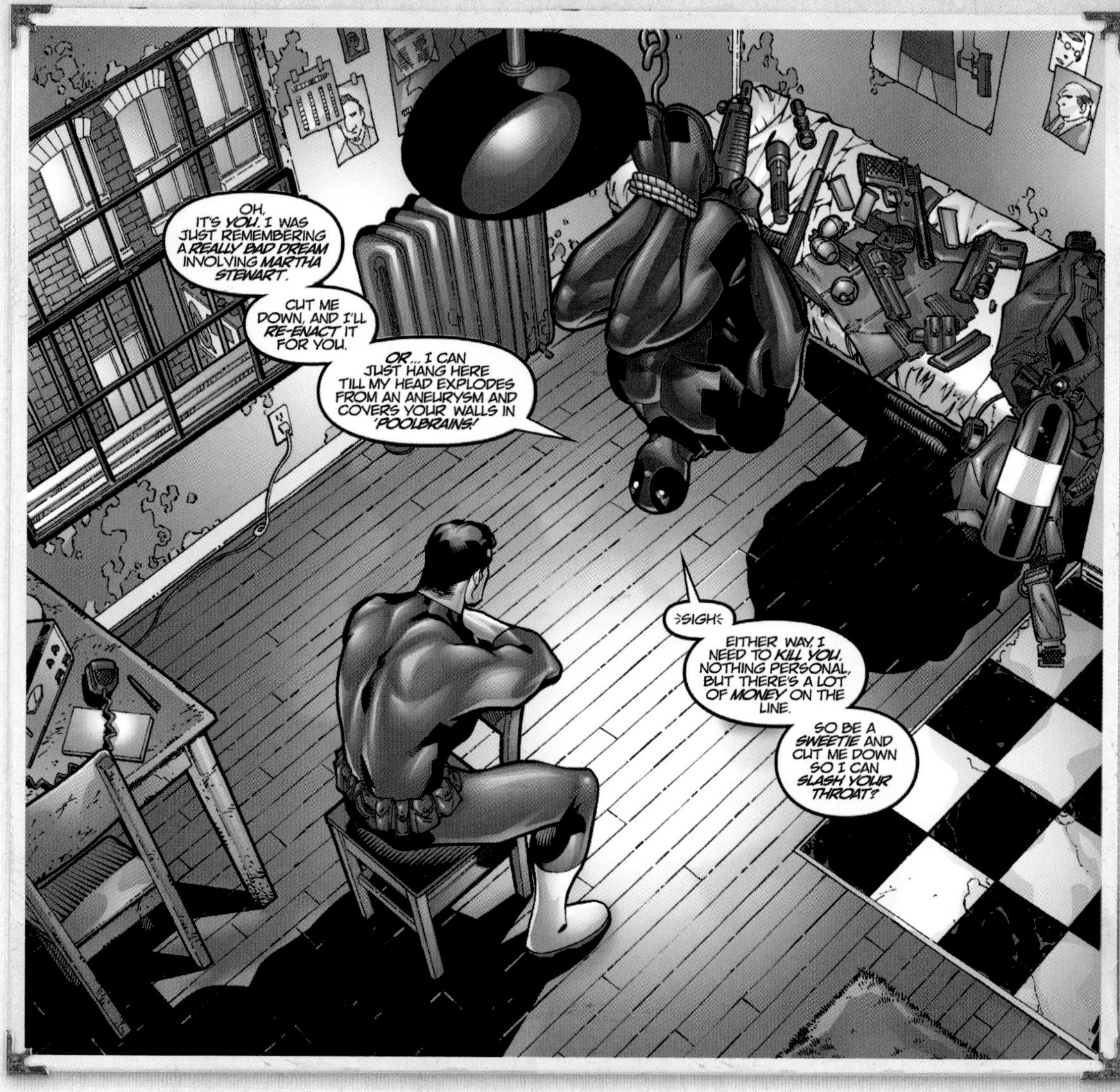
OH, IT'S YOU. I WAS JUST REMEMBERING A REALLY BAD DREAM INVOLVING MARTHA STEWART.
CUT ME DOWN, AND I'LL RE-ENACT IT FOR YOU.
OR... I CAN JUST HANG HERE TILL MY HEAD EXPLODES FROM AN ANEURYSM AND COVERS YOUR WALLS IN 'POOLBRAINS!
SIGH
EITHER WAY, I NEED TO KILL YOU. NOTHING PERSONAL, BUT THERE'S A LOT OF MONEY ON THE LINE.
SO BE A SWEETIE AND CUT ME DOWN SO I CAN SLASH YOUR THROAT?

PUNISHED BY THE PUNISHER

MINE AND DOMINO'S AWESOME SECRET PLAN

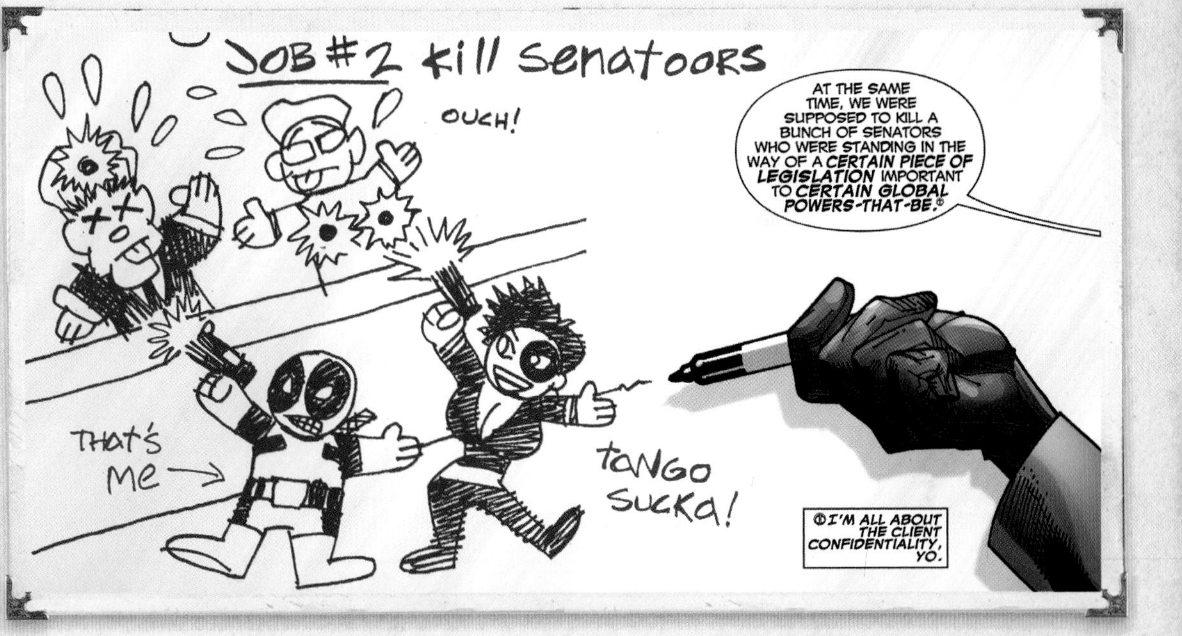

JOB #2 kill Senatoors
OUCH!
AT THE SAME TIME, WE WERE SUPPOSED TO KILL A BUNCH OF SENATORS WHO WERE STANDING IN THE WAY OF A CERTAIN PIECE OF LEGISLATION IMPORTANT TO CERTAIN GLOBAL POWERS-THAT-BE.①
THAT'S ME
TANGO SUCKA!
① I'M ALL ABOUT THE CLIENT CONFIDENTIALITY, YO.

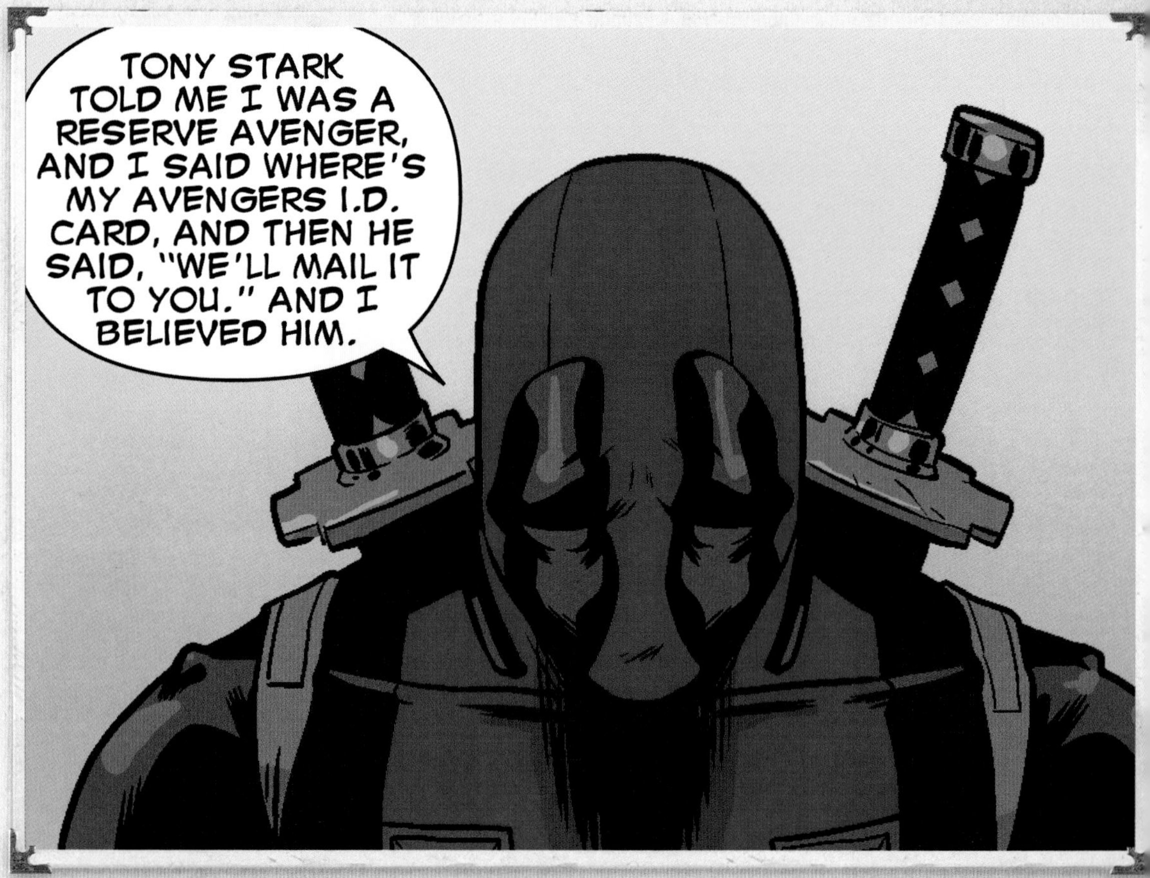
TONY STARK TOLD ME I WAS A RESERVE AVENGER, AND I SAID WHERE'S MY AVENGERS I.D. CARD, AND THEN HE SAID, "WE'LL MAIL IT TO YOU." AND I BELIEVED HIM.

WOLVERINE SCRATCHES MY BACK, I SCRATCH IOU ON A POSTCARD...

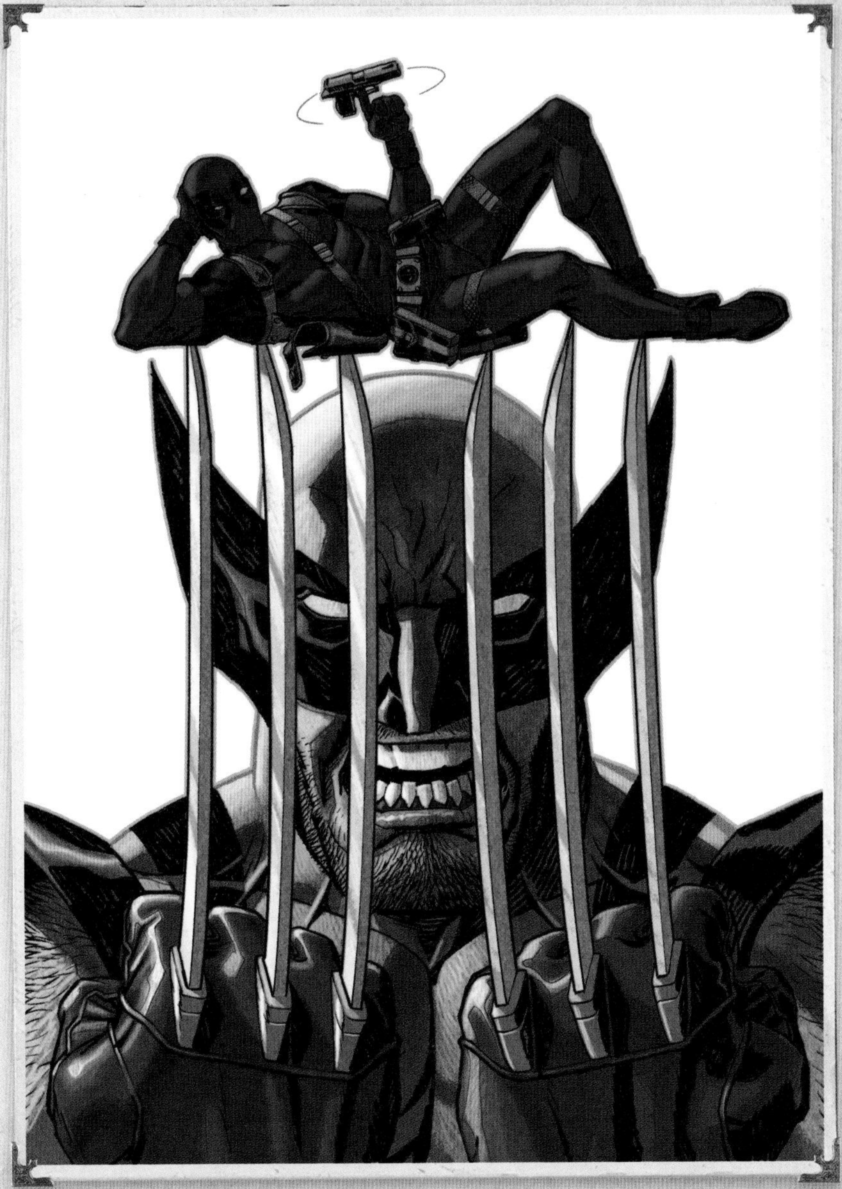

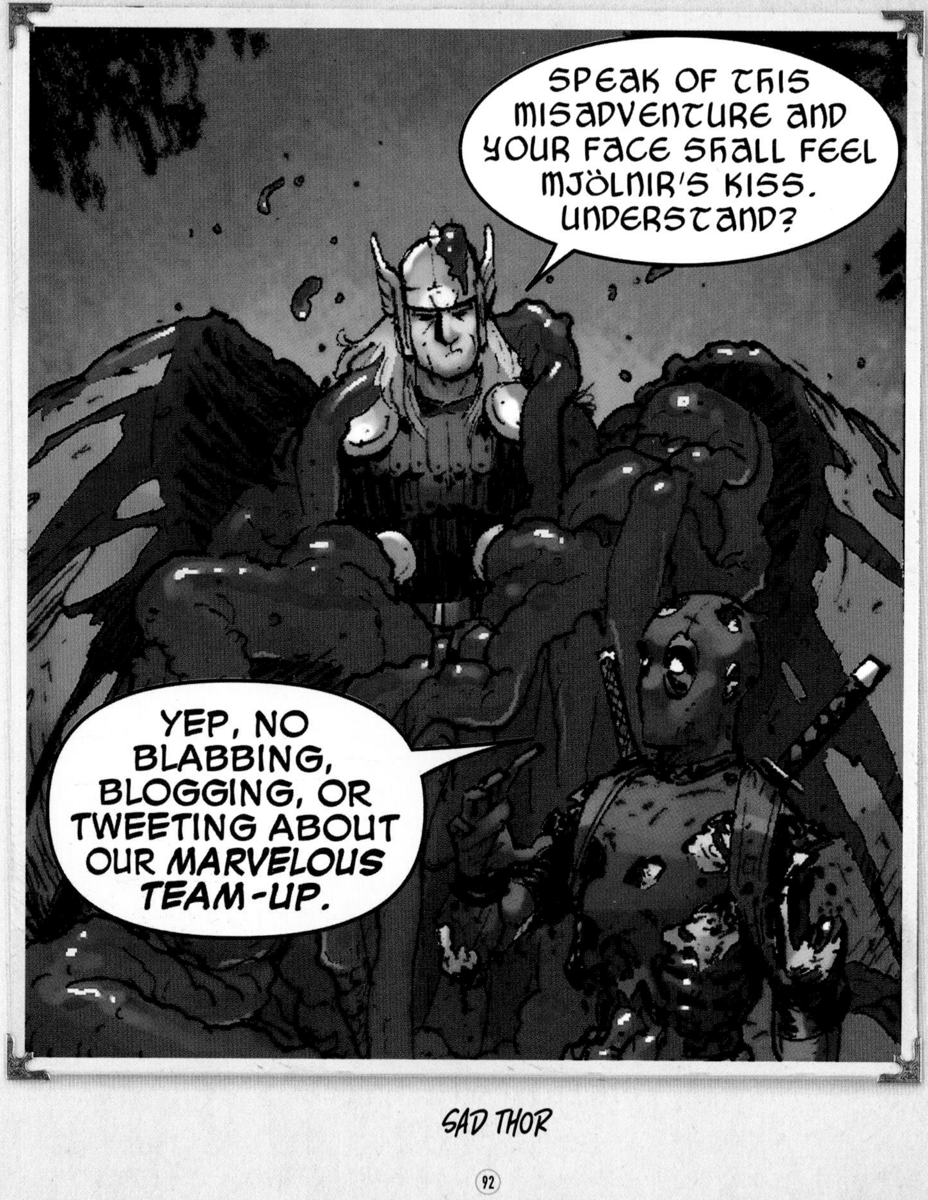
SPEAK OF THIS MISADVENTURE AND YOUR FACE SHALL FEEL MJÖLNIR'S KISS. UNDERSTAND?
YEP, NO BLABBING, BLOGGING, OR TWEETING ABOUT OUR *MARVELOUS TEAM-UP.*

SAD THOR

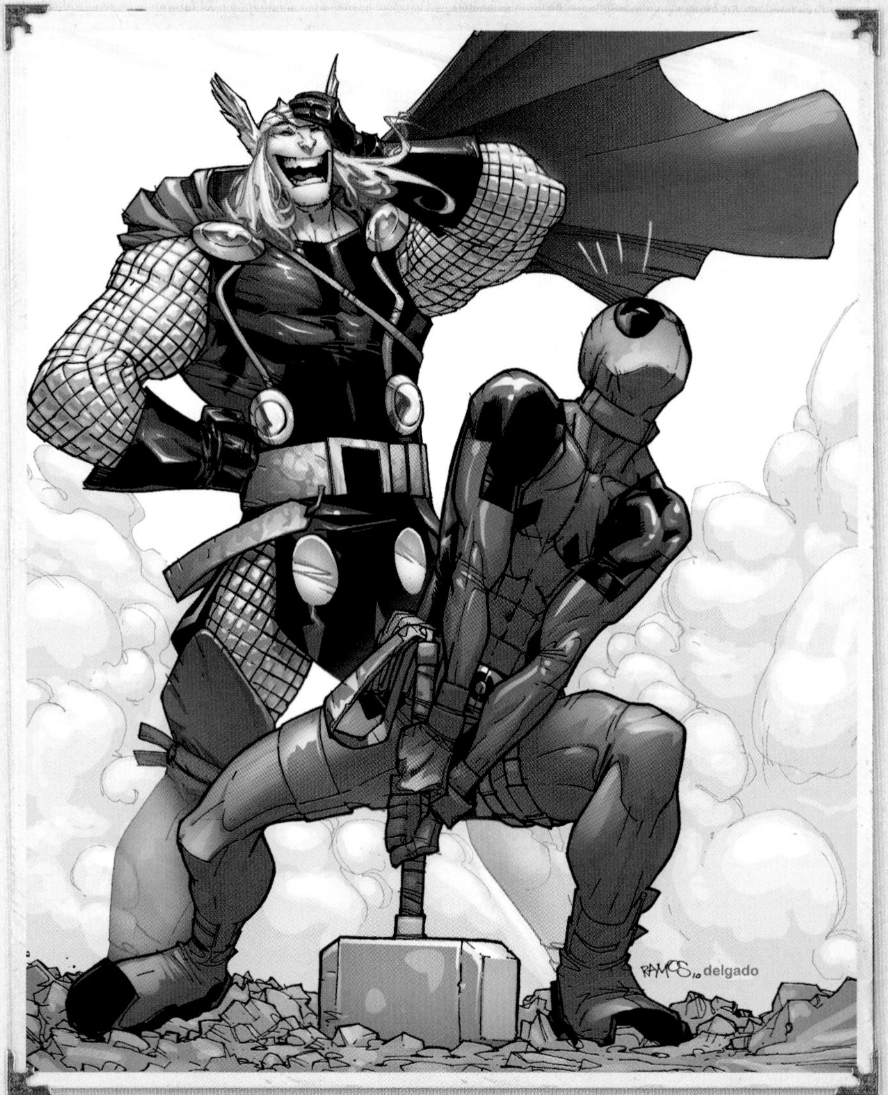
RAMOS 10 delgado

HAPPY THOR

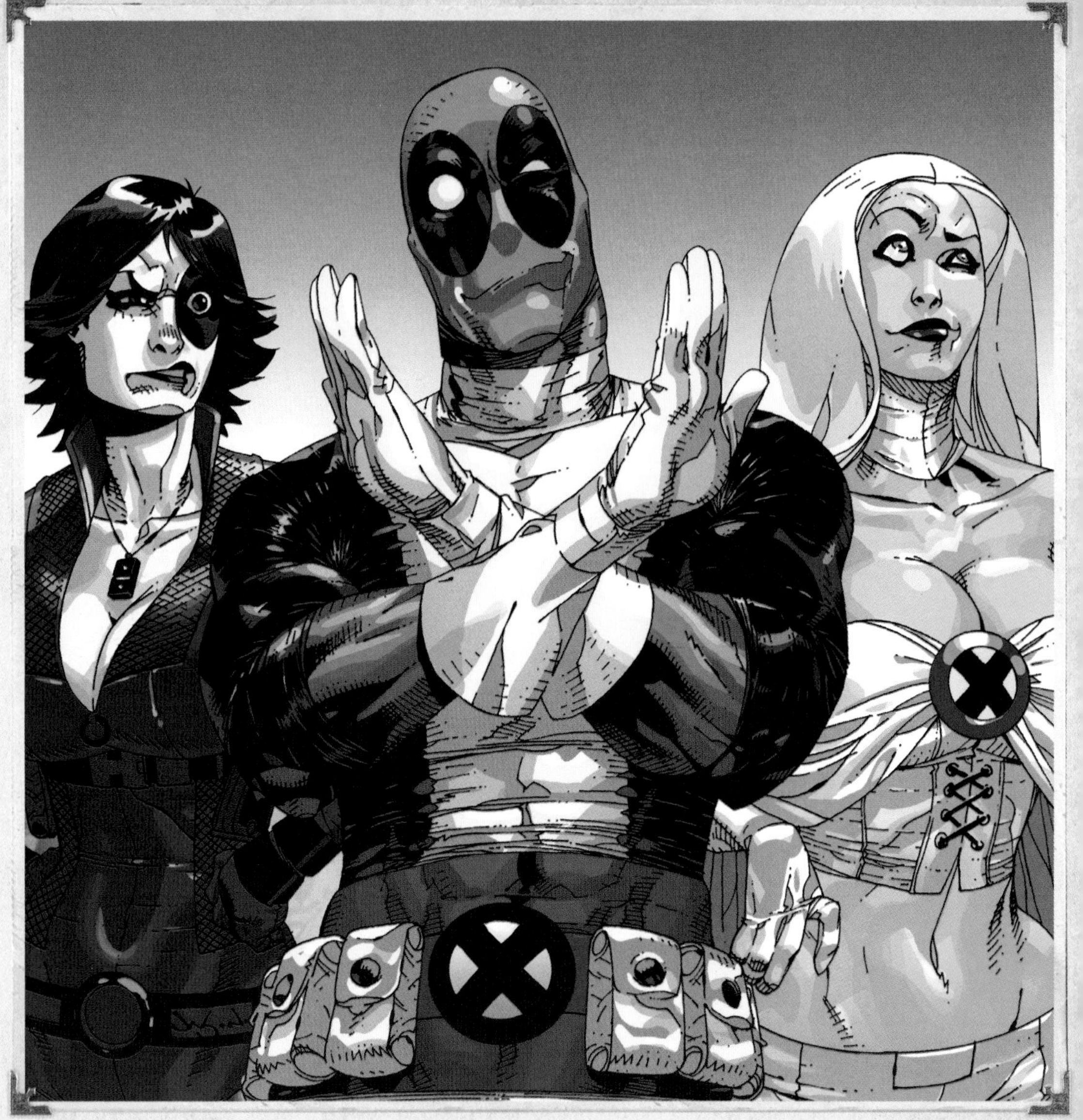

THE X-CHICKS LOVE ME!

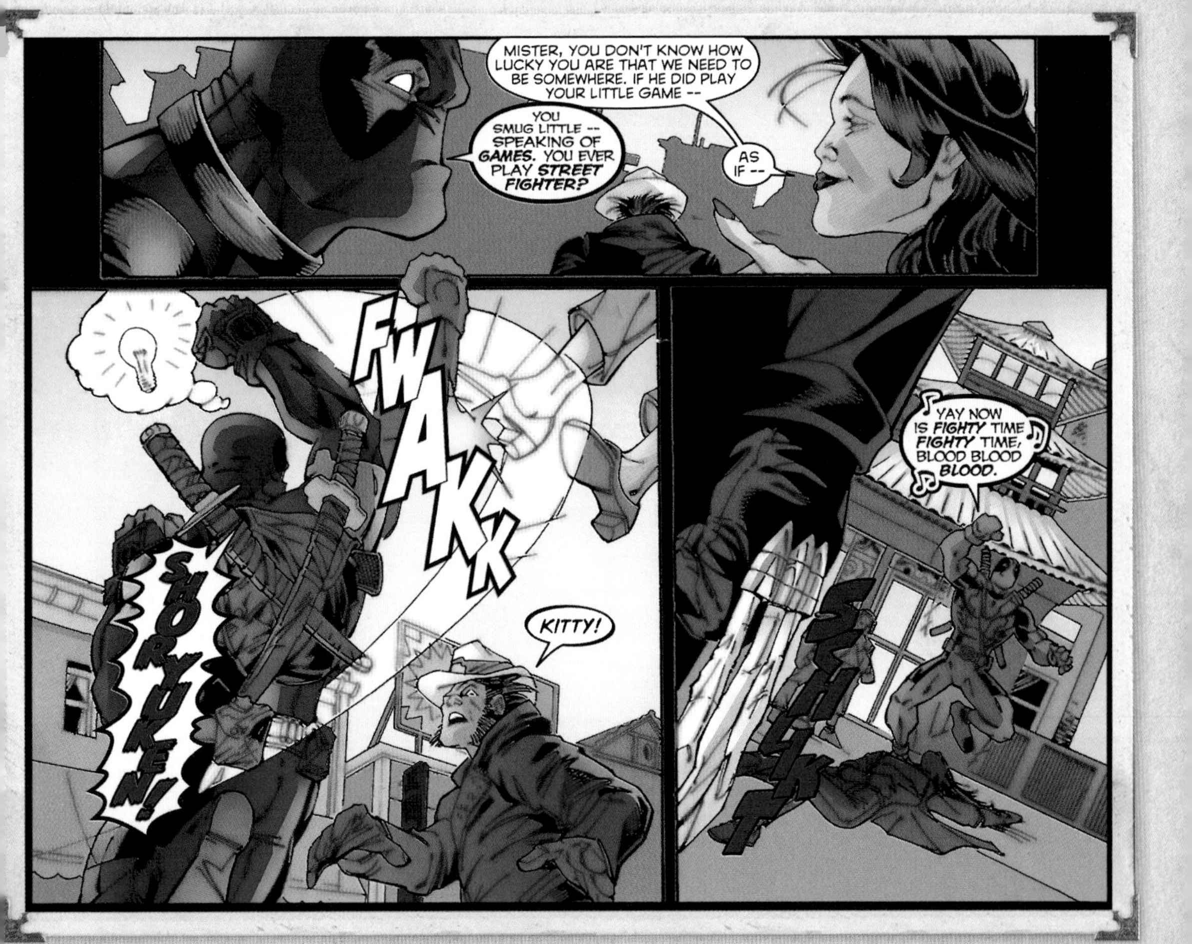
MISTER, YOU DON'T KNOW HOW LUCKY YOU ARE THAT WE NEED TO BE SOMEWHERE. IF HE DID PLAY YOUR LITTLE GAME --
YOU SMUG LITTLE -- SPEAKING OF GAMES. YOU EVER PLAY STREET FIGHTER?
AS IF --
FWAKKK
SHORYUKEN!
KITTY!
YAY NOW IS FIGHTY TIME FIGHTY TIME, BLOOD BLOOD BLOOD.
SCHLIKT

...SEE?

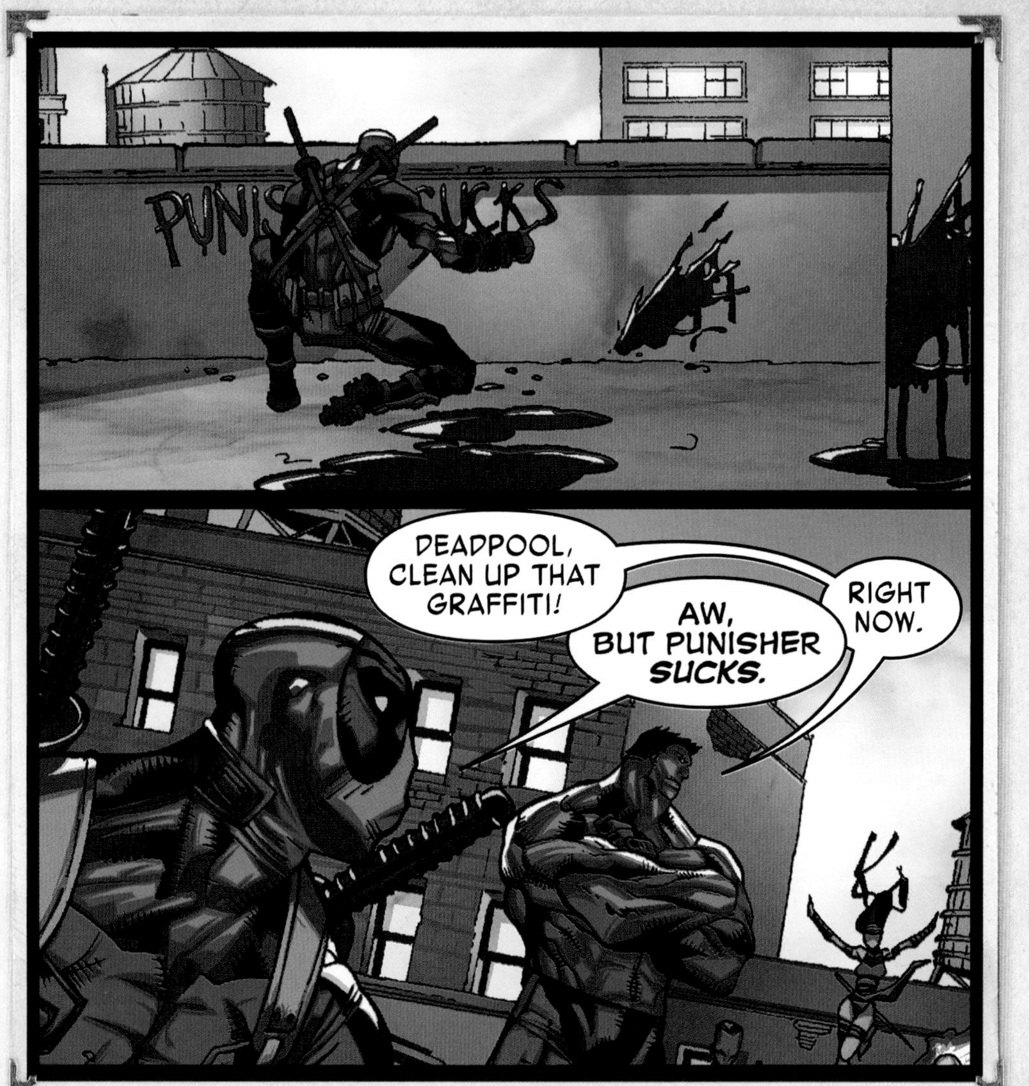
PUNISHER SUCKS
DEADPOOL, CLEAN UP THAT GRAFFITI!
RIGHT NOW.
AW, BUT PUNISHER SUCKS.

THE THUNDERBOLTS DIDN'T LIKE MY STREET ART...

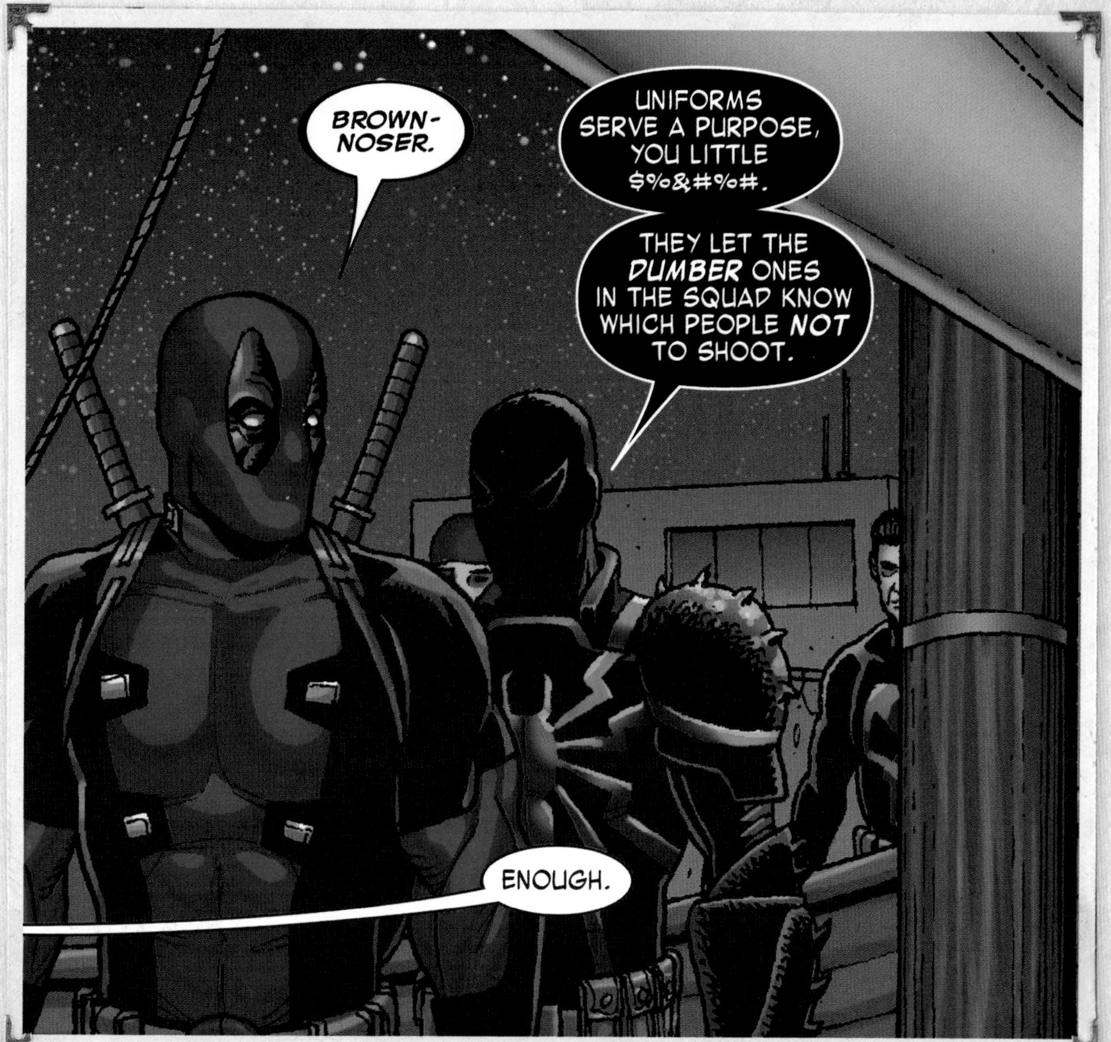
BROWN-NOSER.
UNIFORMS SERVE A PURPOSE, YOU LITTLE $%&#%#.
THEY LET THE DUMBER ONES IN THE SQUAD KNOW WHICH PEOPLE NOT TO SHOOT.
ENOUGH.

...AND THEY STOLE MY COLOR SCHEME!

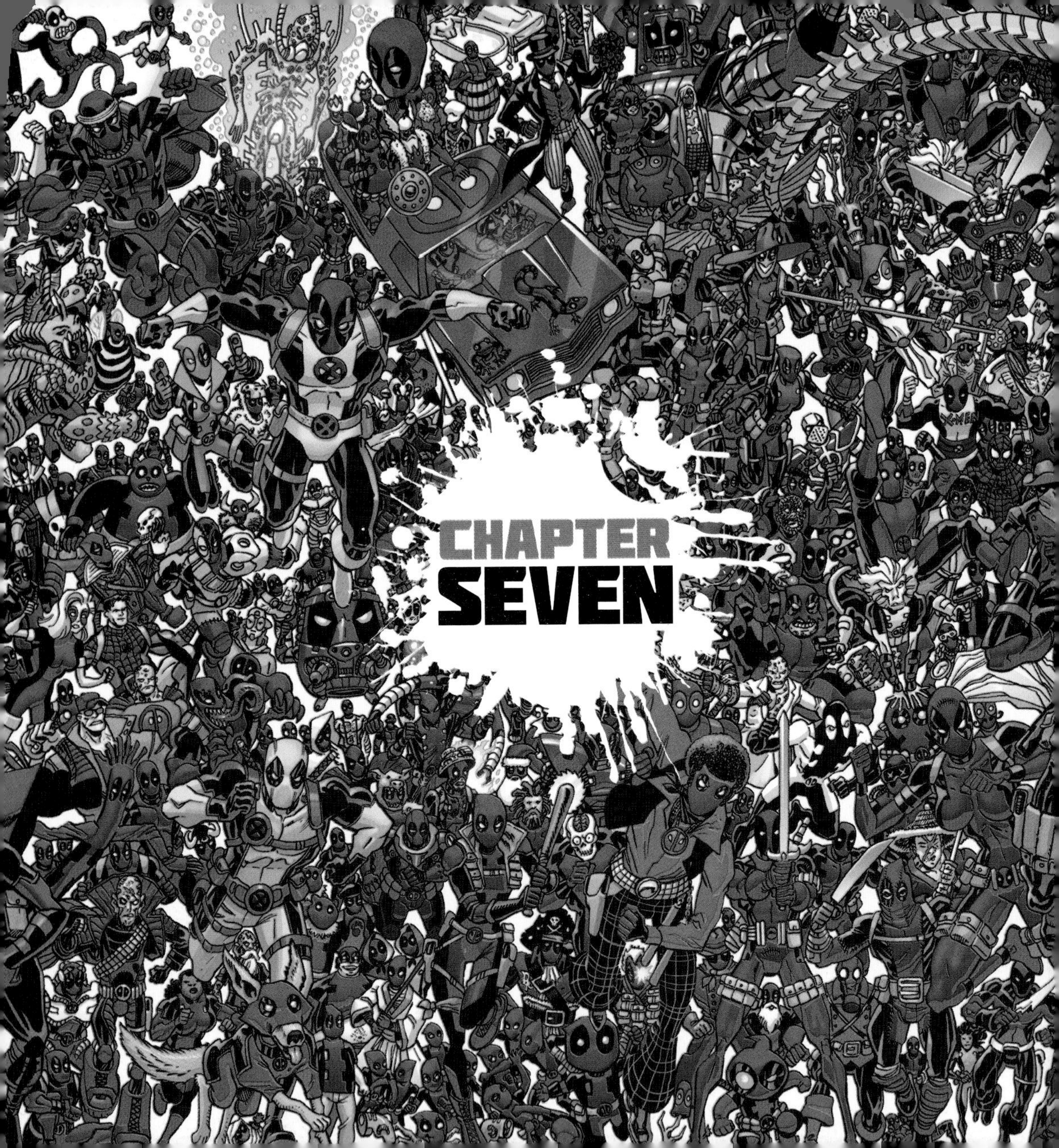
CHAPTER
SEVEN

ONE OF A KIND

THOUGHT THERE WAS ONLY ONE DEADPOOL?
AS IF! I'M TOO BOLD AND BEAUTIFUL TO
KEEP THE WORLD FROM WANTING MORE ME.

TAKE A LOOK AT THE MYRIAD WANNABES,
ALTERNATES, FUTURE-SELVES, AND ENDLESS
D.P. DUPLICATES. JUST REMEMBER, NOTHING
BEATS THE ORIGINAL!

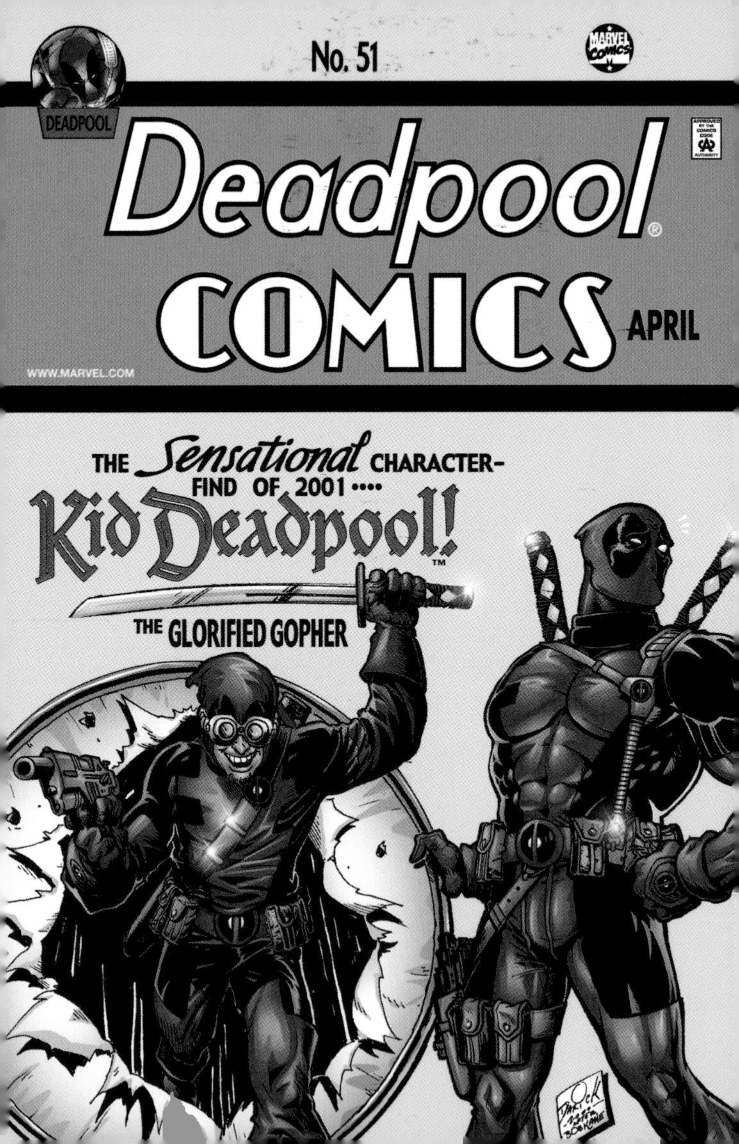
No. 51
MARVEL COMICS
DEADPOOL
Deadpool®
COMICS
APRIL
APPROVED BY THE COMICS CODE AUTHORITY
WWW.MARVEL.COM
THE Sensational CHARACTER-
FIND OF 2001 ....
Kid Deadpool!™
THE GLORIFIED GOPHER

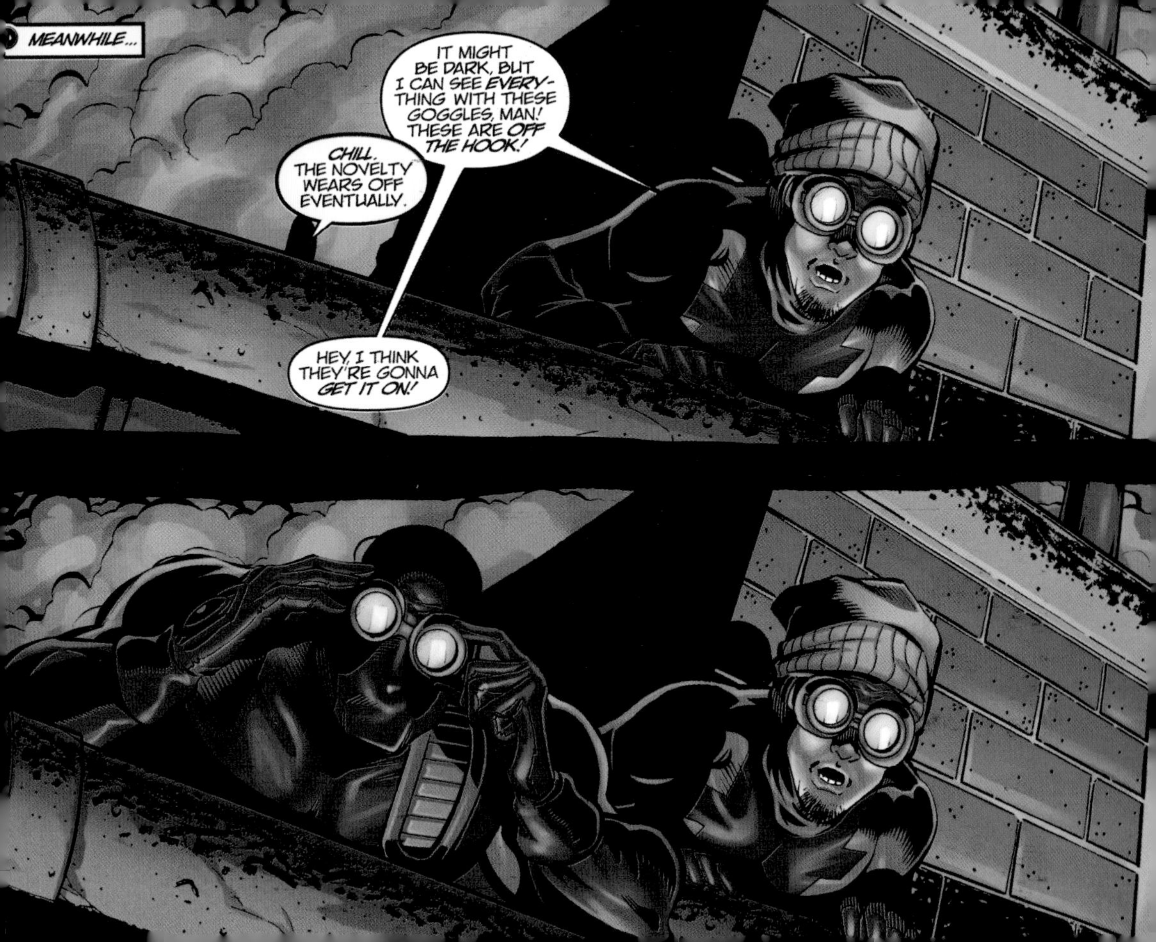
MEANWHILE...
IT MIGHT BE DARK, BUT I CAN SEE EVERYTHING WITH THESE GOGGLES, MAN! THESE ARE OFF THE HOOK!
CHILL. THE NOVELTY WEARS OFF EVENTUALLY.
HEY, I THINK THEY'RE GONNA GET IT ON!

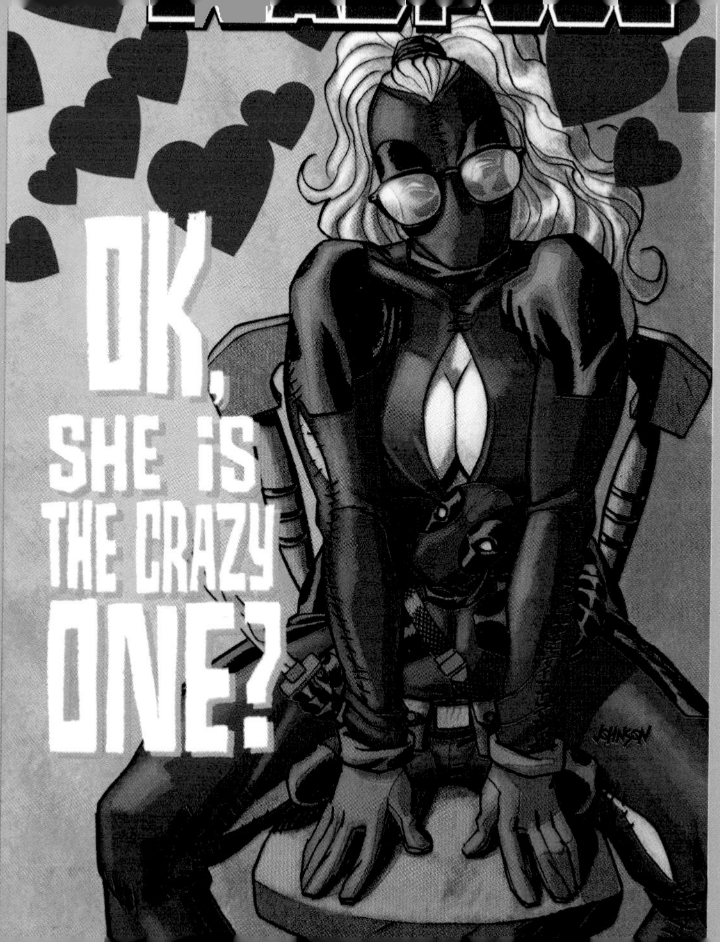
OK, SHE IS THE CRAZY ONE?
JOHNSON

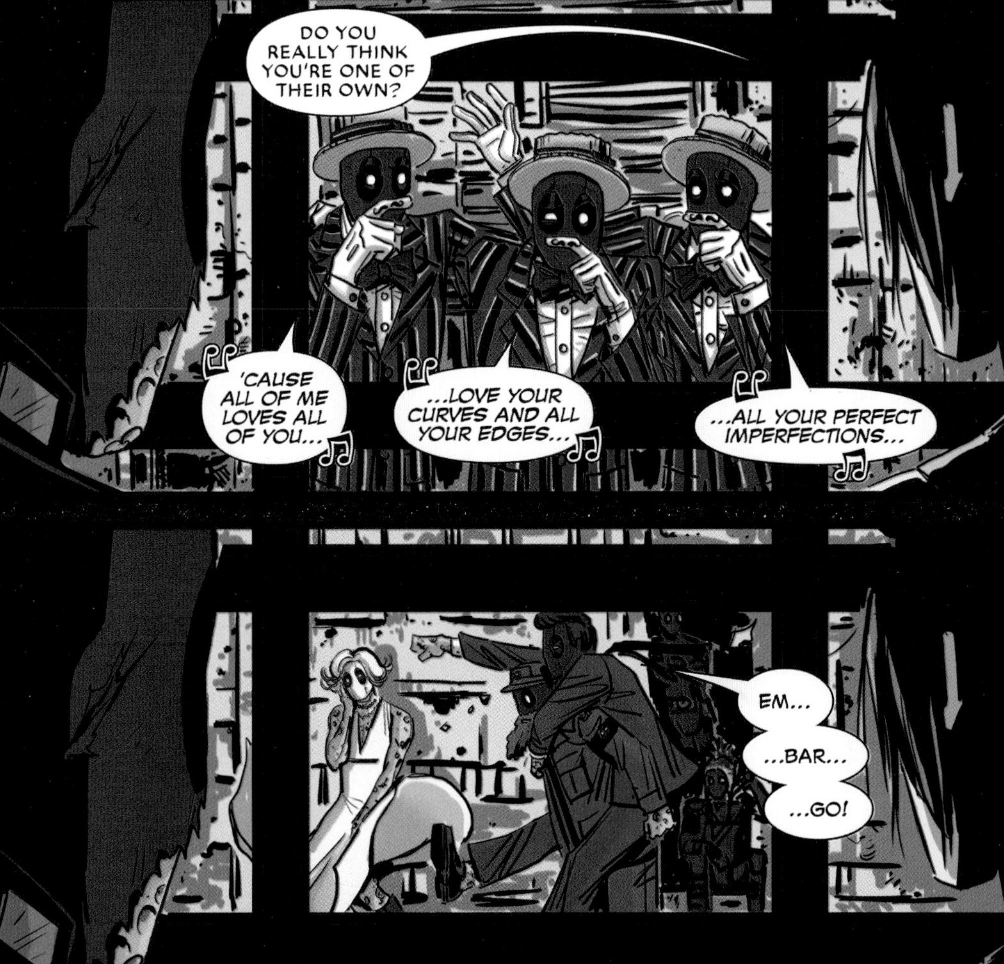
DO YOU REALLY THINK YOU'RE ONE OF THEIR OWN?
'CAUSE ALL OF ME LOVES ALL OF YOU...
...LOVE YOUR CURVES AND ALL YOUR EDGES...
...ALL YOUR PERFECT IMPERFECTIONS...
EM...
...BAR...
...GO!

A WORLD WHERE EVERYBODY IS DEADPOOL - CAN YOU IMAGINE ANYTHING BETTER?!

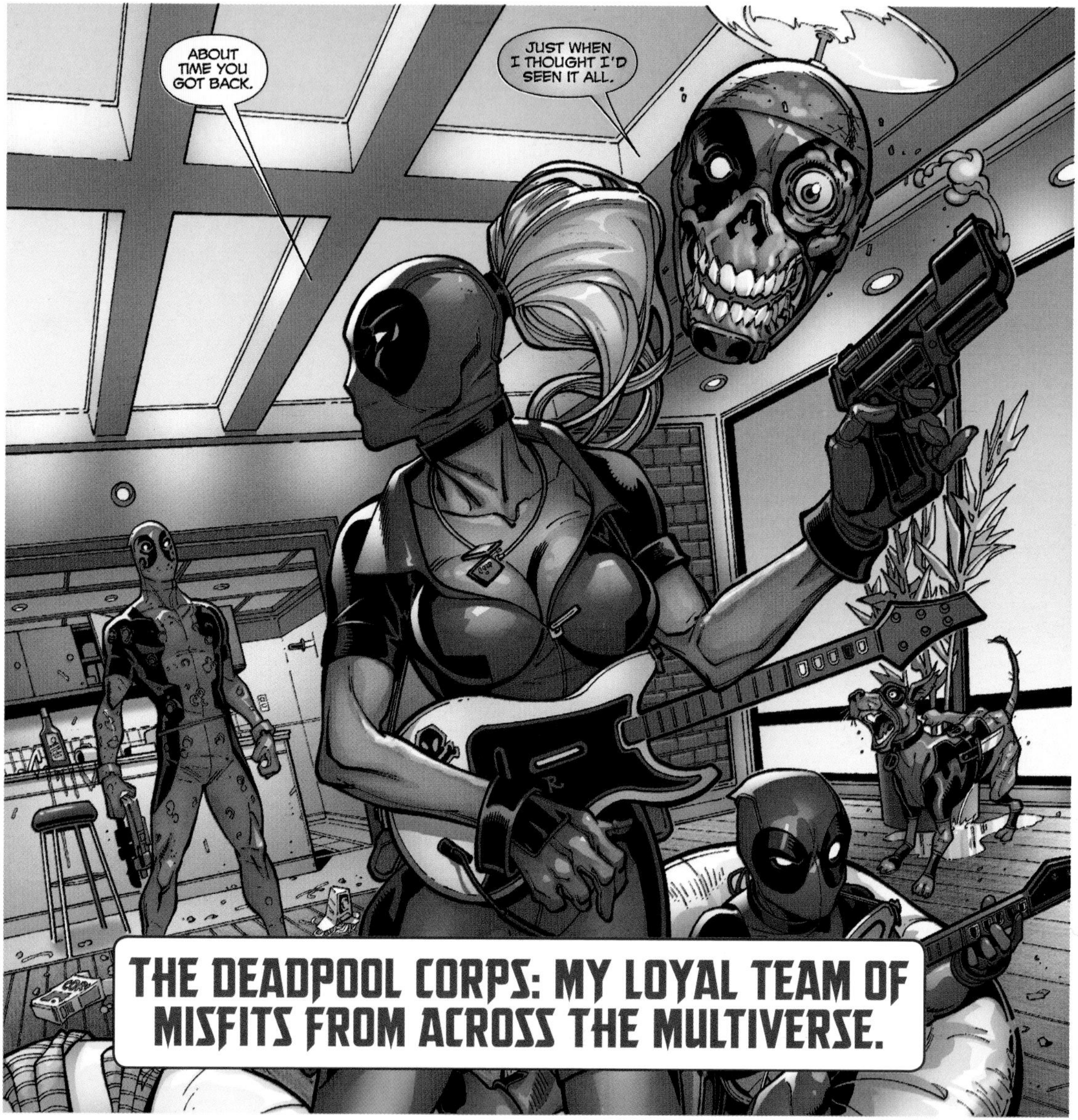
ABOUT TIME YOU GOT BACK.
JUST WHEN I THOUGHT I'D SEEN IT ALL.
THE DEADPOOL CORPS: MY LOYAL TEAM OF MISFITS FROM ACROSS THE MULTIVERSE.

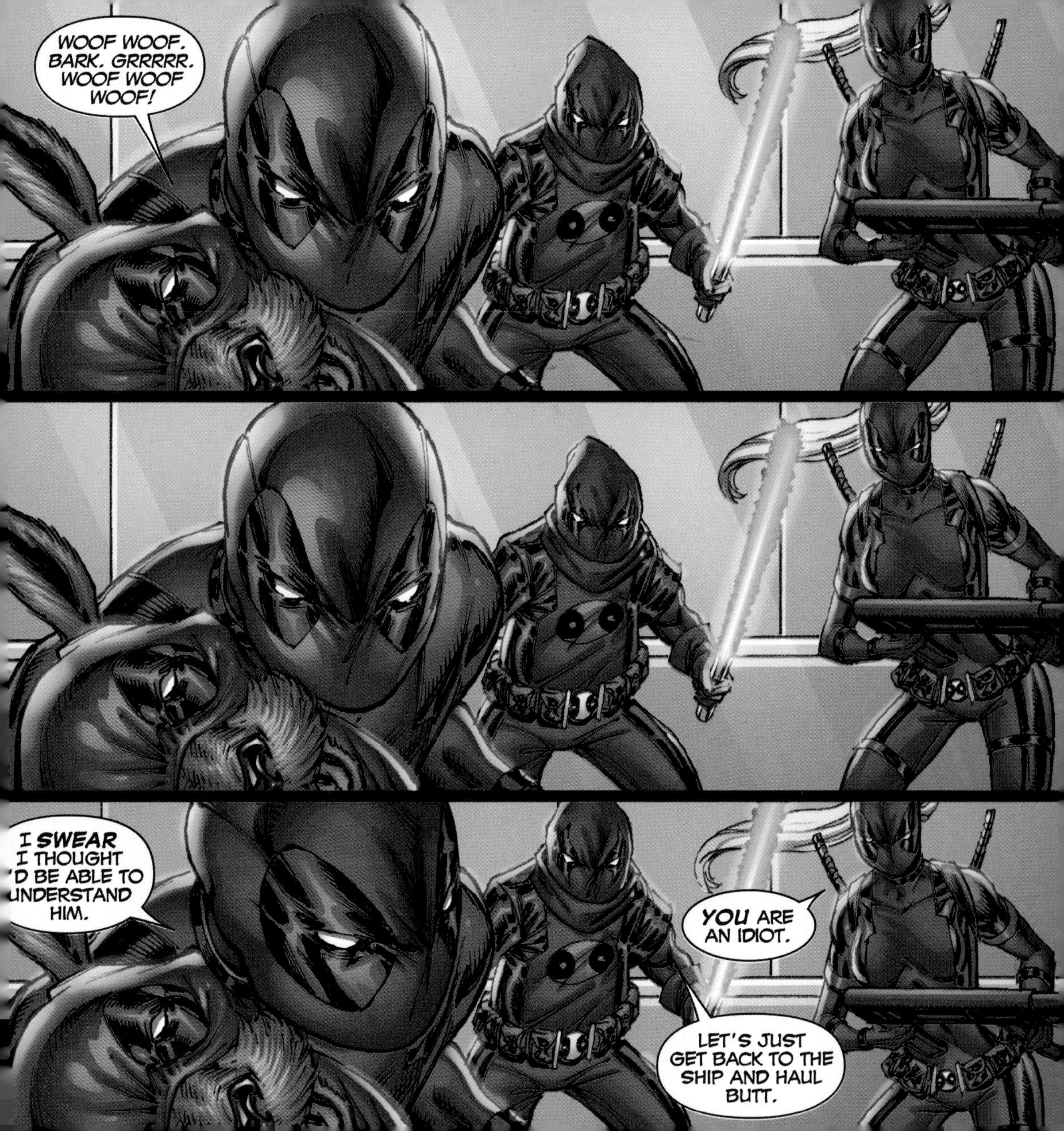
WOOF WOOF. BARK. GRRRRR. WOOF WOOF WOOF!
I *SWEAR* I THOUGHT 'D BE ABLE TO UNDERSTAND HIM.
YOU ARE AN IDIOT.
LET'S JUST GET BACK TO THE SHIP AND HAUL BUTT.

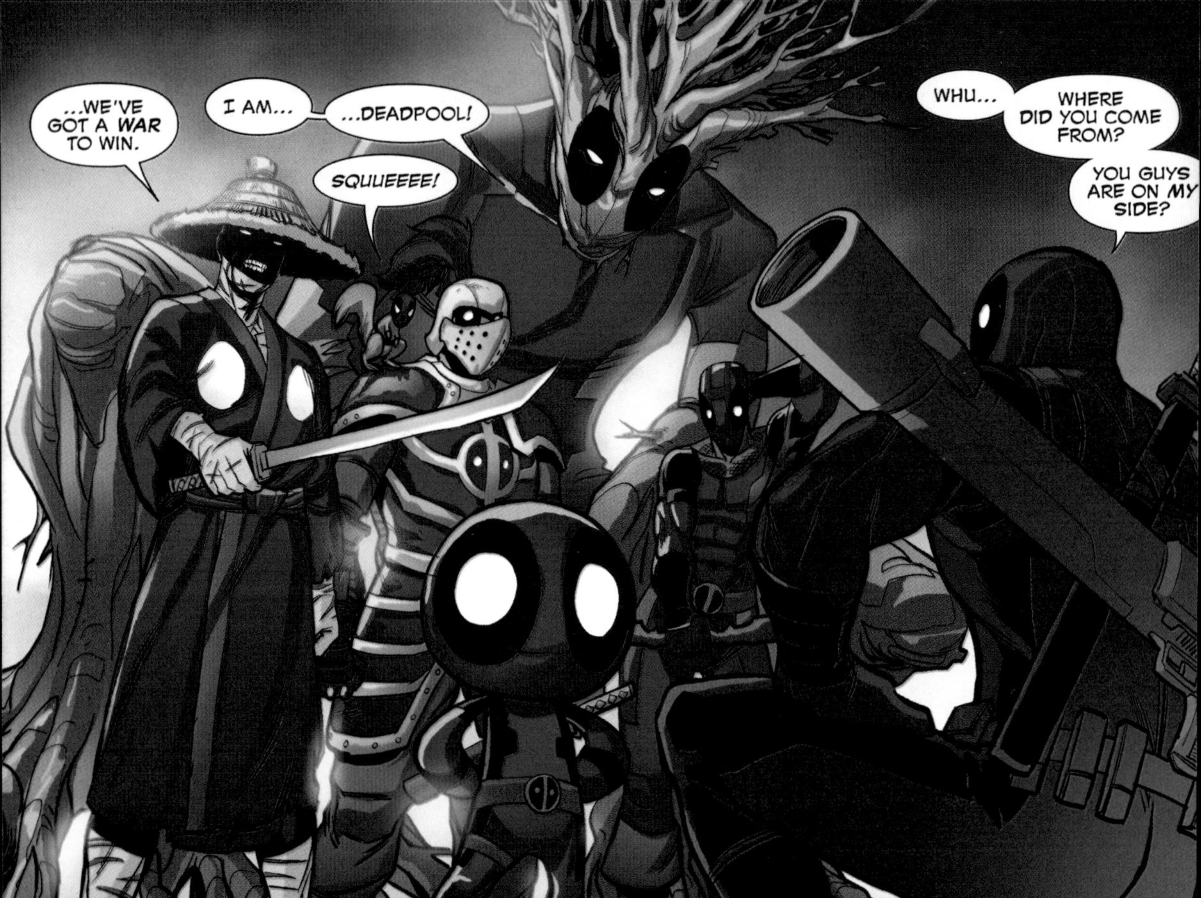
...WE'VE GOT A *WAR* TO WIN.
I AM...
...DEADPOOL!
SQUUEEEE!
WHU...
WHERE DID YOU COME FROM?
YOU GUYS ARE ON *MY* SIDE?

THAT TIME WHEN EVERY DEADPOOL FROM EVERY UNIVERSE CAME TOGETHER FOR... REASONS.

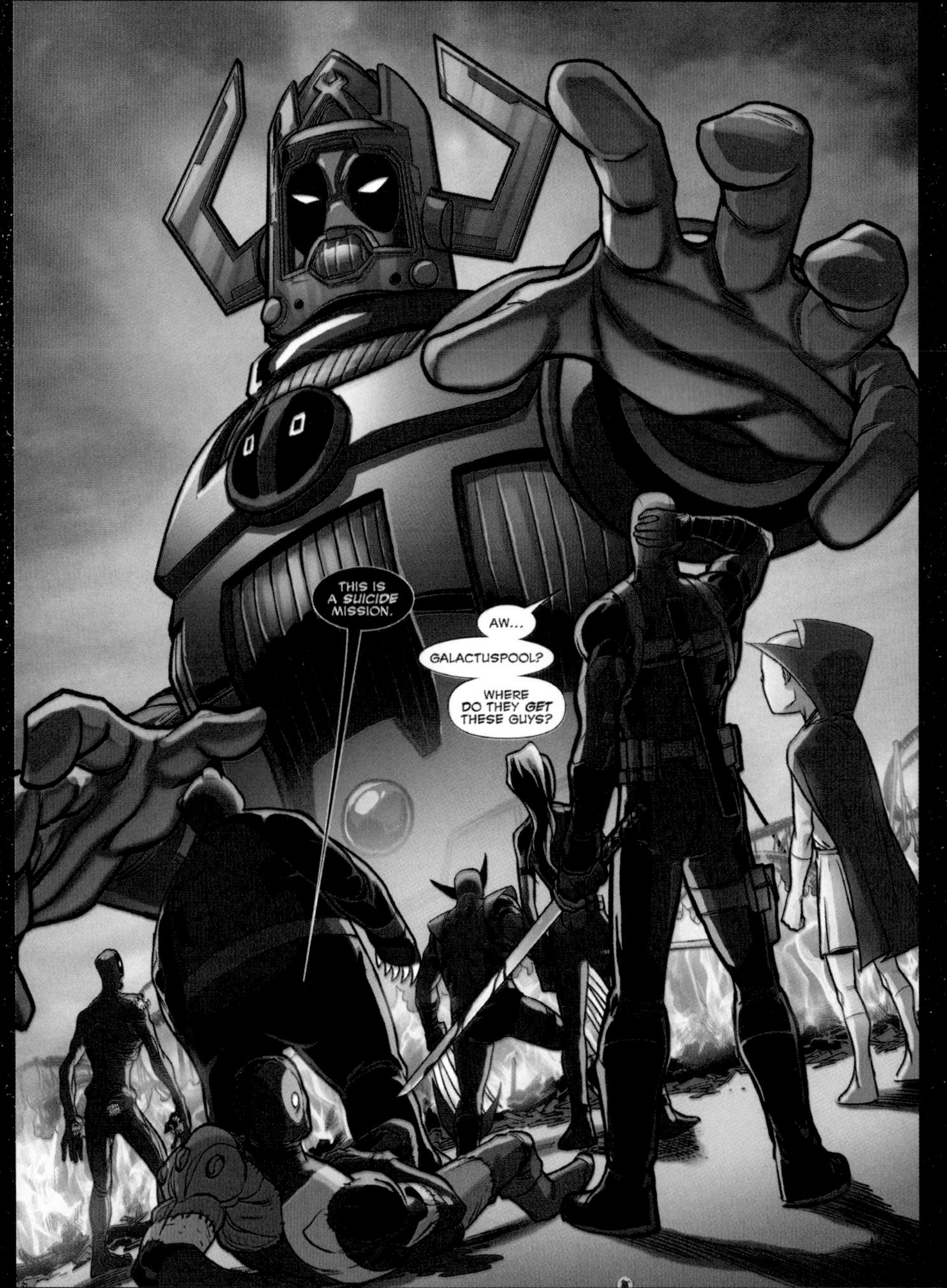
THIS IS A SUICIDE MISSION.
AW...
GALACTUSPOOL?
WHERE DO THEY GET THESE GUYS?

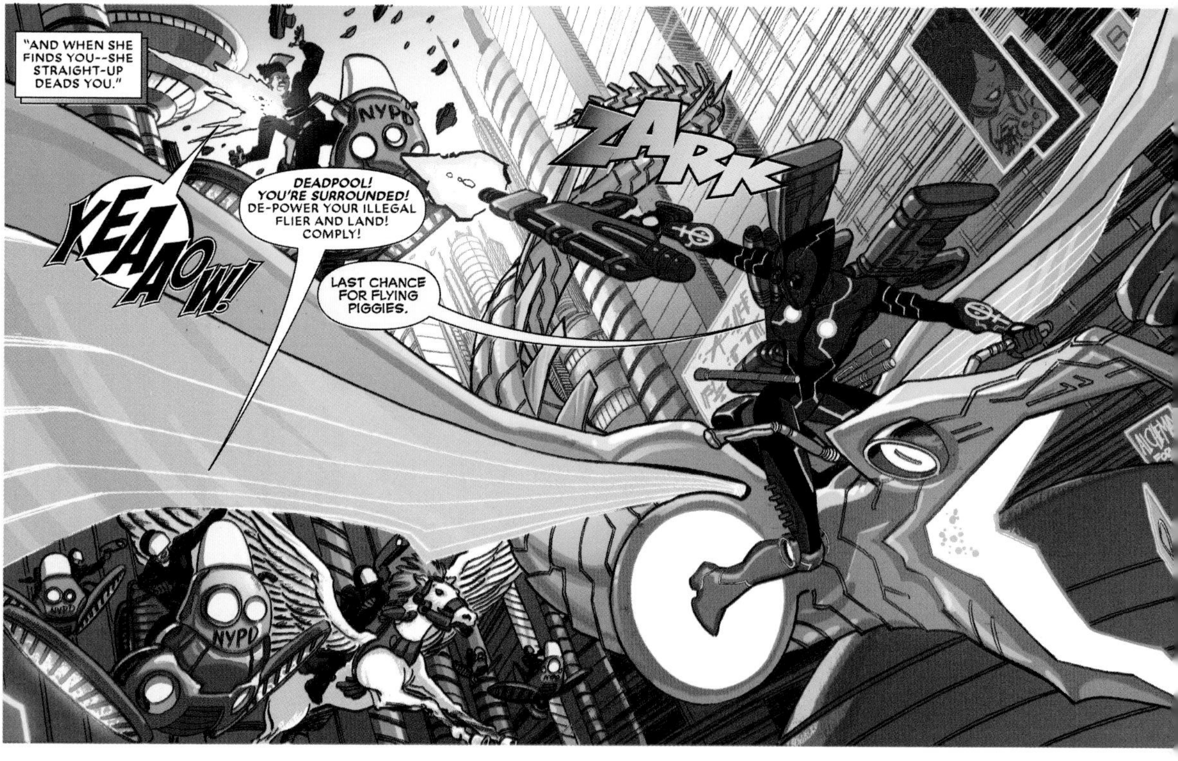
"AND WHEN SHE FINDS YOU--SHE STRAIGHT-UP DEADS YOU."
YEAAAOW!
DEADPOOL! YOU'RE SURROUNDED! DE-POWER YOUR ILLEGAL FLIER AND LAND! COMPLY!
ZARK
LAST CHANCE FOR FLYING PIGGIES.
NYPD

2099 - A GOOD YEAR FOR THIS CHICK...

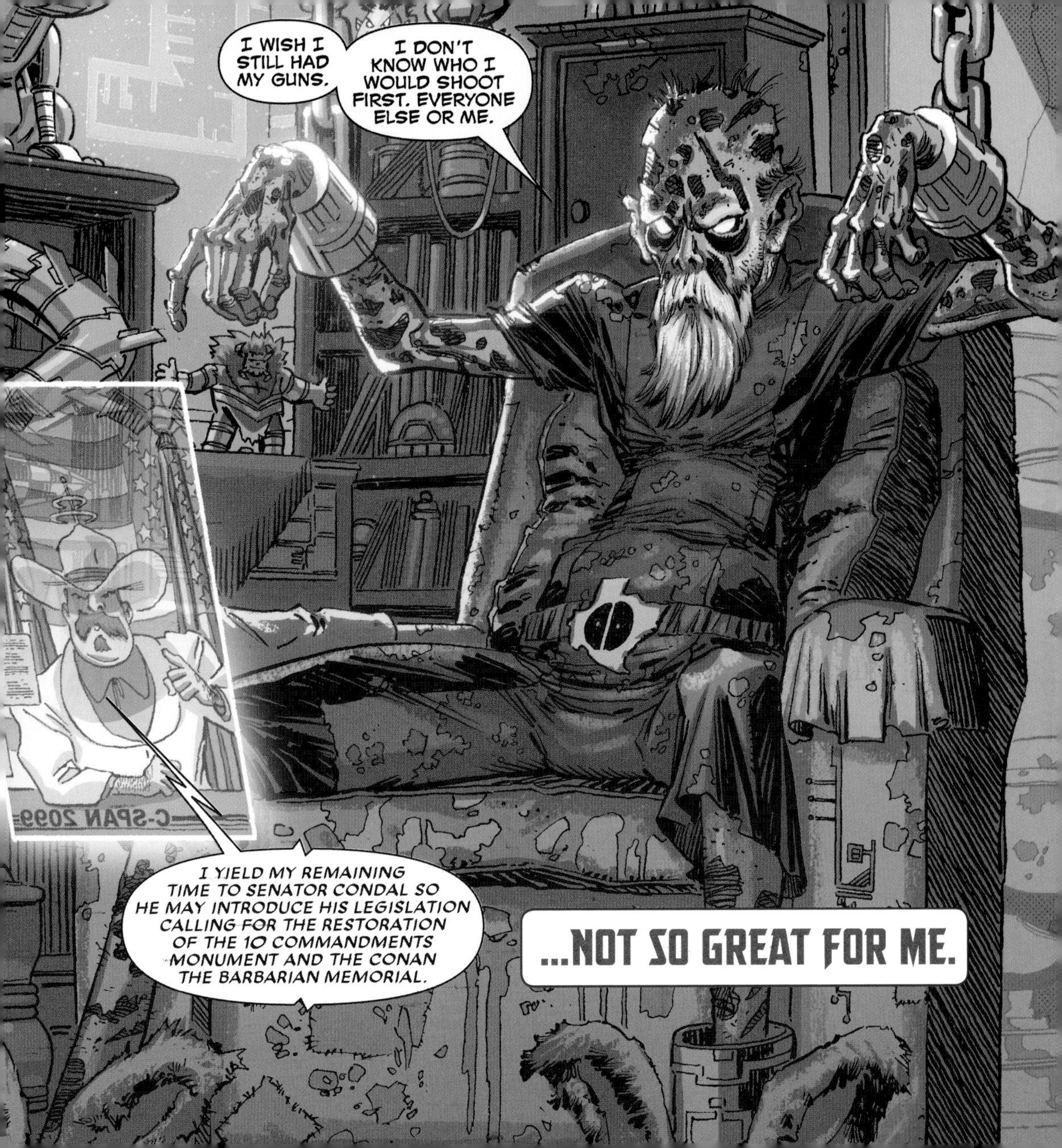
I WISH I STILL HAD MY GUNS.
I DON'T KNOW WHO I WOULD SHOOT FIRST. EVERYONE ELSE OR ME.
C-SPAN 2099
I YIELD MY REMAINING TIME TO SENATOR CONDAL SO HE MAY INTRODUCE HIS LEGISLATION CALLING FOR THE RESTORATION OF THE 10 COMMANDMENTS MONUMENT AND THE CONAN THE BARBARIAN MEMORIAL.
...NOT SO GREAT FOR ME.

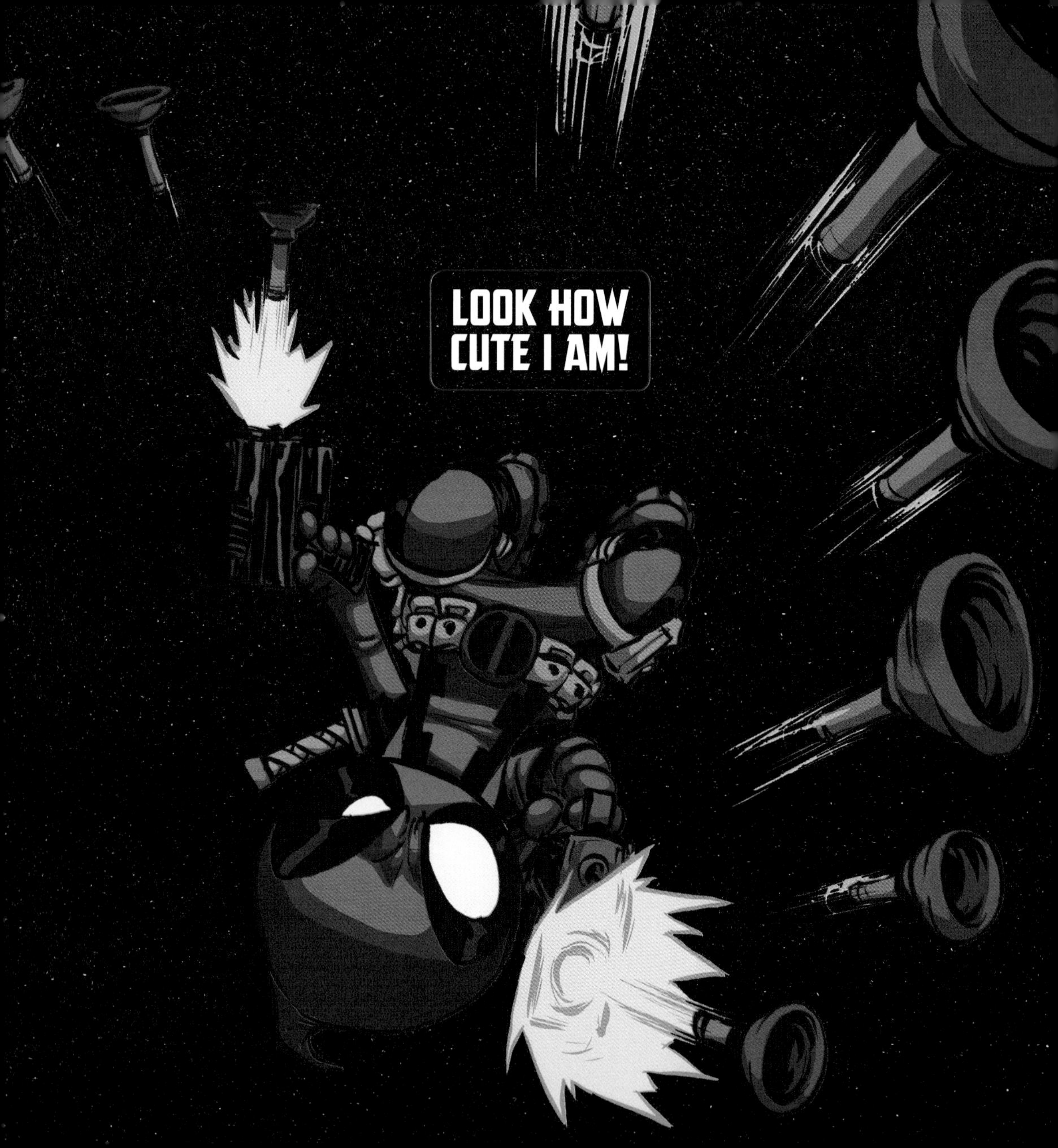
LOOK HOW
CUTE I AM!

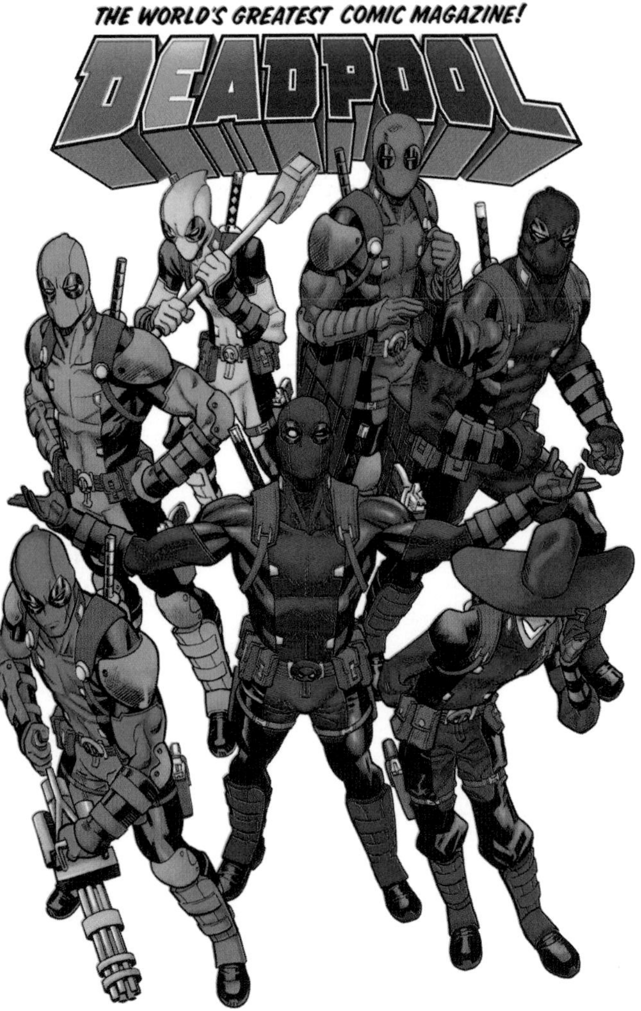
THE WORLD'S GREATEST COMIC MAGAZINE!
DEADPOOL

MY 'MERCS FOR MONEY.' APPARENTLY 'HEROES FOR HIRE' WAS TAKEN...

IS IT STILL FLATTERY WHEN HOWARD THE DUCK IS IMITATING YOU?

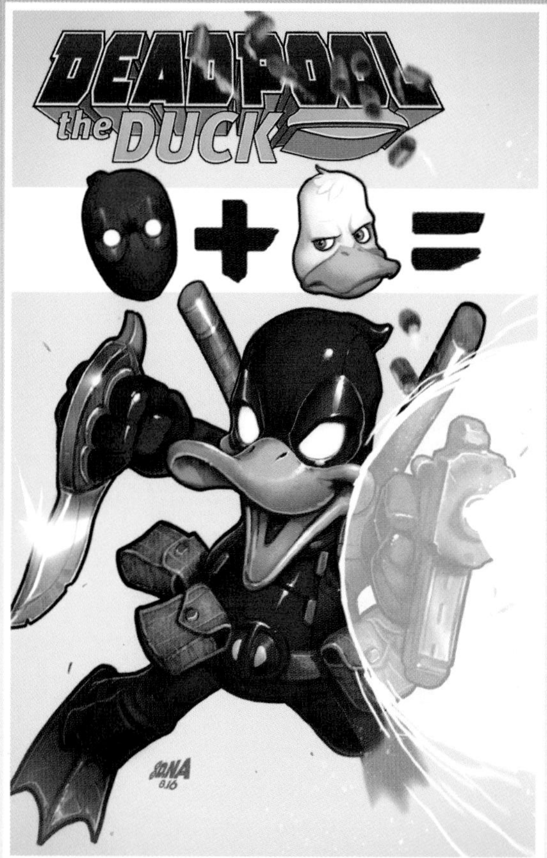
DEADPOOL the DUCK

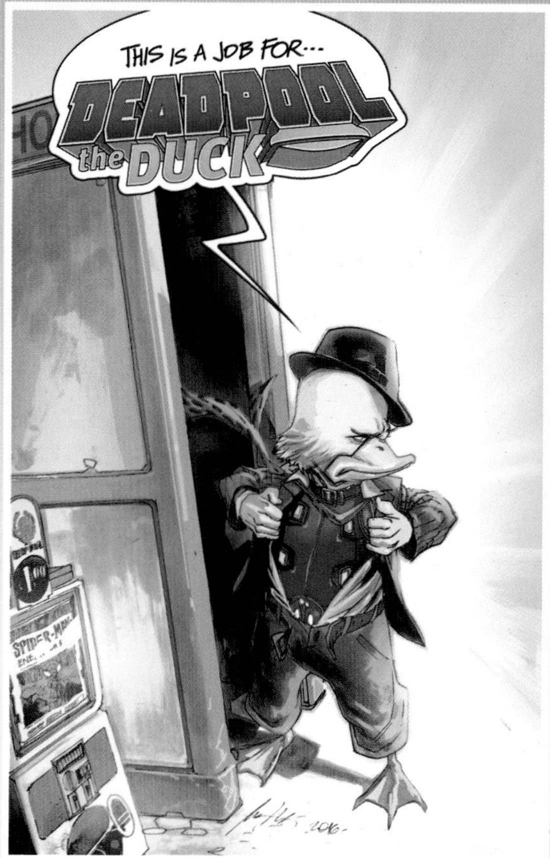
THIS IS A JOB FOR...
DEADPOOL the DUCK

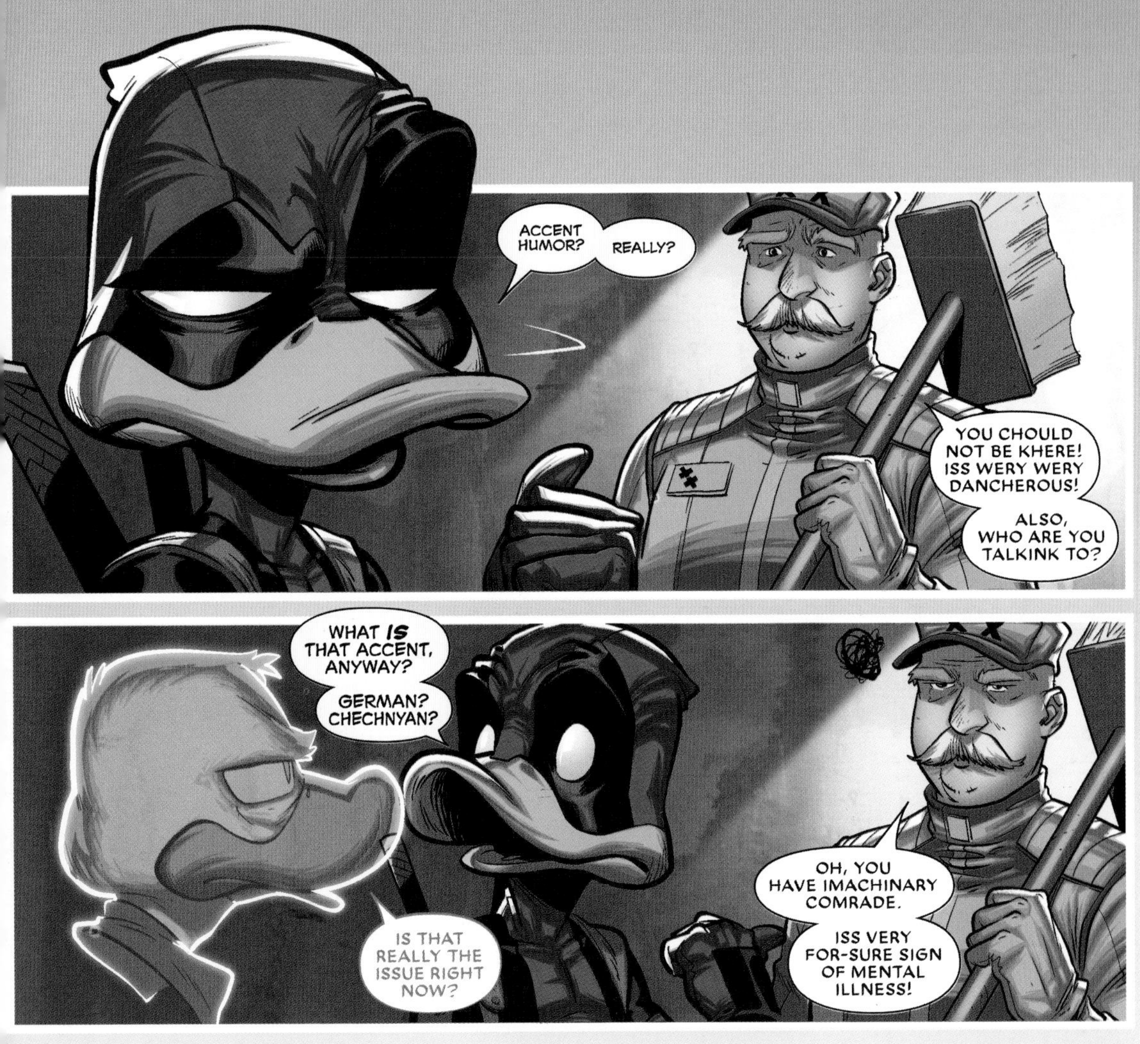
ACCENT HUMOR?
REALLY?
YOU CHOULD NOT BE KHERE! ISS WERY WERY DANCHEROUS!
ALSO, WHO ARE YOU TALKINK TO?
WHAT IS THAT ACCENT, ANYWAY?
GERMAN? CHECHNYAN?
IS THAT REALLY THE ISSUE RIGHT NOW?
OH, YOU HAVE IMACHINARY COMRADE.
ISS VERY FOR-SURE SIGN OF MENTAL ILLNESS!

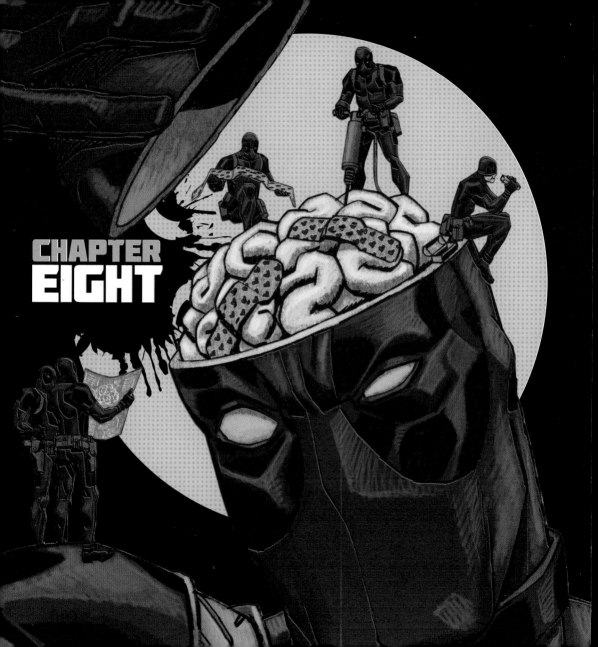

CHAPTER EIGHT

FINAL THOUGHTS OF DEADPOOL

AND SO THE END IS NEAR... THERE'S SO MANY THINGS IN MY HEAD I WANNA SHARE, BUT SEEING AS THE PUBLISHER'S CHEAP, WE'RE GONNA WRAP UP WITH A FEW LESSONS THAT IF YOU PAY ATTENTION WON'T MAKE ANY SENSE AT ALL!

"IT ALL PROBABLY HAS SOMETHING TO DO WITH ME... BECAUSE EVERYTHING DOES!"

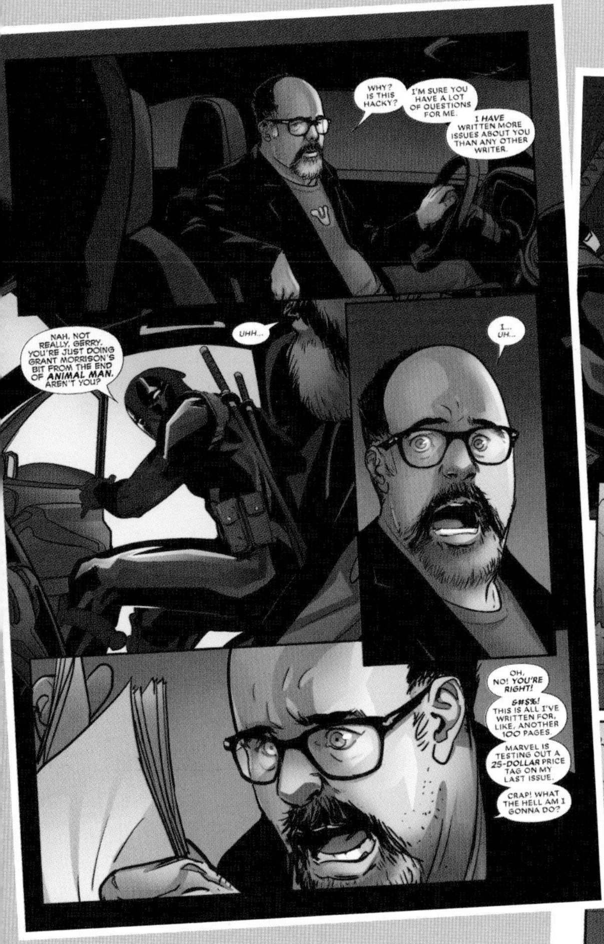
WHY? IS THIS HACKY?
I'M SURE YOU HAVE A LOT OF QUESTIONS FOR ME.
I HAVE WRITTEN MORE ISSUES ABOUT YOU THAN ANY OTHER WRITER.
NAH, NOT REALLY, GERRY. YOU'RE JUST DOING GRANT MORRISON'S BIT FROM THE END OF ANIMAL MAN, AREN'T YOU?
UHH...
I... UH...
OH, NO! YOU'RE RIGHT!
&#$%! THIS IS ALL I'VE WRITTEN FOR, LIKE, ANOTHER 100 PAGES.
MARVEL IS TESTING OUT A 25-DOLLAR PRICE TAG ON MY LAST ISSUE.
CRAP! WHAT THE HELL AM I GONNA DO?

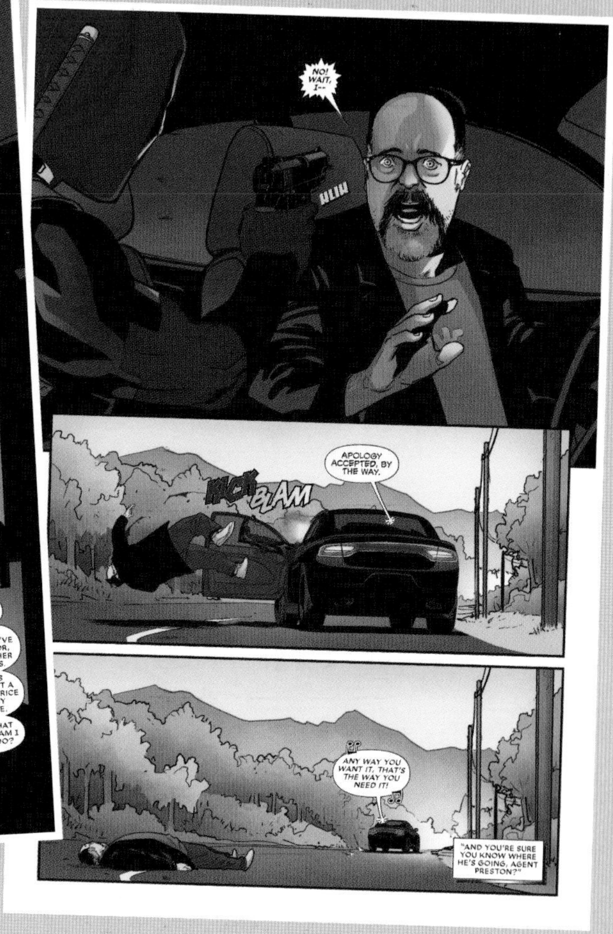
NO! WAIT, I--
KICK
BLAM
APOLOGY ACCEPTED, BY THE WAY.
ANY WAY YOU WANT IT, THAT'S THE WAY YOU NEED IT!
"AND YOU'RE SURE YOU KNOW WHERE HE'S GOING, AGENT PRESTON?"

NEVER MEET YOUR MAKER!

"YOU HAVE FAILED ME BRAIN!"

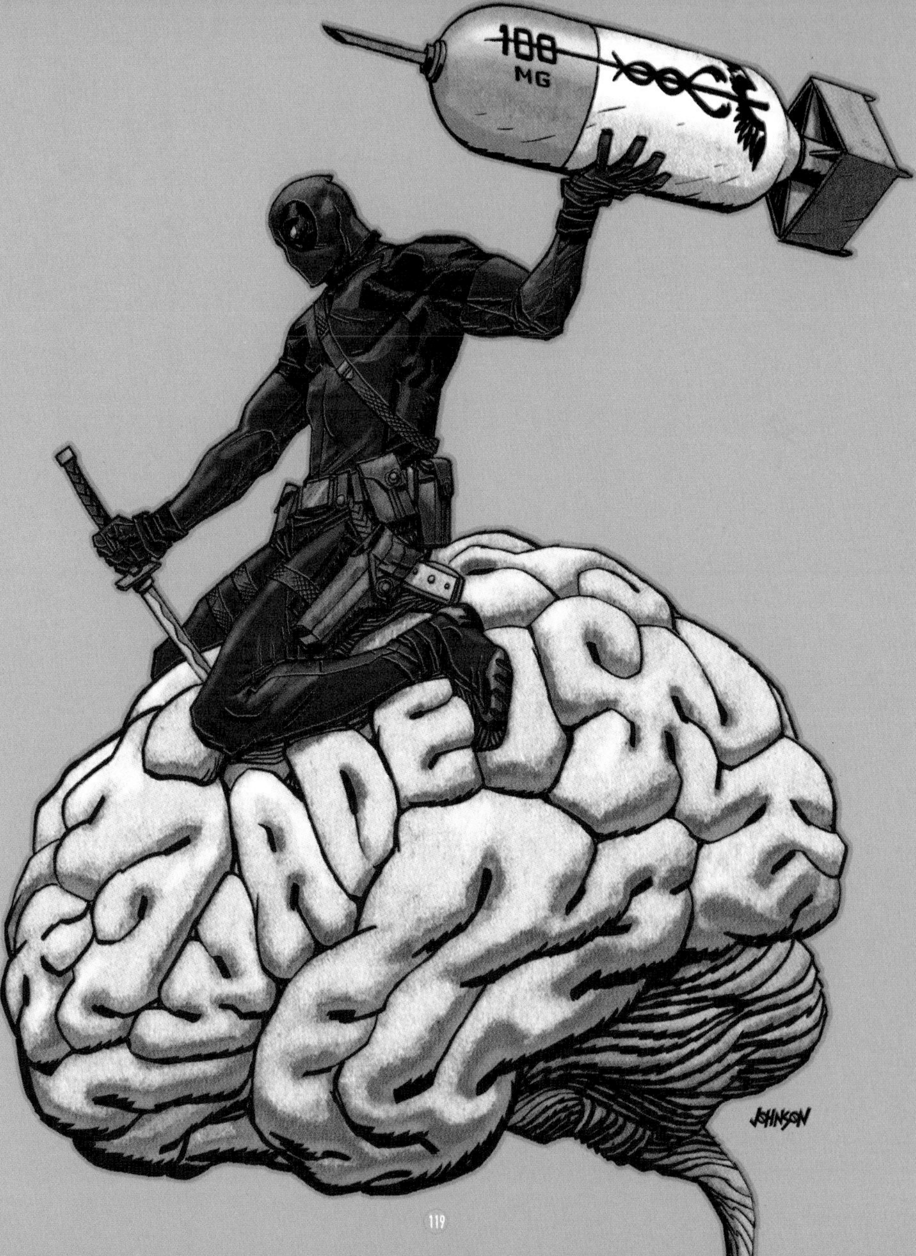
100
MG
JOHNSON

"DON'T SHOOT ANYONE I WOULDN'T."

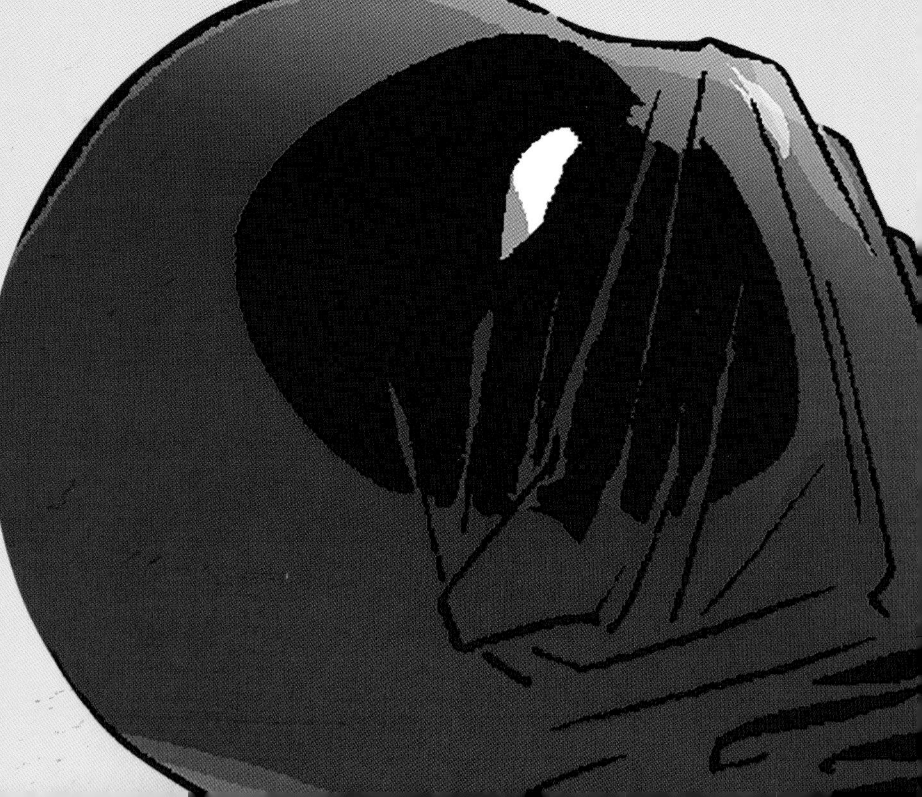

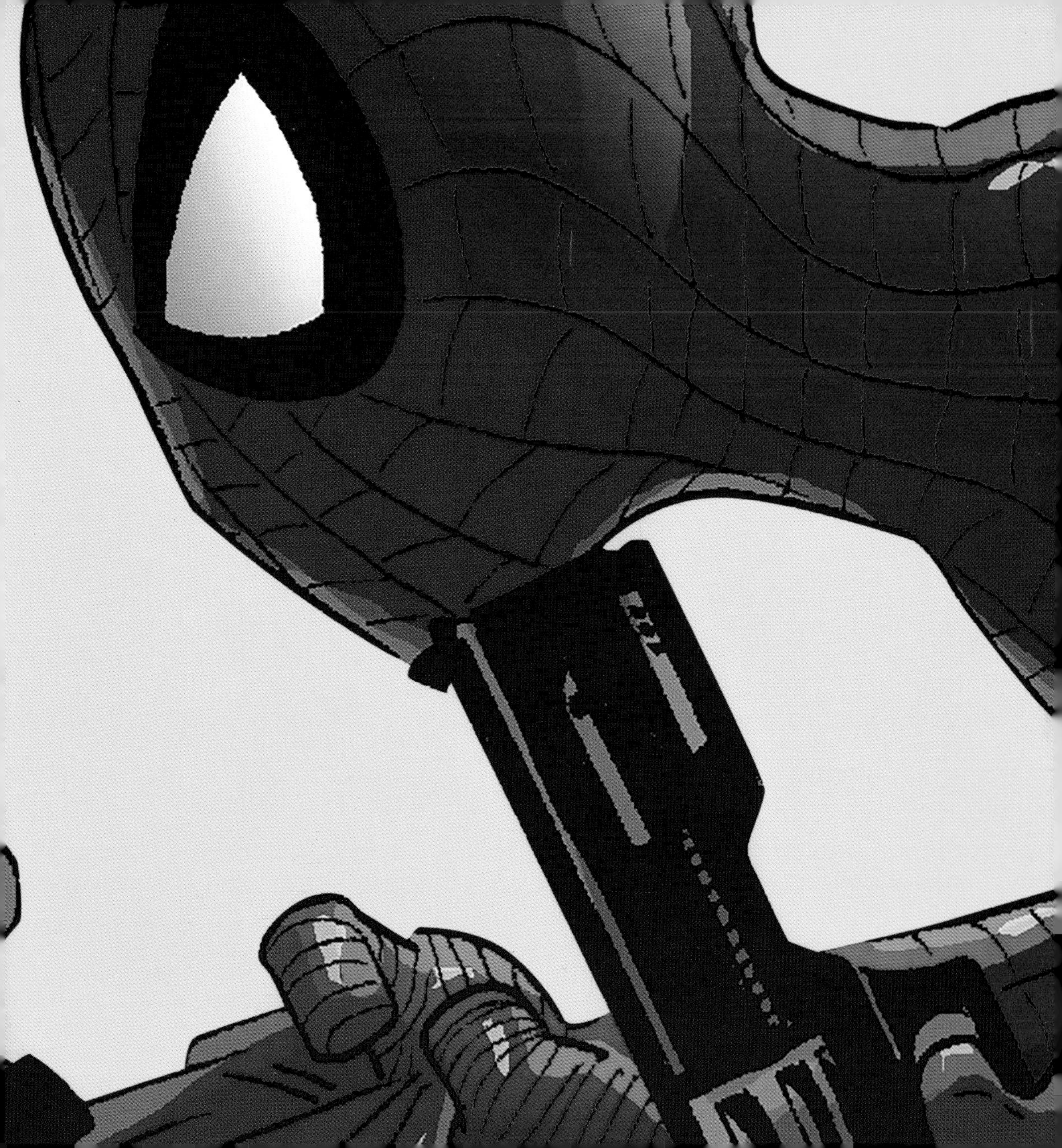

"I'M REALLY GONNA MISS ME WHEN I'M GONE."

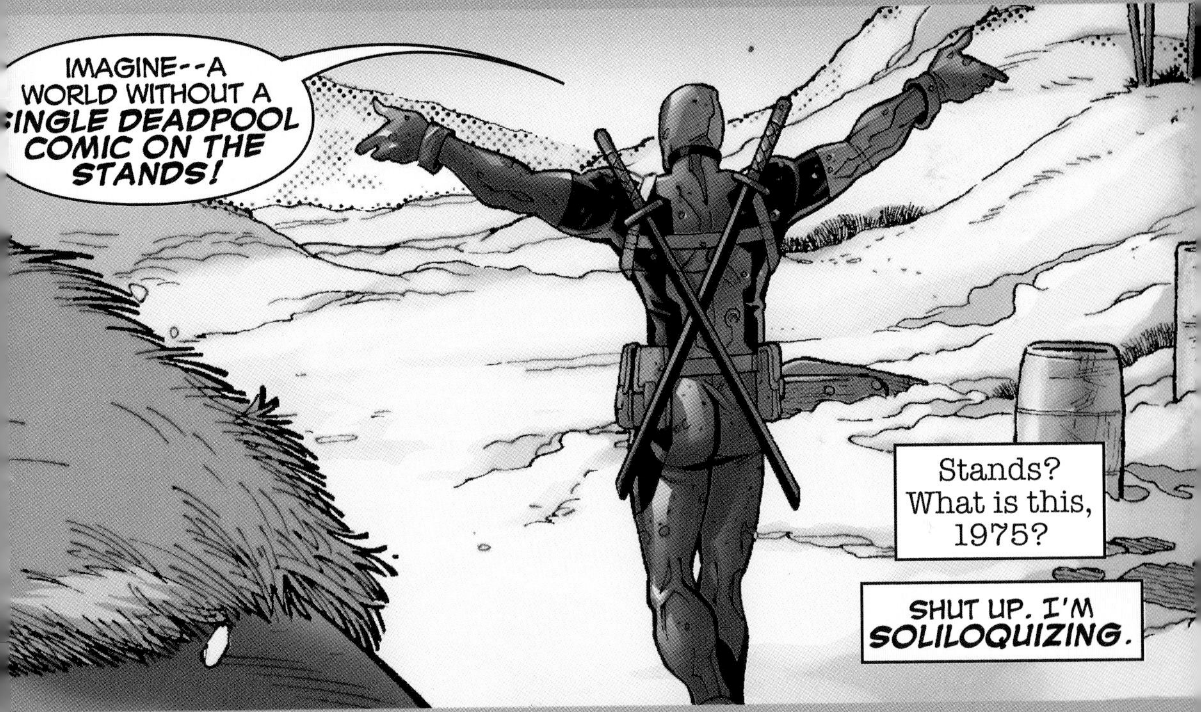
IMAGINE--A WORLD WITHOUT A SINGLE DEADPOOL COMIC ON THE STANDS!
Stands? What is this, 1975?
SHUT UP. I'M SOLILOQUIZING.

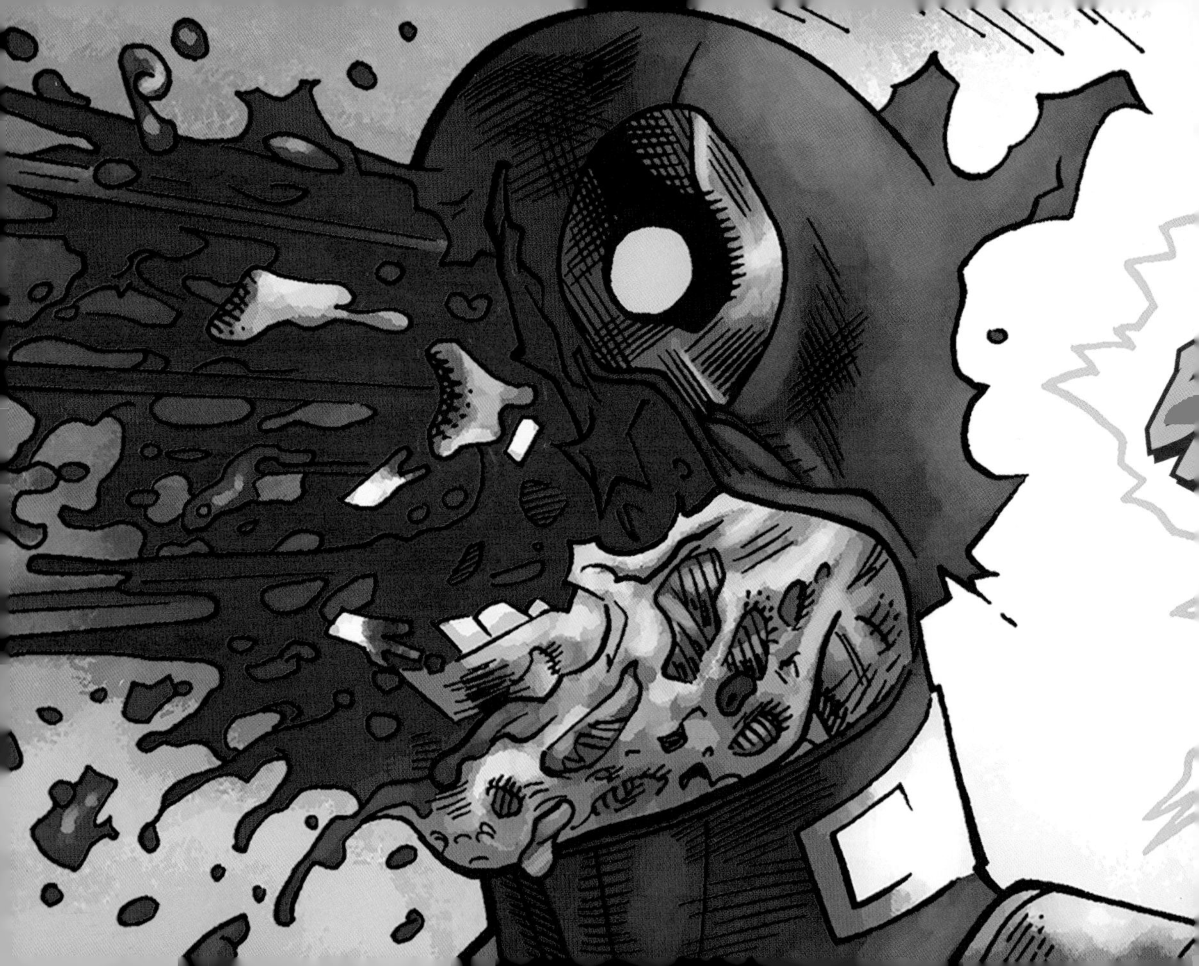

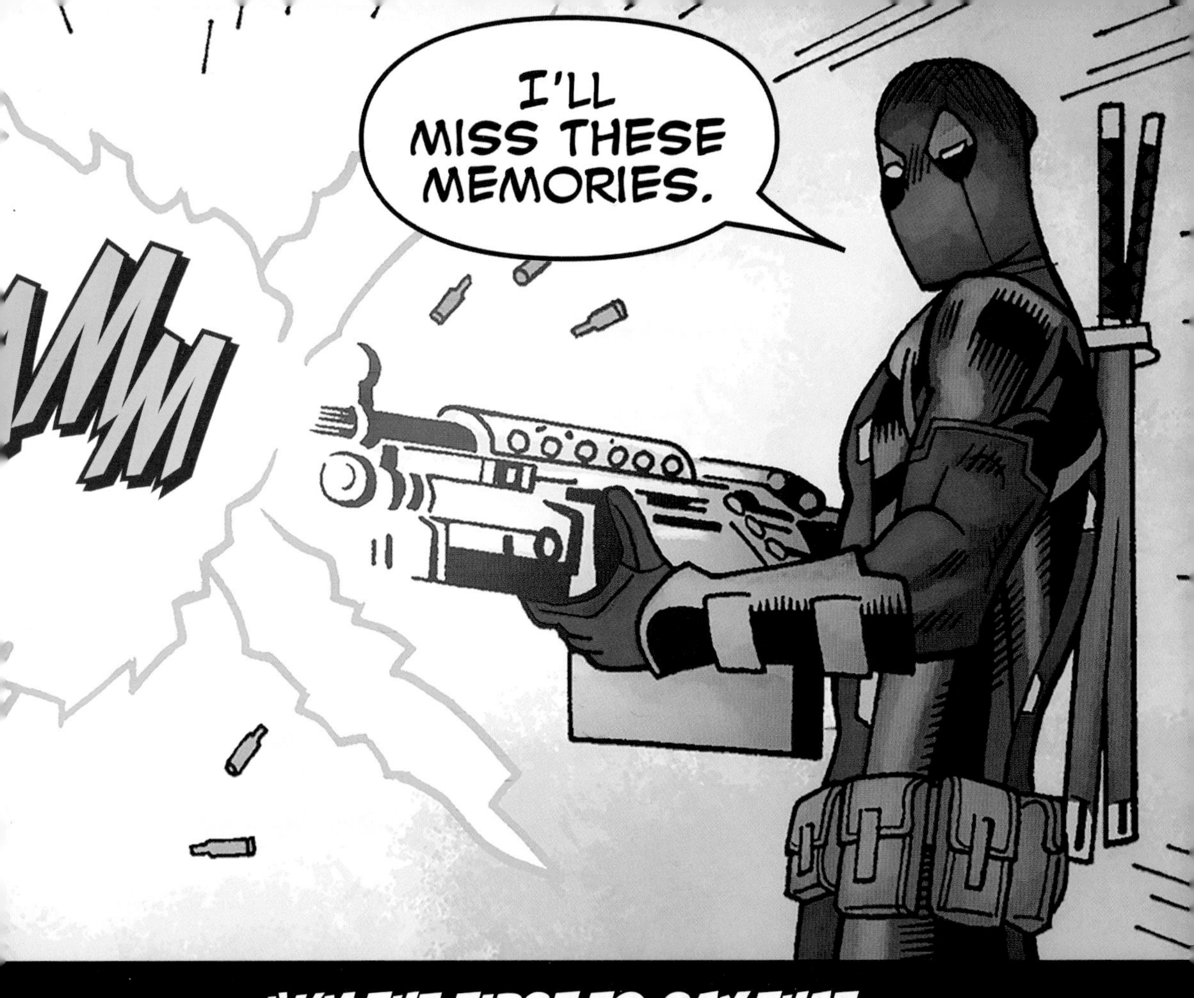
I'LL MISS THESE MEMORIES.

"I'M THE FIRST TO SAY THAT VI LENCE IS NEVER THE ANSWER."

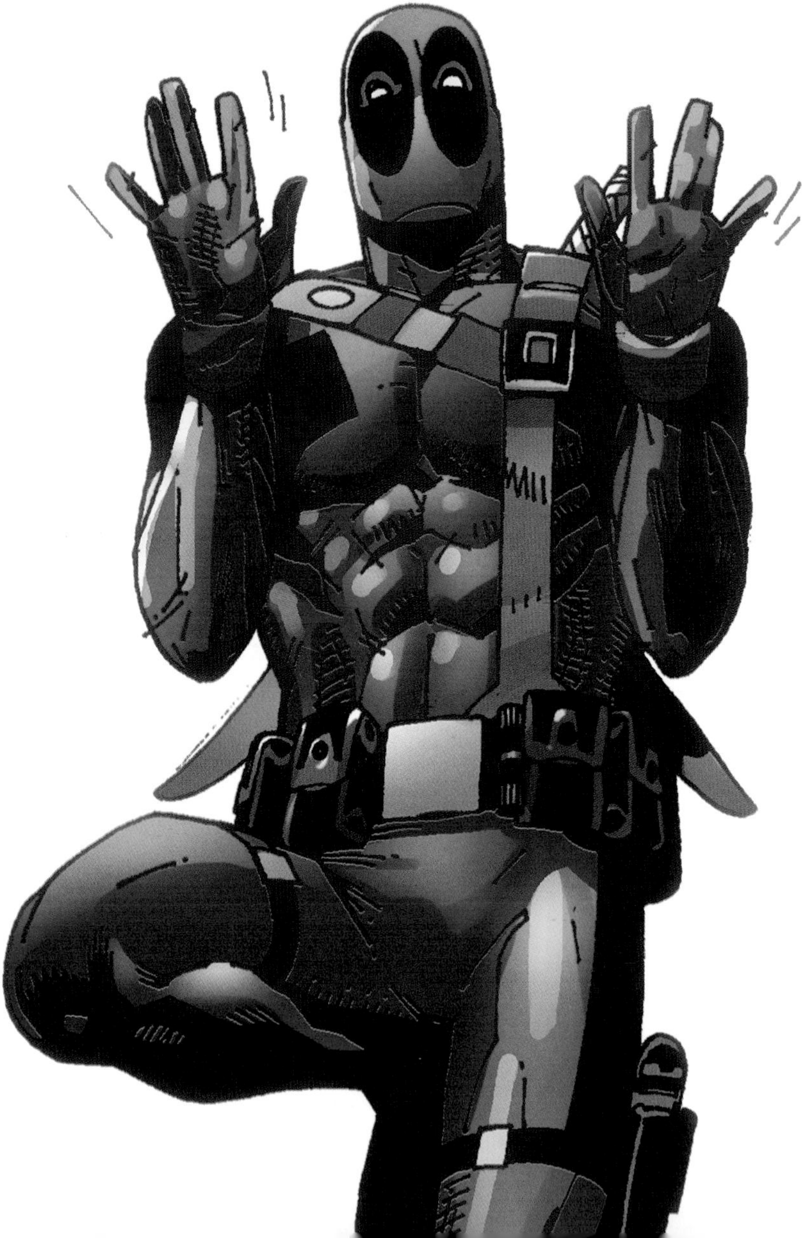

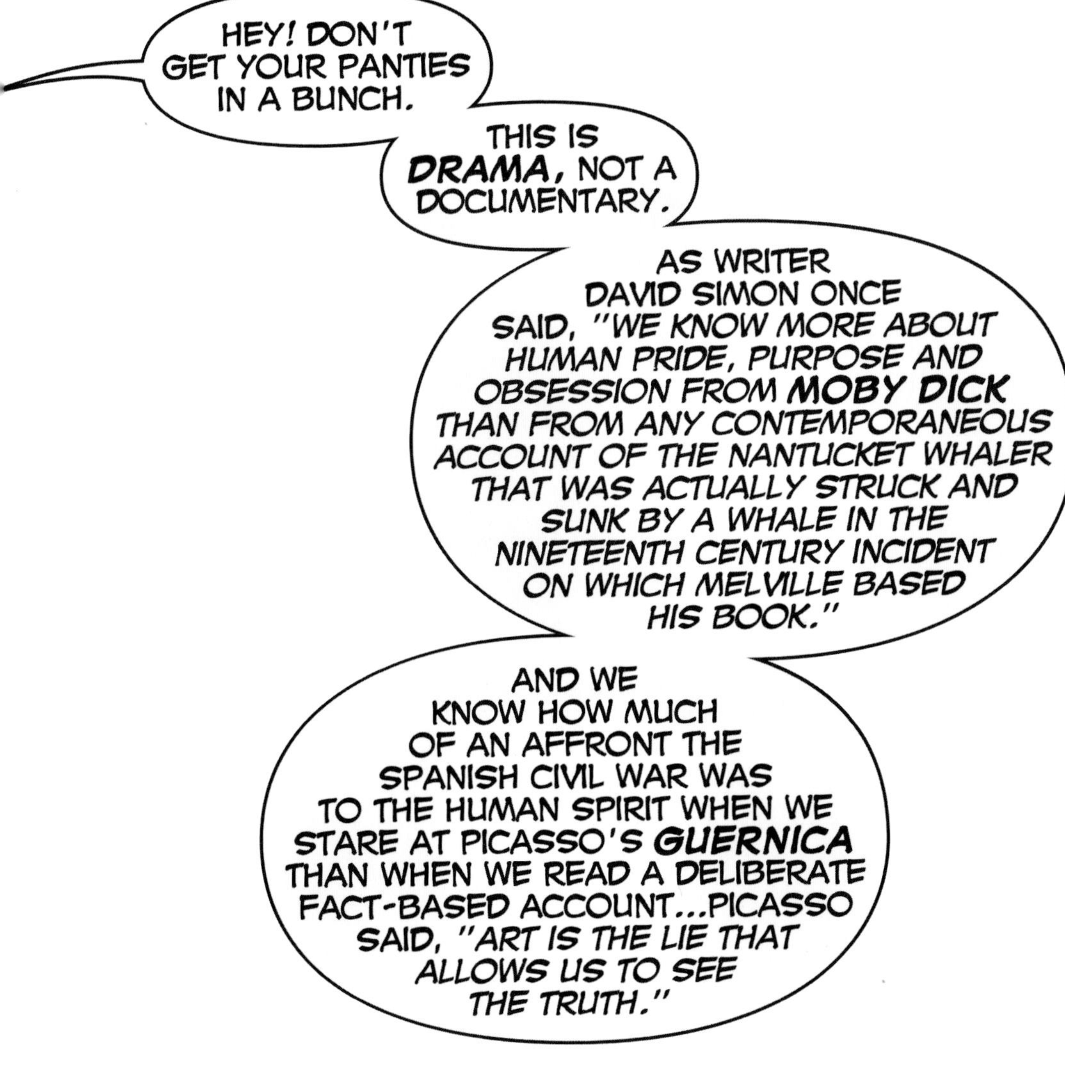
HEY! DON'T GET YOUR PANTIES IN A BUNCH.
THIS IS **DRAMA,** NOT A DOCUMENTARY.
AS WRITER DAVID SIMON ONCE SAID, *"WE KNOW MORE ABOUT HUMAN PRIDE, PURPOSE AND OBSESSION FROM* **MOBY DICK** *THAN FROM ANY CONTEMPORANEOUS ACCOUNT OF THE NANTUCKET WHALER THAT WAS ACTUALLY STRUCK AND SUNK BY A WHALE IN THE NINETEENTH CENTURY INCIDENT ON WHICH MELVILLE BASED HIS BOOK."*
AND WE KNOW HOW MUCH OF AN AFFRONT THE SPANISH CIVIL WAR WAS TO THE HUMAN SPIRIT WHEN WE STARE AT PICASSO'S ***GUERNICA*** THAN WHEN WE READ A DELIBERATE FACT-BASED ACCOUNT...PICASSO SAID, *"ART IS THE LIE THAT ALLOWS US TO SEE THE TRUTH."*

PARTING WISDOM

IF YOU'VE LEARNED JUST ONE THING FROM THIS BOOK THEN I'VE FAILED. SERIOUSLY. AND IF YOU HAVEN'T, TOUGH TACOS. THERE'S A NO REFUND POLICY ON THIS BOOK PAL. AND REMEMBER, IF LIFE DEALS YOU LEMONS, MAKE CHIMICHANGAS, BUT IF LIFE DEALS YOU A ROYAL FLUSH THEN ALWAYS BET ON RED AND BLACK. LATERS!

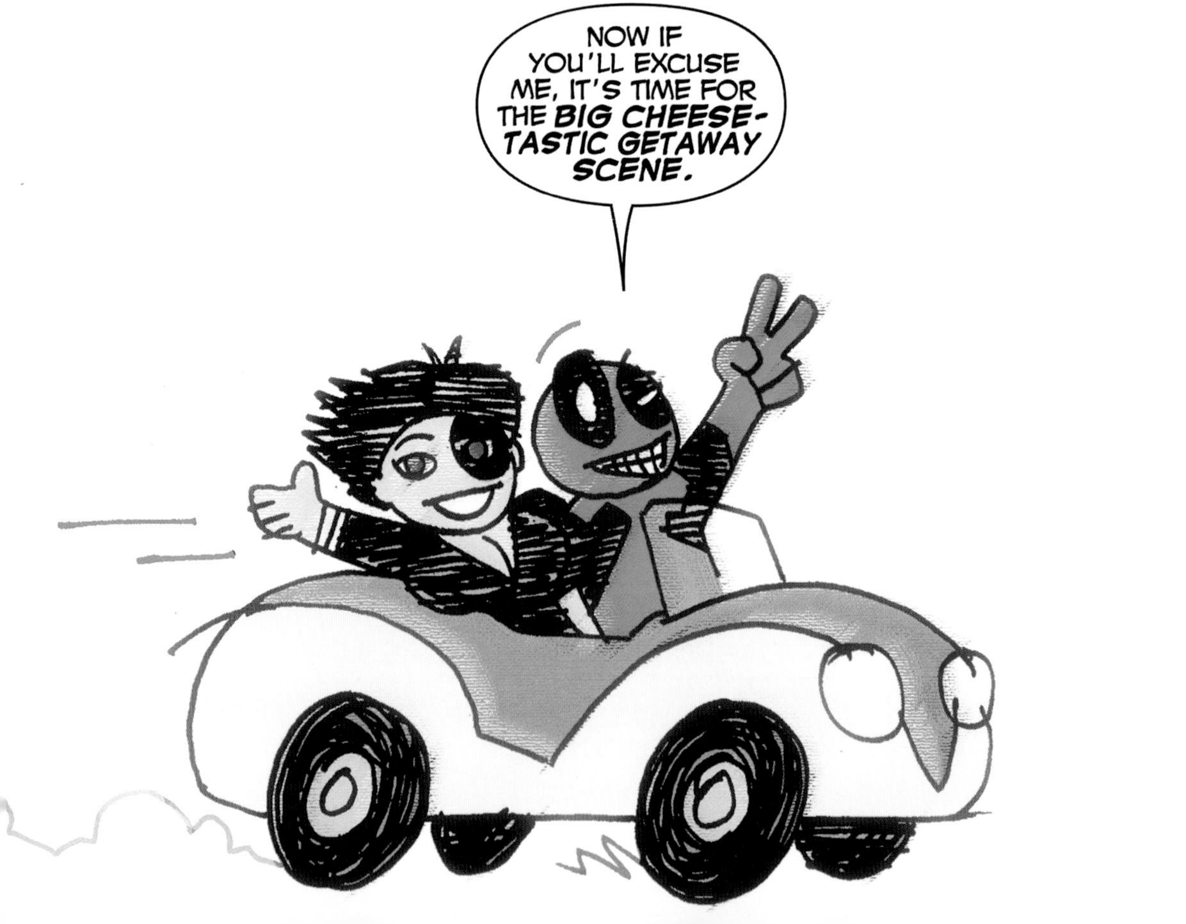
NOW IF YOU'LL EXCUSE ME, IT'S TIME FOR THE BIG CHEESE-TASTIC GETAWAY SCENE.

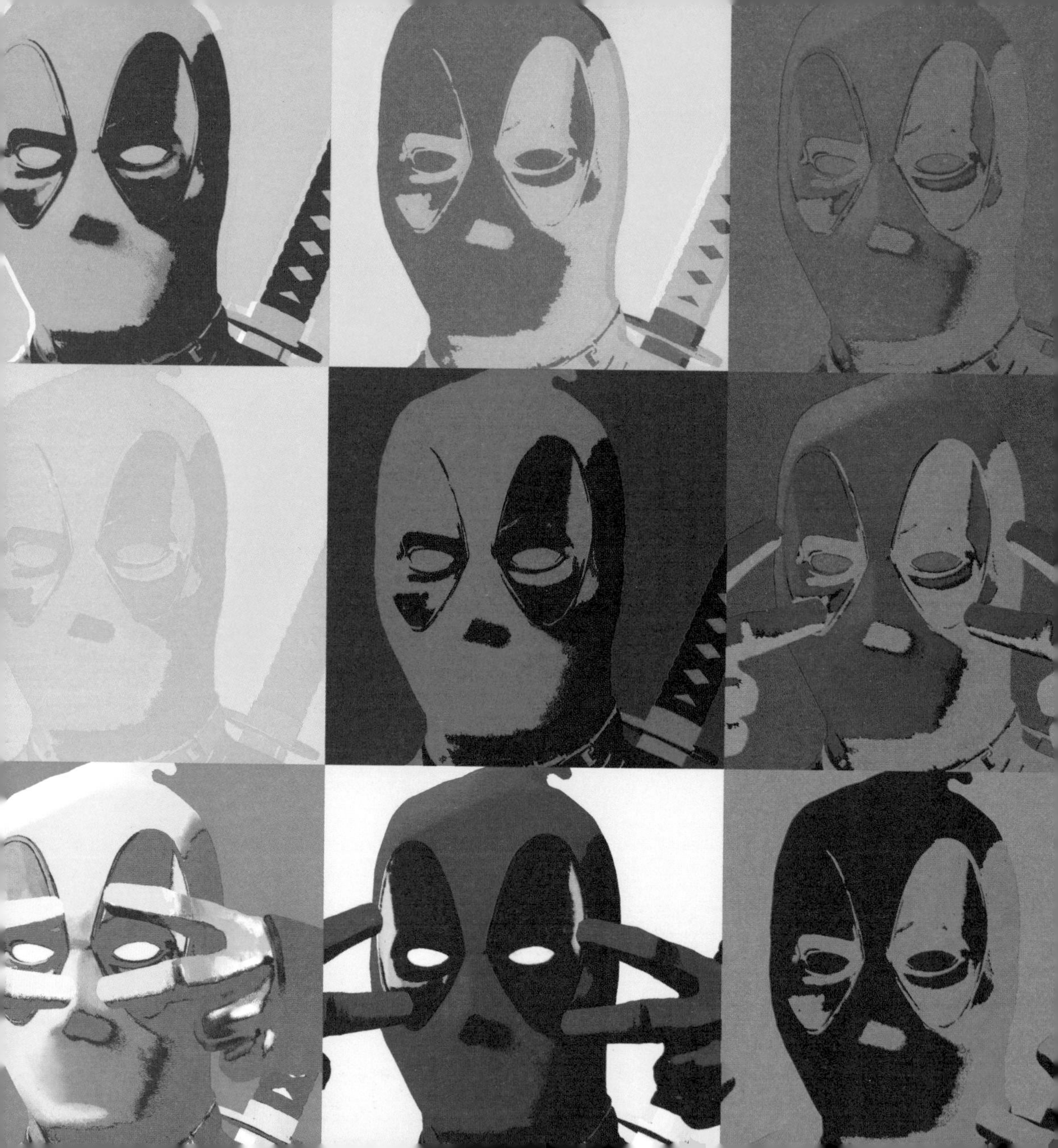